YOUNG AND RESTLESS

YOUNG

AND

RESTLESS

THE GIRLS WHO SPARKED
AMERICA'S REVOLUTIONS

MATTIE KAHN

VIKING

VIKING
An imprint of Penguin Random House LLC
penguinrandomhouse.com

LIBRARY OF CONGRESS CATALOGING-IN-PUBLICATION DATA
Names: Kahn, Mattie, author.
Title: Young and restless : the girls who sparked America's revolutions / Mattie Kahn.
Description: [New York, NY] : Viking, [2023] | Includes bibliographical references and index.
Identifiers: LCCN 2022050008 (print) | LCCN 2022050009 (ebook) |
ISBN 9780593299067 (hardcover) | ISBN 9780593299074 (ebook)
Subjects: LCSH: Teenage girls—Political activity—United States—History.
| Social movements—United States—History.
Classification: LCC HQ799.2.P6 K346 2023 (print) | LCC HQ799.2.P6 (ebook) |
DDC 303.48/40830973—dc23/eng/20230303
LC record available at https://lccn.loc.gov/2022050008
LC ebook record available at https://lccn.loc.gov/2022050009

Printed in the United States of America
1st Printing

DESIGNED BY MEIGHAN CAVANAUGH

What wild and unearned luck to have been born to parents
who believed that there were no limits to what a girl could do
and who once let me shop for a coveted and overpriced
Madame Alexander doll in a feverish haze.

I am so grateful on both counts.
This book is dedicated to them.

I love to see a young girl go out and grab the world by the lapels.
Life's a bitch. You've got to go out and kick ass.

MAYA ANGELOU

How can you say young girls don't get it? They're our future.
Our future doctors, lawyers, mothers, presidents,
they kind of keep the world going.

HARRY STYLES

CONTENTS

INTRODUCTION

n 2017, I wrote an article for *Elle* magazine about the prospect of a women's museum in Washington, D.C. The proposal had been in the works for decades. The pitch had stalled. Under the then president, the federal government did not seem to feel that immortalizing women's contributions to American progress was one of its top priorities. But the would-be institution still had its backers, who were determined to see it realized.

In a show of political spin and blind optimism, some believed a new museum could even be a bipartisan effort.

For the piece, I tailed Congresswoman Carolyn Maloney of New York—one of the museum's most committed advocates. In press releases and at events, the Democrat explained that women's achievements had been diminished and overlooked for centuries. The writers of our historical record have tended to be men. In conventional meditations on power and influence, women were absent. Were it not for the painstaking work of more recent scholars, who knows whether women would ever have begun to be restored to their place in the narrative? The congresswoman wanted to build a shrine to what women had accomplished, and she wanted it on prime real estate.

Because I spent several weeks following Maloney around, I heard her make her case for the museum more than once and to several different constituencies. A stump speech for an institution.

In her remarks—delivered at luncheons and on street corners—Maloney would mention the kind of women who would be included in a museum like this one. She enumerated the credentials of people like Harriet Tubman and Eleanor Roosevelt and the tennis iconoclast Billie Jean King. She name-checked writers and artists, politicians and prize-winning scientists. She invoked the nation's children. Shouldn't there be a museum where little girls could see what their maternal forebears had accomplished?

It was around this point in her presentation that she cited the example of Sybil Ludington, a literal trailblazer at just sixteen.

The name—for me, for her audience—drew blanks. Even now, when I attempt to reconstruct the list of bona fide girls I learned about in school, I don't get far after Sacagawea and Anne Frank. Do fictional girls count? If so, I can add several romance-addled teens to the total.

I heard Ludington's name three or four times before I decided to be a responsible journalist and look her up. I googled and was impressed. Legend had it that in 1777, she outrode Paul Revere as she traveled on horseback over bad roads and in a deluge of rain to warn the troops in her father's militia. The American Battlefield Trust—an organization that exists to fund the preservation of sites of American bloodshed—recounts her ride in a sweeping narrative. It frames her as a brave and headstrong daughter of the colonies who, unlike Revere, was never captured.

I did know Paul Revere—a household name and a staple of lesson plans about the American Revolution. But Ludington had been passed over in the textbooks. She was immortalized on a United States Postal Service stamp printed in 1975, but she has otherwise never gotten her due. I felt a little miffed. A little outraged! "Where was her museum?" I wondered. Where had Ludington been when I memorized the details of the Siege of Yorktown?

I had learned other lessons. Was I in first or third or tenth grade when I internalized what girls were and were not supposed to do? Did I even need to be taught? I had been a superlative and dutiful student. I was rewarded with good grades and effusive report cards. I was a *pleasure to have* in class. I was obedient. I waited to be called on. It never occurred to me that I might want to speak out of turn. People listened to me when I talked. I wasn't conscious of it then, but I must have expected the world to continue to reward that kind of compliance.

As I sketched out the proposal to write this book—a historical account of girls' roles in American protest and a rigorous look at how the tropes of conventional girlhood have made them such able activists—I remembered Ludington and her treacherous ride. It seemed to me that both her feat and her subsequent disappearance from our historical texts summarized in one dramatic anecdote precisely the issues I wanted to consider.

She was a girl who had assumed a set of responsibilities that made grown men balk and whose apparent impulsiveness drove her to greatness. She had a name too few people knew. "Ludington remained obscured," is how the American Battlefield Trust puts it.

Hers was just the kind of narrative I hoped to include. It lent credence to a hunch I had started to formulate: that girls have been a foundational and underappreciated force in moments of American revolution—both literal and metaphorical.

I wanted to explore how girls have shaped the social and protest movements that continue to refine this still-in-progress nation—not because I believe that adults should be more like children, but because I know that in the process of learning how the world works we sometimes forget that we can remake it.

There were more obvious examples than Ludington to reach for— the girls on the forefront of climate activism, the high school students who risked their lives for civil rights, labor reformers and feminist radicals. I would get to them later.

What the Ludington example seemed to offer was something closer to biblical justification. From the founding of the United States, girls had performed these crucial, unsung duties. Ludington was like a prophetess to me. I was a New Yorker with a terrible sense of direction and no driver's license. She was a rabble-rouser before the advent of GPS. I was enthralled.

It took about ten minutes of digging into the research to hit a snag. New work had cast doubt on the idea that Ludington had ever undertaken that pivotal ride. A paper published in *The New England Quarterly* found little evidence of her expedition in contemporaneous accounts or in the books published in the aftermath of the war. Her trip appears to have first made it into the public discourse in 1880. Ludington's descendants provided another account in 1907.

Paula Hunt, who wrote the skeptical article, points to Ludington's exclusion from anthologies of women in the Revolution as evidence that she never rode. I understood the claim, but I couldn't accept it. Ludington's supposed expedition—and her omission from the kind of histories that Hunt cites—resonates because it speaks to the fate of countless women and girls whose stories we don't know. Did her absence from the record prove that she never did embark on that ride, or was it rather that in her era no one had cared to write it down? Perhaps Ludington set forth just as the USPS would have us believe. Perhaps there are discrepancies in our inherited accounts. Perhaps the truth bears no resemblance to the tale as a certain congresswoman tells it.

But Hunt has made one incontrovertible point. In her reconsideration of Ludington, she names the desire to call girls back from historical oblivion. Ludington appealed to people because she could represent their "values and beliefs" about America itself.

Without hard proof or more specific biographical detail, Ludington has been left open to interpretation. She has been made moldable, as adults so often envision girls to be. As the Cold War dragged on in the 1950s, she could function as a patriotic, pro-America teen—a feminine rebuke of Communism. With the rise of second-wave feminism, she was remade as an icon of independence. For one congresswoman, her gumption justified the construction of an entire museum on the National Mall. Who was Ludington? Whom had we needed her to be?

The more I read about her, the more I craved a definitive answer. This was back in the beginning, when I still believed that finding definitive answers was a reasonable aim. I reached out to scholars and experts. I considered whether it might serve me to file a FOIA request with the Postal Service. When I ended up on the phone with the historian Carol Berkin—who specializes in women's roles in colonial America—she admitted she had been hesitant to take the call. She told me the book sounded interesting. But Ludington was not the kind of person she felt belonged in it.

"Because she never did warn the troops?" I asked.

No, she said. Because there were other girls who contributed to the war effort, and Ludington was not perhaps the most deserving of such rapturous obsession.

Berkin has written an entire book about the the roles women held in the battle for American independence and has recorded the stories of several girls who became involved in the war. Some helped soldiers on the front lines. Some sewed at home or worked as spies. But even Berkin, trained as she is in archival research, struggled to follow her heroines after the war ended. She'd been able to pin down each of them to a shining moment, but then the trail went cold. No articles were written about the rest of their lives, let alone books. No reenactments championed their movements.

Berkin had come across a snippet of an account of one girl who had run into battle to deliver ammunition to the front lines. She could have been killed in an instant, but she believed in her cause and was willing to die for it. So she saved those soldiers—and that's all we know about her. "She just disappeared from the written record," Berkin said. She tried to track her down but found nothing. "It's as if she never existed, because there was nothing more that she was called upon to do."

It turns out that, whatever she did or didn't do, Ludington was indeed emblematic of the stories and themes I wanted to explore in this book. The metaphoric asterisk next to her sole noted achievement is a reminder that the real contributions girls have made to American social movements have too often been minimized or recast to suit even the best-intentioned political aims. She exemplifies the extent to which the impulse to turn girl activists into celebrities—or influencers, in modern parlance—neutralizes them and reduces their causes to matters of personal triumph, rather than attempts at structural progress.

She has kept me circling around the same questions that motivated this research: What has made girls such effective organizers in protest movements, from civil rights to climate justice to Black Lives Matter? Why do we champion girls who "look the part" and discard those who don't? And what does the attention we lavish on precocious girls tell us about our societal view of just-as-impassioned grown women?

Years after I first encountered Ludington, I profiled the climate activist Greta Thunberg for the cover of *Glamour*, where I was then an editor, those same questions still rattling around. For the piece, I interviewed several other prominent climate organizers. In New York, I talked to Alexandria Villaseñor, the founder of an organization called Earth Uprising, who skipped school to camp out outside the United Nations before she was old enough to vote. I called Luisa Neubauer, who advocates for divestment from fossil fuels in Berlin, and Anuna De Wever, who helped lead school strikes in Belgium.

"We like to tell people our movement doesn't have leaders," Isabelle Axelsson told me. She was eighteen at the time and had planned a series of school strikes with Thunberg in Sweden. What she meant was that people had their roles and each person complemented the rest—that while Thunberg was famous and so adept with the media, others preferred to work behind the scenes. She needed me to know that, lest I think climate activists themselves were as delusional as the press seemed to be and indeed that the future of the entire planet did rest on the shoulders of one determined girl.

Axelsson admired Thunberg; she didn't sound a single jealous note. She just hoped that the focus on Thunberg wouldn't overshadow the other work. She didn't want those who paid attention to Thunberg and who commended her speeches to mistake taking part in the spectacle for activism. Axelsson knew that cheerleading for a girl with verve could feel to some adults like an act of protest. But trumpeting Thunberg—the future!—was not the same as protecting the planet. We all have responsibilities—to the world, to one another. It is not enough to tell a girl she can do whatever she sets her mind to. It is not enough to clap because Thunberg tweets.

Axelsson told me about her peers in the movement, enumerating their varied skills, and I took down their names. The list was a roll call of impressive girls. Girls leading and speaking and agitating. Girls behind the microphones. Girls handing out the flyers.

When I interviewed De Wever, I asked what she made of the apparent overrepresentation of girls in the climate movement. I can still remember the lilt in her voice when she replied. The movement overflowed with girls. She chalked up their dominant presence to the demands that it was making of its activists. To address the climate crisis, nations and individuals would have to consume less, share more, and help one another. Some researchers have proposed a link between a willingness to act on climate and gender, finding that women are socialized to value altruism and compassion and in general to be more aware of risk.

There is no one answer to the problem of climate change, but we know this much: People will need to make hard choices in the service of a better and more stable future. That means operating in the name of the greater good.

In making the case for such an approach, organizers have no choice but to be vulnerable. To admit to fear. De Wever felt she and her peers had been raised to care for others, to be empathetic, to communicate, and—sometimes to disastrous effect—to seek approval. Those qualities made them excellent activists.

The more I read, the more people I interviewed, the clearer it was to me: The norms and social strictures that have failed women have also made some of them resolute organizers. The same conventions that were meant to rein them in have helped them crack the world open.

"This thing with men," De Wever said back then, with an exaggerated exhale. The world told them to compete and to strive "to be better and higher and earn more and produce more."

"We don't need to do that right now," she continued. "We need to rethink and take a step back. And I think women might be better at that."

When I started to work on this book, I wanted to understand how the activism that girls practice has worked—what distinguishes it and makes it unique. I opted not to use a strict age range to decide who was eligible for inclusion. Most of the stories to which I was drawn involved activists in high school and college. A few centered on girls who were ten or eleven or twelve at the time of their protests. Young, unmarried women in their twenties make occasional appearances— deemed girls per the conventions of their era.

The term "girl" is a freighted one. I think we can reclaim it. Several of the people featured in these chapters were dismissed as "mere" girls—the designation turned derisive. Dozens were underestimated. For some, girlhood was an evident and obvious asset, one that the activists themselves wanted to hold on to. Others could not wait to shed it.

Instead of a concrete definition or a litmus test, I have tried to focus on activists for whom girlhood was a motivating factor—those whose girlhood pushed them into the streets or helped them be heard. I hope I will have made a compelling case for the latitude.

With *Young and Restless*, I wanted to dissect the social forces that have made girls a cultural fixation but seldom earned them respect or power. I start with the girl laborers in the Lowell mills, who invented themselves in dress and gave themselves an adolescence before the term existed. Later, I trace the careers of girl abolitionists and student suffragists and delve into the lives of civil rights activists who became plaintiffs and protesters and Freedom Riders. I have tried to tease apart stories about second-wave feminism, which have tended to focus on disillusioned and rebellious housewives, so that I can see the girls who had their own notions about what it might take to be recognized as complete and autonomous people.

The book ends in the present. Raised in the era of Me Too, Time's Up, YouTube stars, mean tweets, and K-pop fandom–driven social media ambushes, this latest generation of girls has learned fast to hone a public voice and weaponize it. Their power can't be tabulated in "social impressions." It is felt in statehouses and town halls. It influences legislative priorities, magazine lineups, and cable news. It has for the first time in decades put the NRA on the defensive, climate deniers on their heels, and status-quo politicians on notice.

The social media—Twitter, Instagram, TikTok—that amplifies Gen Z's efforts is new. The fact that girls dream of a better world and move to realize it is not.

This book charts American girls' crusades and puts them in context. It examines the set of tools girls wield to achieve their aims—friendship, gossip, a taste for drama. It looks at the evolving response to teenage organizing—from indifference to condescension to suppression, fascination, and fetishization. And it considers how the experience of activism is different depending on the kind of girl who attempts it.

I haven't aimed to be comprehensive. (The book would need several volumes to even come close.) I chose instead to draw attention to the stories of girls whose experiences best represented to me the possibilities and perils of "girl activism."

A warning now: You will read these stories and be tempted to use words like "hero" or "icon" to describe the actions of the girls featured here. You will want to sing their deserved praises and wonder what we might do to be more like them—to channel their spirit and zeal. You might be tempted to declare that *if girls were in charge, the world would be a better place.*

But girlhood does not confer innate goodness. While I decided to focus on the stories of girls in progressive social movements, thousands of ferocious, charismatic girls have mobilized over centuries to oppose access to equal education, civil rights, women's liberation, reproductive justice, racial justice, and LGBTQ+ rights. I mention a few prominent examples in these pages, but know that there are countless more in portraits of plantation families or photos of the crowd that surrounded the Little Rock Nine in 1957. Their convictions are part of this narrative of girlhood too. Those girls also understood how their faces and bodies and dress and voices might be used to advance their own political agenda. Their stories could fill another book. It would explain so much about how we arrived at this moment in our divided America.

I do not believe that girlhood is a simple force for good in the world. I have come to think of it instead as an aperture. The people who look out and see the world through it have a perspective that others cannot access. How girls interpret the landscape that unfolds before them is their decision.

We obsess over it as a universal age. But there is no one experience of girlhood. Girls can be disrespected and condescended to, and some are still luckier than others. To be recognized as a girl or as a child at all is to be accorded a certain amount of space and time and freedom. Such liberties have not been made available to all girls—not to those whose motives we question, whose bodies don't fit our conventional standards, who are trans, who are immigrants, who are poor or marginalized, who have no choice but to take on the responsibilities of adulthood even as children.

For them, girlhood is out of reach or zoomed past. The historian Nazera Sadiq Wright calls it "premature knowing"—being forced to grow up. The fact that some of these girls claimed what would have otherwise been denied to them and used the framework of childhood to call for change is an act of tremendous courage. I hope I have honored it here.

While I worked on *Young and Restless*, dozens of people asked me versions of the same question, some with an arch smile, some in earnest, all interested in the same phenomenon. Based on the interviews and research I'd done, did I believe it was true—that the kids *were* all right? Would girls save us?

The process of writing this book has filled me with hope and admiration. Over and over, impatient girls—brimming with the determination that adolescence affords and armed with the sense of dutifulness that daughters are raised to heed—have stepped into the breach. But the question of whether girls can rescue us from our worst impulses, whether girls can compensate for our failures with the qualities we ascribe to them—sweetness, charm, righteousness? That's not the question I set out to answer.

This book is an attempt to understand the unique contributions that girls have made to America's social and protest movements and to isolate the qualities girls bring to their activism. Will girls save us? Or is it possible that we might build a better world for them?

We can marvel at our indefatigable girls. We can also help them grow up.

1

MATERIAL GIRLS

DREAMERS AND SCHEMERS AT THE
DAWN OF A LABOR MOVEMENT

From a distance, the chanting must have sounded like a school-girl's clapping game. It had the same singsong cadence and the same tune. The structure, the tempo—if we had traveled back in time to hear it ourselves, we might have felt a wave of nostalgia. Youth!

That morning in October 1836, it wasn't some classroom jailbreak that crowds on the streets were witnessing. The girls had shown up for their shifts as usual, walking in groups from their boardinghouses to the factories that housed the massive, still-new machines. But beneath the routine, an adolescent discontent was simmering. The corporations that controlled the mills had just cut wages. Worse—as the mill girl Harriet Hanson remembers in her 1898 memoir, *Loom and Spindle*—their bosses had also eliminated the housing subsidies that reduced their cost of living, leaving the workers to furnish an additional twenty-five cents for rent each month. Hanson estimated that the combination amounted to at least a dollar less for the girls each week—about half their salaries. Mill work had once seemed like salvation; this kind of humiliation demanded a response.

When the appointed hour arrived, at least fifteen hundred workers funneled out of the mills and marched down the streets of Lowell, Massachusetts. No placards or signs, just a procession of girls still dressed in their work clothes, calling out slogans and lobbing barbed couplets in the direction of their overlords. One participant delivered a speech, becoming the first woman ever to speak in public in Lowell. Others riffed on a then popular verse, oozing the dramatics of girlhood: "Oh! Isn't it a pity, such a pretty girl as I— / Should be sent to the factory to pine away and die?"

It wasn't recess or a performance, but a protest. Its organizers were farmers' daughters. Some were still in grade school. Their walkout modeled what collective action could look like on a scale that New England had almost never seen, realizing a tactic that would later become essential to the burgeoning labor movement. It would be decades before men deserted their coal mines to win a 10 percent wage hike in 1902, and several more before women and girls left their counters at the Woolworth's department store in downtown Detroit to demand a forty-hour workweek in 1937, but the lack of precedent seemed not to faze the so-called ladies of Lowell.

It was 1836 and not the most obvious historical moment for a female-led uprising. Women couldn't vote in a single state in the union. In Massachusetts, women lost their legal identities at the wedding altar, stripped of the right to hold deeds in their own names, write their own wills, and enter binding agreements. Girls had few rights and few prospects. But the Lowell girls were different. Some alchemic combination of dreams, friendship, and finances drove a workforce to its feet. For one incandescent moment, the Lowell girls were in revolt.

THE FIRST TEXTILE FACTORIES opened in the United States in the 1820s, and their establishment marked the start of a new era in American manufacturing. Their mastermind was the merchant and industrialist Francis Cabot Lowell, who'd seen, on a recent trip to England, how advanced British factories had become.

Across the Atlantic, machines were now capable of outproducing families and small shops. Individuals couldn't hope to compete. When he returned to America, Lowell set out to build his own mills, which would adapt and improve on the power looms he had visited abroad. His death in 1817 didn't slow the pace of the business; factories were built all over the state, drawing on power generated from its rivers. In 1823, one of the most prominent was erected in Lowell, the town named in his honor. Over time, Lowell's partners moved north and incorporated more land on the banks of the ferocious Merrimack River. Within two decades, the area was home to more than twenty-five factories and eight thousand textile workers, most of them women and girls. The influx was so rapid and pronounced that the town of Lowell soon had the second-largest population in the state.

Unlike their fathers and grandfathers, the girls who traveled to Massachusetts to operate the mills did not come with patriotic zeal and plans for war. The oldest of those first hires were in their twenties. Girls found work too; Harriet Hanson was ten. Not one would have expected to have what we would now call a career. There were no ladders to climb or balances to strike between work and home. No one set out to "have it all." The girls' ambitions were far more modest. When the factories opened their doors, a full workweek paid about two dollars. The salaries could amount to a small fortune for the good girls of New England. Some used their wages to support their families. Others took themselves on shopping excursions in town. Girls bought gold watches, new skirts and dresses, clothes for their siblings, food for their mothers, books, and magazines. Their income paid for their education. It paid for sweets.

The mills were not a social project. But the decision to hire the girls who would make up the nation's first large-scale industrial labor force was cast in almost moral terms—another stroke of Lowell genius. While he was in England, Lowell had seen the barbaric conditions in which children were made to work. Factories were decrepit and dangerous. Kids got sick and died. Their families—desperate, often starving—were helpless. The operation might have turned a profit, but it didn't look good. Lowell decided that his mills would be run without such crude labor. Instead, he'd hire girls—a touch older—and treat them better. Trust an American to make the inherent woes of capitalism look at least a little more presentable. He theorized that opportunities in the mills would accrue to the girls' benefit—in actual dollars and cents as well as in something harder to name. It wasn't reckless endangerment, but self-improvement. The daughters of rich men had their finishing schools and their etiquette lessons. Now the daughters of farmers would have factories. Lowell would create the low-paid internship of the era. When the novelist Anthony Trollope published his book *North America* in 1862, he describes the town's workforce as "taken in, as it were, to a philanthropical manufacturing college."

In one sense, "college"—with its implication of a time-bound education—was an apt metaphor. Lowell had never intended to hire a permanent workforce. Mill girls were meant to age out of their duties, with married life waiting for them on the other side of their efforts. Lowell envisioned the job as a holding pattern, meant to fill the still-amorphous time between childhood and womanhood with work, education, and a little cash.

In turning to girls, Lowell solved several problems at once. Other mills relied on skilled labor to produce finer material than Lowell planned to churn out. Those workers expected to be paid more and required specialized training. In Rhode Island, another magnate had attempted to institute an apprentice approach and, when that failed, hired entire families to work together in his mills, from little children to elders. But he couldn't hold on to his workers. His habit of designating whipping rooms for corporal punishment could not have helped with retention. What Lowell understood was that farmers—suspicious of the massive new mills and of committing to weaving work that was coded as feminine—were not eager to trade in the freedom of running their own land for spinning thread. Moreover, the same men needed something to do with their daughters. Girls were an able population, and it was accepted as a simple fact that those who weren't occupied with honest, respectable toil and chores were liable to give in to temptation, drain their parents' resources, and otherwise burden those around them with their whims and habits. Girls were a problem. Lowell had a solution: Send them here.

In mill towns, houses were built to accommodate them. Schedules and rules were constructed to overemphasize to parents that their children would be protected and *monitored* even fifty or a hundred miles from home. Churches were built. Housemothers were hired. Within the decade, daughters poured in. When one arrived in Lowell or in other towns like it, she'd meet hundreds more just like her. Soon she might recruit relatives or friends to join her, creating a small clutch of allies in what could be a competitive environment.

For girls who had been raised on isolated farms in an era that predated even the establishment of a federal Department of Education, the mills created a unique and delicate social experience: the closest the workers could get to something like high school. In Lowell, working and living and sleeping and eating happened with peers instead of families. Learning happened like that too. The mills were not a prep school, but time there could serve as a launchpad. The mill worker Laura Nichols came to the factories with her future in mind. She labored in Connecticut until she saved the then enormous sum of fifty dollars. After that, she quit and enrolled in a still-new school for women: the fledgling Mount Holyoke College. Nichols graduated in 1854, a member of one of its earliest classes.

If parents now see independence as a value worth instilling in their children, the earliest American child-rearing books—released just as the mills were opening—begged to differ. The aim was not to raise freethinking, liberated children but obedient ones. The influence of peers could be corrosive, threatening to compromise critical ties between parents and children as it bolstered those between friends. In Lydia Child's formative *The Mother's Book*, the popular writer expresses her particular distaste for the "new custom" of holding parties for children that their friends attended. The whole concept validated the idea that children should spend time with and define their social lives in terms of their peers: unacceptable. Books aimed at older kids stressed that the transition from childhood to adulthood would leave them vulnerable and open to outside influence, and it was best for them to follow instead in the well-trod footsteps of their elders. These books, with titles like *Lectures to Young Men* and *The Young Lady's Companion*, urged them to be vigilant and measured in the face of "various impulses, wild desires, [and] restless cravings." It cautioned them against reckless behavior, like, for example, walking off their jobs.

The books anticipated—and did nothing to stave off—an imminent cultural shift in which children realized that the impressions and values of their peers were far more consequential than the opinions of their parents.

In Lowell, the future had arrived. The girls had the shared hobbies and peer orientation that Child feared. The work gave them common interests, and while their income didn't quite endow them with political capital, it did grant them social and commercial relevance. Lowell's technological innovations put the mills on the map. Its workers turned it into a spectacle. Such is the effect of cramming thousands of pink-cheeked white girls into a few square miles: Men will come to stare.

The writer James Fenimore Cooper declared that no one could compete with the allure of an American girl between the ages of fifteen and eighteen—an unfortunate age bracket for a grown man to single out for its appeal. In June 1833, President Andrew Jackson visited the area, and the girls dressed in white, wore colored sashes, and held parasols to march in a welcome parade in his honor. In the crowd, someone marveled at this "mile of girls." The poet John Greenleaf Whittier would later become disenchanted with mill life, but he too was at first mesmerized. The sheer number of *girls*! "Acres of girlhood," he wrote. He compares them to "flowers gathered from a thousand hill-sides and green vallies of New England"—buds blooming with promise, primed to be plucked and swept up into a bouquet.

In his book *The Belles of New England*, William Moran writes that the mill girls were members of "a class of women the nation idolized." While wealthier women were shut up behind closed doors, these laborers were beginning to capture the national imagination in public view. That perch earned them fans, but it also made their status precarious. In working outside the home, American girls became visible, scrutinized, idealized, and sometimes suspect. Fears about sex and fallen women turned up as much in the press as in the era's fiction. The historian Lori Merish contends that "seduction narratives about Lowell women were a staple of the sensationalist press." The "determinist narratives" traced with some measure of zeal a woman's decline "from seduction to unwed motherhood to prostitution and often death." These at-odds attitudes—were the girls the pride of their fellow citizens or proof of national ruin?—had a consistent through line: Girls were precious and valuable and pure. The risk of their defilement, with its consequences for the nation, was real.

Charles Dickens—a vocal critic of the gruesome English factories—visited the mills to assess similar worries and found them put to rest. In the crowd of laborers, some of whom were "verging upon womanhood," he claimed to see not one in need of his rescue. No face gave Dickens "a painful impression." He observed their "serviceable bonnets, good warm cloaks, and shawls," and the fact that there was even a coatroom in the mills for girls to store their belongings before heading into work. The workers had retained "the manners and deportment" of women, "not of degraded brutes of burden."

No doubt his report calmed the nerves of New Englanders, who were consumed with the idea that mill work might render some of their finest specimens undesirable or, per the experts in American childhood, ungovernable.

With the anxieties of a nation somewhat quelled, corporations didn't have to make the hard sell to would-be workers. Nathan Appleton, who had been a partner to Lowell and continued running the business after Lowell's death, took tremendous, rather paternalistic pride in the entire operation. "Here was in New England a fund of labor, well educated and virtuous," he said. And like Dickens—albeit with a greater stake in the outcome—he was determined to prove that earning their own keep would not "deteriorate the character" of his unblemished workforce. The message worked. Broadsides advertised jobs for girls and women between the ages of fifteen and thirty-five. Locals swarmed.

Harriet Hanson started in the Lowell mills in 1835, having moved to the area in 1832. She spent over a decade on the rolls, supporting her mother and her three siblings after her father died. At first, she worked for nine months and attended school during the other three, as the corporation operating the mills mandated. After she turned fifteen, she worked full time.

In her book, she describes the decision to look for work as her own choice—an "urgent request" that her mother granted despite Hanson's age. It sounds the explanation of a dutiful, protective daughter. But Hanson would have had her own motivations for leaving home for the mills. With her mother responsible for keeping the children together, Hanson's home had been converted into a boardinghouse. That meant "unrelenting household labor"—as the historian Claudia Bushman puts it in her book about Hanson—for the Hanson children, who were expected to help attend to the forty or so people living with them at any given time.

So the prospect of working in the mills didn't just mean cash. It meant a break. Hanson's work as a "doffer" required her to spend about fifteen minutes per hour replacing the bobbins on the looms. The remainder—relative free time—time opened her up to a world outside the domestic sphere.

It sounds odd to the modern ear that Hanson would have found more leisure working in factories than laboring at home. But when she joined—and let it be known that this particular version of mill work would not last—being a mill girl did mean escaping the domestic grind.

The factors that drove Hanson to the mills were common. Dead fathers meant almost certain financial hardship for families who had depended on their income. And sending a child to the mills meant one fewer mouth to feed at home. But no one explanation accounts for the sheer number of girls who descended on Lowell—or for their eventual rebellion. Newspapers extolled the virtue of honest workers. Personal narratives like the one Hanson later published recounted losses that compelled children to find work. Some girls wanted to escape broken families or abusive relatives. Others savored the small freedoms that their labor secured them.

In the beginning, the press was so fawning and the girls were described as so appreciative that it's hard to point to the precise moment it all went sour. What laid the groundwork for the strikes? Where had unhappiness festered? Conditions had started to deteriorate, which did not help. Utopian visions were colliding with corporate realities. And then there was the shopping.

In his review of the letters that female textile workers sent between 1830 and 1860, the historian Thomas Dublin finds that most of the girls came to Lowell with a definite plan for their wages, expressed in detail in their correspondence. In his breakdown, he identifies three of the most common line items: education, dowries, and clothes. Some girls did work to support their families, as Hanson had. But Dublin writes that in contrast to European women, whose work outside the home was considered an extension of their households, American mill girls did not believe their income was owed to their families. Their work, their cash.

It sounds like semantics, but it represented a monumental shift. Now when wages were reduced, the injustice was not just practical and financial but personal. Young women had come to view their recompense as a deserved reward for their own hard work. Spending it was in that sense a form of self-actualization. Being denied it was a violation of what some were just starting to think of as their rights.

In histories of the Lowell mills and the girls who worked in them, this point—this revolution!—gets short shrift. The strikes are flashier. But the books and the articles and the poems that the girls would go on to publish seem more revealing. Credit to Dublin, the rare man who understands just how crucial the matter of financial liberation would have been to a group of American girls and how much havoc a reversal of that fortune had the potential to wreak.

Dublin stands apart because people tend to think of girls and their material preoccupations as frivolous. Conventional thinking mandates that if we are to learn from the stories of the mill girls, we must avert our gaze from their embarrassing wants. At best, such fixations are distractions. At worst, the prospect of them is a threat.

Fears about shopping-obsessed girls date back to the seventeenth and eighteenth centuries, when colonial women started to demonstrate an enthusiastic appetite for British imports, and panicked men worried about where such an investment in self-presentation could lead. That same uneasiness recurs in stories about girls who seek to control their own appearance, often manifesting as disdain. We who are not so skeptical of girls and their talents tend to just ignore their shopping habits. Isn't there so much else to focus on?

But to accept the premise that shopping is beside the point is to miss—or dismiss—the fact that even an exploitative marketplace can foster a certain kind of power in its consumers. In the dawning awareness of the value of their dollars, girls were able for the first time to think of themselves as independent constituents.

The streets in Lowell were lined with shops that confirmed their purchasing power: satin, silks, and lace for sale on Central Street. Fine hats at the corner of Merrimack and Kirk. Boots and shoes at the

American House Block. When the stores were closed after hours, the process of self-improvement continued. Girls were invited to attend lectures on literature and art. Season tickets were issued for a nominal fee. The boardinghouses were low on amenities, but included in the price of room and board was access to libraries. Hanson writes in her memoir that word of their existence traveled. Without the work and the "advantages to be found there," she writes, some girls would have been stuck "in secluded parts of New England, where books were scarce." At one point, Ralph Waldo Emerson came to deliver a speech to the mill girls. So did Edgar Allan Poe. A Harvard professor recalled how the girls would take notes when a lecturer spoke, their attention so focused and rapt that he claimed never to have seen another group compare—not even his own esteemed students. The farms had been quiet; the town bustled.

These twin pursuits—material and academic acquisitions—stemmed from the same desire: to participate in self-invention. Fashionable dress and bookish interests became obsessions for women in search of their own identities. Affluent women kicked off the trend, defining themselves according to the contents of their bookshelves and closets. Wageworkers in Lowell could follow in their well-heeled footsteps. The girls now shared the expectation that developing as a person was an enterprise that required material investment.

In 1845, one worker articulated just that: "What expansion of mind!—what awakening of dormant powers!" she wrote. "Wellington was not prouder, when he gained the field of Waterloo, than I was with that gown." With dollars to spend, the operatives got to work.

OF COURSE, it wasn't all mood-boosting dresses and slumber parties. Despite the relative leisure that girls like Hanson savored compared with children who grew up on farms, bells tolled at five a.m. Curfew was not until nine p.m. Tasks were repetitive and monotonous. The noise was inescapable, and the air was thick with dust and thread and cloth. People died in the mills or were wounded. Girls boarded up to six to a bedroom, and for all the praise that would be heaped on the Lowell model, the exhausting workweek did not leave much time to pursue other interests, let alone to dress for them.

The appeal of the mills had been that it did not take particular or specialized knowledge to do the work. The low barrier kept the dream of earning potential alive for thousands of otherwise unskilled girls. It also meant that workers had little clout once on the rolls. Turnover was a constant, and replacements arrived all the time. Workers who were dissatisfied with the job or its conditions had no recourse. And mills faced growing pressure to increase their output. With the mushrooming of factories came fierce competition between them as overproduction drove down the price of finished cloth. The profits that the first industrialists had raked in became inconceivable, and workers bore the brunt. Conditions deteriorated. Wages were slashed. Recognizing the limitation of their individual power, the girls reached for a more collective tool. A unilateral withdrawal. A walkout.

Because Lowell had been the model and the jewel of the mill towns, conditions tended to be better there than in smaller satellites. When the discontent started to bubble over, it hit those less distinguished mills first. In Dover, hundreds of girls walked out for the first time in 1828—a reaction to a harsh fine that would dock wages for workers who came in after the opening bell stopped ringing. In 1829, sixty weavers left their looms in the Taunton mills in response to an announced wage cut, forcing a partial shutdown across the factories.

Lowell survived the decade without disruption, but in 1834, overseers announced wage cuts. Reductions were supposed to be gradual and rolled out over time, but it was clear that the workers had been underestimated. The girls were incensed at the mere prospect of their implementation. Faced with an incandescent workforce, the bosses decided to effect the full cut at once—the "let's-get-it-over-with" school of management. The response was no less furious. Meetings were held. Plans were drawn up. The *Boston Evening Transcript* reported that one of the workers suggested mass resignations, which would induce a run on the local banks. She was fired, but when word of her dismissal got out, a procession of eight hundred girls marched in a show of support. Enough withdrew their savings that the Lowell Bank had to reach out to Boston branches to keep cash in circulation.

That same weekend, workers issued a proclamation, staking out their position: "Our present object is to have union and exertion, and we remain in possession of our own unquestionable rights. We circulate this paper, wishing to obtain the names of all who imbibe the spirit of our Patriotic Ancestors, who preferred privation to bondage, and parted with all that renders life desirable—and even life itself—to procure independence for their children."

It was quite a declaration for citizens who did not in fact share in the same "unquestionable rights" as their brothers and fathers, and who, as women and girls in their teens and twenties, would not live to see the Nineteenth Amendment ratified. The protest turned out to be a short-lived albeit bold war of independence. Within the week, most of the strikers had returned to the mills. A few did quit their jobs. The factories had no trouble maintaining their output.

When another protest erupted in the fall of 1836, the overseers were not quite as fortunate. Hanson recalled how word spread through the mills in advance, as transmissible and potent as the best gossip. The action this time would attract almost double the number of workers, totaling between twelve hundred and fifteen hundred deserters. The looms would have to be powered down that October, unable to function without their girl minders.

In the room where Hanson worked, some waffled. Was it a good idea? How much trouble would it cause? Hanson remembered her horror. After all that talk! "Not one of them having the courage to lead [it] off, I . . . became impatient, and started on ahead," she wrote.

Brimming with what she later called "childish bravado," Hanson told them she would walk out even if she had to do it alone. She marched through the door, not waiting to see who would join her. Behold the real-time awareness that a girl has more power than she thinks. In *Loom and Spindle*, the moment still seems to shimmer: "As I looked back at the long line that followed me, I was more proud than I have ever been since."

Hanson was eleven.

For weeks, the mills remained understaffed. Protesters formed the Lowell Factory Girls Association, a de facto union for mill workers, to capitalize on the momentum. The new organization circulated a proper constitution, complete with a stirring preamble. The text testified to the shared aims of its members. It pledged a "females irrefragable vow" that each worker would undertake to help her neighbor. It insisted that workers "administer to each others wants, to prevent each others back-sliding—to comfort each other in sickness, and advise each other in health, to incite each other to the love and attainment of those excellences, which can alone constitute the perfection of female character."

Here was a worker and a new kind of American girl. Hear her roar.

INDEED, PEOPLE HEARD. In Lowell, girls read and wrote to understand themselves. Bored doffers stationed around the mills pinned poems to their machines and hid paper scraps in their workstations to scribble on. Since books were forbidden in most factories, pieces of paper or newsprint became the workaround—a self-guided enrichment course for those who knew where to look.

One worker tore up the works of John Locke and carried a page or two at a time into work, reading his words until she mastered his thinking. Another memorized the Bible. Some wrote their own stories, imaginations whirring.

In retrospect, it seems inevitable that such creative impulses would inspire the Lowell workers to do what thousands of underresourced, underappreciated teenagers later would. In 1840, the mill girls started a zine. It was called *The Lowell Offering* and came out of a merger between two existent magazines—one that a local preacher named Abel Charles Thomas had started, and one called *The Operatives' Magazine*, which two mill girls edited. Once the two publications joined forces, the girls took over, and *The Lowell Offering* became the nation's first magazine with an all-female staff—an apparent improvement over the previous management. In her memoir, *A New England Girlhood*, which chronicled her own time in the mills, the writer Lucy Larcom noted that "people seemed to be more interested in it after it passed entirely into the hands of the girls themselves."

The Offering was not some mouthpiece for the risible proletariat. Although the issue of lower wages remained ever relevant, the magazine tiptoed around topics that could offend the corporations. Its tone was sentimental, romantic, sometimes maudlin, and often fanciful. The girls who produced it did not, however, see it as a superficial diversion. Larcom wrote that *The Offering* was proof that she and her peers were thinking people who cared about "solid and serious matters." In certain stories, writers nodded to their less-than-agreeable working conditions. Later, another worker-led publication called *The Voice of Industry* would be far blunter in its criticism.

The Offering toed the line. But it is impossible for a girl-led publication to be less than radical. Its existence argued that girls have voices deserving of their own platform. *The Offering* found thousands of readers in New England. It courted a wider audience too—one that included men. Charles Dickens was an admirer. The preacher William Ellery Channing and the famed newspaper editor and publisher Horace Greeley were both patrons. Its writers must have seen no reason that even the old and grown and male should not be readers and supporters of their work.

Larcom started as a doffer at the Boott Mills in Lowell in 1835. She was, like Hanson, the daughter of a boardinghouse keeper and a dead father. Her mother had also taken the job to keep her children together. Larcom was eleven when she walked into the mills. She was twenty-one when she quit. In that decade, she took German classes and algebra lessons. She attended "improvement circles," in which girls convened between dinner and curfew to discuss books and debate issues like abolition and women's rights. Of course, she wrote for *The Offering*.

The magazine's prospectus made its intentions plain. The staff described its enterprise as essential to the maintenance of still-new and fledgling democratic ideals:

> Other nations can look upon the relics of a glory which has come and gone—upon their magnificent ruins—upon worn-out institutions, not only tolerated, but hallowed because they are old. . . . We have other and better things. Let us look upon our Lyceums, our Common Schools, our Mechanics' Literary Associations, the Periodical of our Laboring Females; upon all that is indigenous to our Republic, and say, with the spirit of Roman Cornelia, "These, *these are our jewels.*"

The historian Sylvia Jenkins Cook, who studies the relationship among fashion, reading, and women's burgeoning identities, writes that Lowell girls used *The Offering* to make sense of the incongruities inherent in their own circumstances, signaling "their acute consciousness of the larger changes" that their unique position "represented for them as workers, women, and authors."

At once producers and consumers—both under the surveillance of others and observers of their own experiences—girls found the magazine gave them a space to explore their tenuous social place.

One writer composed a meta piece in which she considered possible subjects for a submission and so made fun of the themes that came up again and again in the pages of *The Offering*: "There were 'the beauties of nature,' the pleasures of home, hope, memory, the stars, the ocean, the birds and flowers," she wrote. She dismissed each one. What could she add to the discussion of such well-trod topics? She wanted to write something *new*.

Another contributor composed a satirical letter about how hard it was to live up to expectations of workers as "mind[s] among the mills." How much did a girl need to prove?

In a forerunner to those popular staples of women's media in which women detail their spending habits for a week, an editor ran an article in which she invited four workers to discuss their planned uses for a week's wages. Their responses included: a shawl, reading material, depositing it in a savings account, and making a charitable donation.

There were no lifeguard jobs in 1835 and no opportunities to make friends with the other waitresses at the local diner. Hanson and Larcom labored at a time when teenagers as we now know them did not exist. There was no appreciation of the developmental epoch between childhood and adulthood. The idea of adolescence as a period of distinct developmental growth would not come into being until a researcher named it in 1904.

The mills were not high school. But working in them did more than appeal to the kind of girl who might not even have had the language to describe the relative independence—financial and social— she craved. It helped to create her.

HERE IS THE PLACE to note that the 1836 strike failed. Did it seem as if we were hurtling toward our spirited girl-power conclusion? All that pomp and circumstance didn't take. Work hours were not reduced. Conditions did not improve. Hanson is frank in her memoir: "So far as results were concerned this strike did no good."

For Hanson, the consequences were grave. Hanson's mother was fired from her boardinghouse, with a representative from the corporation telling her that while no one could have expected her to prevent the girls who happened to live under her roof from walking out, she should at least have controlled her own daughter.

Workers who mounted similar protests throughout New England did not fare much better. It didn't help their cause that those who participated had few friends in the media. In 1828, when laborers "turned out" of the Cocheco Mills in New Hampshire, *The Dover Enquirer* blamed the action on "some imaginary grievance" and ruled that "*turned out* to their cost, as well as disgrace." The newspaper added that the girls' half-mile procession "presented one of the most disgusting scenes ever witnessed." After the demonstrations in Lowell, strikes were planned in Lawrence and Nashua; those too were busts.

The most substantial concession the Lowell girls won was the kind of rhetorical consolation prize well known to precocious girls. After the 1836 walkout, a Lowell mill boss reported that the workers "manifest *good spunk.*" That quasi-compliment did not lead to material improvements. Soon the alliance the girls had established fell apart. The supposed values on which the mills had claimed to be built faded too.

Newspapers started to question whether New England's finest belonged in factories at all. Was there not someone less photogenic capable of doing the job? In 1846, a reporter visited the Lowell mills and noted that the girls laboring in them would become wives and mothers. The American project depended on them. The writer frames "the preservation of their constitution" as "the highest public importance." In 1847, the same newspaper covered the debate over a labor law in New Hampshire and insisted that girls needed to be better "shielded from the life-long evils which result from . . . severe or protracted toil." Were the mills the best incubator for the future of the nation?

Putting good white girls to work had forever been a tightrope walk. The girls had to be exalted without being allowed to amass real power or influence. And for the sake of the PR push, as much distance as possible had to be placed between the girls and the enslaved people who produced the cotton that the mills wove. But there was no circumventing the truth: the work was compromised. When the mills first opened, a popular song protested too much. After two stanzas about the girls' overall health and cheerfulness, the last reads:

> *O sing me a song of the Factory Girl!*
> *Link not her name with the SLAVES.—*
> *She is brave and free as the old elm tree,*
> *That over her homestead waves.*

Let the capitalization be a clue: Anxieties abounded about the relationship between the work girls did in factories and the brutal conditions enslaved people were forced to endure to produce their raw material. The public picture of the workers as chaste and respectable coupled with their unimpeachable whiteness was supposed to help "manage the racial intimacies of the cotton textile trade," as Lori Merish has written. Alas, the stain was evident.

Whatever moral character the mill owners might have wanted to claim, their margins were dependent on slave labor. In a poem, Larcom later questioned how complicit she had been:

> When I've thought,
> Miss Willoughby, what soil the cotton-plant
> We weave, is rooted in, what waters it,—
> The blood of souls in bondage,—I have felt
> That I was sinning against light, to stay
> And turn the accursed fibre in cloth

Elsewhere, workers probed the idea of their supposed specialness. It no longer felt so notable to be a mill girl. In *The Voice of Industry*, one worker wrote, "This talk about the continued prosperity, happy condition, and future independence of the producing class of this country, as a class, is all fiction, moonshine."

A poem submitted to the magazine reads, in part:

> And amidst the clashing noise and din
> Of the ever beating loom,
> Stood a fair young girl with throbbing brow,
> Working her way to the tomb.

Their growing despair did not stave off further wage cuts or reduce their hours. But the squeeze did push the New England–born workforce to look for opportunities elsewhere. Protest is an investment of time as well as resources. Most girls lacked both and left the mills after a few seasons.

Not long after the first failed strikes, cities grew and industrialization created a permanent and urban working class. Girls who were working at fifteen or nineteen would often still be working at thirty or forty. Fewer people thought of those women as the wives and mothers of the nation. The share of women workers in the mills in Massachusetts fell too. Women accounted for 80 percent of all workers in 1831. That number was reduced to 62 percent in 1865. Hanson wrote that "after a time, as the wages became more and more reduced, the best portion of the girls left and went to their homes." Others found jobs in newer industries that were "fast opening to women," like teaching and nursing. The "old guard" moved on. Even the improvement circles that had once been a staple of the sales pitch to would-be workers disbanded.

In 1949, the writer Hannah Josephson released a book about the New England mill girls. She observed that workers paid the price for the factories' struggles. The workers "fought a dignified campaign to regain their old standards." But when it failed, the girls left. Or as Josephson puts it: "retired from the scene."

In 1845, *The Offering* published its last issue. In 1846, the militant reformer Sarah Bagley, who had cofounded *The Voice*, moved on from the labor movement. She opened a telegraph office and became one of America's first women telegraph operators. The reformer association she had championed waned in significance without her.

With the end of the decade came the end of the experiment in Lowell as it had been conceived. It was a bleak conclusion and most discouraging for the immigrant and working-class women who now labored under deteriorating conditions. (Fewer writers were wringing their hands over what negative effects the work might have on these women.)

Still, the first recruits to the mills made their mark. For a little less than two decades, a generation of girls learned, worked, wrote, socialized, slept, ate, and resisted within a few square miles. The close quarters bred if not deep friendship then insistent, shared determination. When someone was sick, another worker would cover her loom so that no one missed wages. In their limited free time, the girls traveled in groups to shops, church, and lectures. Thomas Dublin attributed the formation of such tight-knit communities to one simple, unusual factor: These insular worlds developed in a place in which women lived and worked together around the clock. It was a remarkable arrangement.

Before Lowell—with the exception of the wealthiest women's tearooms and parlors—there were almost no spaces in which girls could gather as a group. After Lowell, that irreducible, maddening unit— the girl gang—would become a fact of the adolescent female experience and a fearsome force in American life. In his introduction to a collection of writings on life in the New England factories, the labor historian Philip Foner notes that it became clear to the girls that corporations were capitalizing on them—good girls, whose hard work would be rewarded with an education. "It did not take long for them to realize," he writes, "that a favorable image was no compensation for exploitation."

We know as much as we do about the Lowell mill girls because some made sure we had a record. In their written work and in their speeches, the workers expressed their opinions and aspirations. In the grand tradition of judgmental teenagers, some expressed their scorn. Hanson remarked that the clothes as much as the dialects of one recent set of Lowell recruits were "peculiar." Their dresses were made of the "plainest of homespun" and cut in an outdated pattern. The girls looked like the kind who might have "borrowed her grandmother's gown," she added. The snark still oozes cool-girl frostiness. But the jab is also revealing: Lowell girls did not have to wear hand-me-downs.

Born in an era in which ministers instructed women to be silent if men were present in church, girls who labored in Lowell in that first phase of its existence grew up with a keen sense of themselves—of the power of not just their appearances but their voices and their dollars.

That nerve remained with them. Sarah Bagley—who was older than Hanson and Larcom when she started working—recalled how repetitive tasks gave her the mental space she needed to think and strategize. With machines roaring, the mills became for her a "pleasant place for contemplation." She did not make small talk. She schemed. Charged with "but one kind of labor to perform," she felt as if her mind had been left "free for reflection on other matters."

She was not alone. Alumni of *The Offering*—who represented a fraction of the mill workforce as a whole—made a disproportionate mark in the fields of art, education, and literature. Larcom and Hanson had both been involved in the magazine. Larcom became a teacher, poet, and author, and later cofounded a student magazine after taking a job at Wheaton College. The journal continues to publish. Harriet Hanson Robinson became an ardent and active suffragist, instrumental in the founding of the New England Women's Club and the Massachusetts chapter of the National Woman Suffrage Association. The mill worker Harriet Curtis wrote novels and became a political commentator and newspaper correspondent. Eliza Cate published eight books. Other contributors became educators. Abba Ann Goddard was a writer and served as a nurse in the Civil War.

In 1978, two books would anthologize the work of the mill girls.

The women's liberation movement was in full swing. Books about women who had stood up for themselves had an obvious audience. But so few women's histories had ever been recorded. The mill girls—in their determination both to build a new world and inhabit it and to narrate their own efforts—still resonated. "Here and there among these diversified documents we glimpse the first seeds of the . . . evolving feminist," wrote a reviewer in *The New York Times*. "There is talk of sisterhood, of the need to unite, of the battle to maintain self-respect in the face of imminent defeat." He—and it was indeed a man who had been tasked with evaluating the merit of their work—called *The Offering* an "invaluable tool." The magazine had "provided its contributors, editors and readers with a voice and sounding board where before there had been only a void."

Hanson's and Larcom's memoirs present two of the most enduring accounts of mill life, and both writers went on to make peace with their working past. It had not all been good, but it shaped them. Their books are not contemporaneous diaries, recording the small humiliations, triumphs, injuries, and boredom of their adolescence, but reflections. Suffering is alchemized into grit. Childhood trials produce women of value. The retrospective lens helps. The mills made them. Others were left broken.

Well over a thousand girls and women marched out of the factories in 1834 and 1836. We know the names of only a handful. Some became suffragists or abolitionists or poets like Larcom, building on a foundation of outspokenness and imagination learned as girls. Hundreds more lived lives we will never know about. What power did the girls have in the end? The power to walk out but not the power to grow up into independent adult women. The power to earn a taxable income but not the power to vote.

In the mills, weavers used to breathe in lint as they sucked thread through the wooden shuttles that fed into the looms. The phenomenon was called the "kiss of death," quite a name for an affliction that befell women and girls whose "virtue" was supposed to be protected at all costs. A doctor who saw mill workers reported that some of his patients vomited up balls of cotton. Per one report, 70 percent of mill workers died of lung-related diseases, compared with 4 percent of Massachusetts farmers.

In the decades that followed, the situation for laborers worsened. Technological inventions encouraged faster and cheaper production. There were more strikes, more tragedies, more crackdowns. In 1911, the Triangle Shirtwaist Factory fire publicized the brutal work conditions of a labor force made up of an overwhelming number of women. It produced indelible photos of girls leaping to their deaths to escape the flames. *The New York Times* reported that five of them on the Greene Street side of the building had jumped together, "clinging to each other, with fire streaming back from their hair and dresses."

Yes, the mills gave some workers the chance to test their mettle. The enterprise also showed owners that much of the power remained theirs. The mills were not schools. Their aim was not humanitarian or philanthropic, no matter how the PR apparatus tried to spin it. But in an era that offered girls zero opportunities to be heard in public or even to find their own voices in private, the factories offered something concrete. The mills became a place to explore ideas about labor and worth, to test and narrate notions of desire and romance, to develop independent identities.

For the most fortunate workers, the mills were more than a job. When Harriet Hanson left to wed the journalist and abolitionist William Stevens Robinson in 1848, she did not see it as quitting. In her memoir, she writes she had been given an "honorable discharge." She had trained. She had served well.

Scores of mill girls opted not to return to their childhood farms after their stints in the mills ended. Most, like Hanson, married. Some became schoolteachers or entered seminaries for women—forerunners to the women's colleges that would open later. Larcom went on to befriend the poet John Greenleaf Whittier, who had once found the Lowell girls so captivating.

When she wrote about her time in the factories, Larcom tried to explain what the experience meant to her: "I felt that I belonged to the world, that there was something for me to do in it, though I had not yet found out what. Something to do; it might be very little, but still it would be my own work."

2

THE MOUTH ON THAT GIRL

ANNA ELIZABETH DICKINSON
AND A NATION AT WAR

She was called America's Joan of Arc—a title bestowed upon her before it became clear that she too would be made to suffer for her visions. Like her namesake, she could drive grown men into battle and make her disciples cower. She did not claim divine inspiration. But she did speak with all the fervor of an evangelist.

Anna Elizabeth Dickinson was born in Philadelphia in 1842, the fifth child of committed Quaker abolitionists. Her life was a series of achievements we now trumpet on magazine covers: She defied the conventions of her era and wrote and published under her own name. She scored a clerk's position with the United States Mint at eighteen, a rare professional achievement for a woman at the time. She became the first woman ever to address the U.S. House of Representatives. Dickinson was paid for her speeches. She was a relentless advocate for abolition and a devout Republican—a pundit long before the advent of cable television. She was so popular that she outearned not just famous activists but Mark Twain. She had a presence and a mission. The word "precocious" appears in the first dozen sentences of the most comprehensive biographical treatment of her to date.

No wonder. The term was invented to describe someone like Dickinson. She overcame circumstances that would have sunk a less determined child. Her father died when she was a toddler. He had a heart attack in the middle of an abolitionist meeting. It was said that his speech was so vehement that it killed him. His death thrust Dickinson's mother into immediate financial precariousness. With her limited choices, she did as Harriet Hanson's mother had: She took in boarders to support her children and keep her household solvent. In a moment of desperation, she operated a small school out of the living room.

Dickinson concluded her formal education in her teens. She needed to work. Later, Dickinson would exchange letters with the progressive journalist Ida Tarbell, who expressed interest in her career at a time when most spurned her. In looping script, Dickinson recalled her determination to stand on her "own feet" and added that she had been unwilling to wait for someone to give her permission to strike out on her own. She told Tarbell she believed even then that "a girl could and should make her own way in the world as surely as a boy."

The independent streak was her birthright. Dickinson had grown up in a house that welcomed outspoken visitors. Frederick Douglass and Robert Purvis had sat in the parlor; her parents' home was a stop on the Underground Railroad, providing haven to enslaved people escaping the South. In Philadelphia, her parents weren't outliers. While local elected officials proposed their share of racist laws, the area was and remained a nerve center for the abolitionist cause. It was notable too for the number of women who participated in the operation. In 1833, twenty-nine women, most of them Black or white

Quakers, formed the Philadelphia Female Anti-Slavery Society. Lucretia Mott was a member; so was Angelina Grimké. The association became one of the first interracial organizations to recognize Black women as leaders. Others soon followed. The network bolstered a class of women who were used to writing their own charters and constitutions, setting their own ground rules, and being heard.

Dickinson, a product of that milieu, wasted no time in speaking up for herself. Her first published opinion writing was printed in response to an article in *The Liberator*, William Lloyd Garrison's esteemed pro-abolition newspaper. The piece described what had happened to a schoolteacher who'd voiced his own abolitionist views in Kentucky. For the crime of his pluck and honesty, he had been tarred and feathered. Dickinson was furious. She noted with disdain that the barbarians were residents of a state that believed itself to be liberal and evolved, even as it continued to sell human beings within its borders. In her letter, she seemed at least as irate about that kind of posturing as she was about the incident itself. It was so sanctimonious. So hollow! Was Kentucky a bastion of fair-minded thinking? Or did its citizens just like to think so?

"It is an established truth, that where the press is free, the people are free, and that, where freedom of the press is not known, the people are the slaves of despotism," she wrote. The fate of this teacher was evidence. A state that insisted on policing speech and shutting down opposition was doomed, no matter the high esteem in which it held itself.

"How long will Northern men watch this struggle between Freedom and Slavery?" she demanded. "How long will they see their rights trampled on, their liberty sacrificed, their highest and most lofty sentiments crushed beneath the iron heel of oppression!"

She signed the letter "Anna E. D." and made no secret of her gender. She did not, however, include her age. She was thirteen.

We can't know what Dickinson was thinking when she wrote to *The Liberator*. Perhaps she saw the era for what it was—a time of limited but tantalizing opportunities for a select bracket of American women.

Dickinson was born into a world of strict social norms. Gender roles were considered immutable. Women had jobs to the extent that finding a husband and bearing children were jobs. Some were permitted to teach. Some had hobbies. But speaking to audiences crammed into loud lecture halls was not part of their mandate. How then to explain the fire-breathing female activists who were racking up ticket sales and embarking on multistate tours? The women who headlined events and sat with men in front of packed auditoriums?

The existence of these barnstorming women would seem to rebuke the tired norms. But in fact, the old inflexible theories made their careers possible. Women were deemed gentler and more pious than men. The fairer sex was endowed with better morals and more compassion. That conviction gave reform-minded women some latitude to have a presence in the public arena. It gave them social cover and served girls like Dickinson well. If women and girls were born with a superior set of values and if their task was to raise the next generation of American citizens, it was more than their right to speak up. It was an obligation.

Women, armed with their feminine wiles and the goodness that men seemed to believe was innate to them, seized their moment. Black and white women gave speeches. Christian and Quaker women organized activist circles and battled for labor reforms. Some set out to improve access to education. Others submitted letters to their local newspapers or wrote books. Harriet Beecher Stowe published *Uncle Tom's Cabin*. The memoirist Harriet Jacobs composed *Incidents in the Life of a Slave Girl*, choosing to tell it from the perspective of a spirited Black girl—an orientation that set her book apart from narratives of enslaved people, which tended to be anchored in and around the lives of men. In *Incidents*, horrific circumstances force its heroine to grow up fast. Jacobs must have known what she was doing when she wrote about the childhood she had been denied. In a letter to the *New-York Daily Tribune*, she explains what drove her to record her own experiences: "The truth can never be told so well through the second and third person." She wanted to be clear. She found her narrator in a plainspoken girl.

In her speeches, Dickinson did not dwell on her personal life, but she knew as Jacobs did that an orator or a writer needed to forge a direct connection to her audience. Resonant arguments depended on an emotional core. Dickinson had no trouble summoning her feelings.

The decades leading up to the Civil War were boom times for orators. Rhetorical flair was not a mere skill worth developing but a civic good. Politicians like Daniel Webster and Charles Sumner built public personas on the basis of their speeches. Universities instructed their students in the art of debate. Public speaking became such a popular form of entertainment that even small towns hosted forums so that citizens could parse pressing political issues.

White men dominated the field, but women started to seek a platform too. Sarah and Angelina Grimké spent their lives calling for abolition, managing to offend both Southerners who were opposed to their cause and Northerners who didn't believe women should weigh in on political matters. Sojourner Truth, the preacher, and Frances Ellen Watkins Harper, a poet and author who had been born to free Black parents, also carved out careers for themselves as popular orators, with Truth accepting a spot on a speaking tour with the English abolitionist George Thompson and William Lloyd Garrison in 1851.

Dickinson did not have such a well-orchestrated debut. It was 1860, and she had just turned seventeen when she noticed an advertisement for an upcoming lecture titled "Woman's Rights and Wrongs." She declined to tell her mother she was going and headed to the venue to listen to someone she later recalled as a "bristling dictatorial man" in one breath declare that his daughters were equal to men and in the next maintain that girls like them had no future in the public realm.

Dickinson was furious. She exploded out of her chair and wagged a "slim finger in his face." She didn't offer a counterargument or defend women's abilities. She instead tore into the man himself. "In Heaven's name, sir," she called out, "what else is to be expected of such a father?" Her rebuttal was heated and personal, flouting normal debate protocol. She so offended the speaker that he fled the hall in the middle of her outburst. But the rest of the room must have been impressed, because Dickinson was soon invited to speak at other events around Philadelphia.

Dickinson was welcomed into the same venues that noted abolitionists like Lucretia and James Mott headlined. Some newbies would have taken their cues from their fellow speakers, careful to follow their lead. Dickinson seemed to relish outflanking them. Journalists seized on her performances, comparing her zeal and bold ideas with the sober presentation and rehearsed lines her elders favored. "However erratic, enthusiastic, or impractical her sentiments," wrote one reporter, her audience received them "with the closest attention." "Her greatest oratorical talent," writes a historian in 1944, "was the sarcastic scorn" with which she treated her opponents.

Dickinson was an unequivocal trailblazer. But no matter how she felt about their politics and their compromises, she benefited from the people who had come before her. The abolitionist speaker circuit had developed several decades earlier, with movement leaders establishing a robust network of newspapers, clubs, and organizations to elevate their cause. Abolitionists were still "political outsiders," as the historian Manisha Sinha writes in *The Slave's Cause*. But revolutions in communication and transportation made it easier for their ideas to circulate and break into public consciousness. Sinha calls their strategies—lecturing, building institutions, founding their own publications—"a blueprint for subsequent radical movements," not least because their approach allowed people to derive an actual income from their convictions.

There were risks, of course. The kind that adolescents don't have a reputation for being able to anticipate. Garrison, who first published Dickinson in *The Liberator*, found gallows and nooses outside his house, was pelted with rotten eggs and garbage in public, and almost died at an event in Boston when thousands of anti-abolition demonstrators showed up and mobbed him. A carpenter hid Garrison in his shop, saving the man's life. Threats of violence and retaliation dogged outspoken abolitionists, Dickinson included.

The stakes of her crusade were clarified in the aftermath of her first substantive solo address. In 1861, she delivered a lecture titled "The Rights and Wrongs of Women"—a throwback to her showdown in Philadelphia. It scandalized critics with its claim that men and women were intellectual equals, and received a mixed reception in the press. But within a few weeks, both Dickinson and the newspapers had to turn their attentions to other urgent concerns. The Civil War broke out that April. Dickinson was desperate to share her perspective on the crisis. She got several invitations to speak and didn't hold back behind the podium. Her remarks at one event were so caustic that she lost her job at the United States Mint. She was in a sense a representative of the federal government, so it didn't look *great* when she used her lecture time to attack a Union general whose performance had failed to impress her. The recent battle at Ball's Bluff had been lost "not through ignorance nor incompetence," she said, "but through the treason of the commanding general, George B. McClellan." The line earned her hisses from the crowd, but she doubled down, repeating the charge three times.

Her dismissal from the Mint turned out to be a minor setback. Dickinson soon sped off for Massachusetts, where Garrison had organized a speaking tour. She was an instant hit. Fellow abolitionists—men in particular—championed her. Crowds loved her, even when she scandalized them. "[I]ndeed," she wrote home in one letter, the masses "have almost devoured me."

Within a matter of months, her reputation preceded her. She was called a "prophetess." Her audiences arrived "wanting to be impressed," and people "who came in this spirit," one social historian declared, "dispersed, convinced."

In a lookback on Dickinson's career published in 1936, a writer noted with awe how much fervor she could draw from her crowds—tears, laughter, cheers, the whole room "listening with breathless suspense." The piece also took note of her looks: dark, thick hair, cut short; thin nostrils; "Napoleonic" jaw. When she lectured, she had a "peculiar carriage of the head and shoulders," with her face "pitched forward and downward, which mark the combative temperament." Dickinson wore plain clothes and no jewels. She was described not at all like a woman of refinement or taste; not maternal or empathetic. But she didn't need to be. She was still a girl.

Without a full-time job, she was also a girl in need of work. Dickinson's mother depended on her, and their correspondence is punctuated with references to financial concerns. Touring became an imperative. Dickinson took on more speeches, which meant more appearances and more travel. Even her supporters fretted. The abolitionist Samuel May recorded his worries in a letter to reformer Elizabeth Buffum Chace, who had hosted Dickinson when she stopped in Rhode Island. "It must be a great trial and even danger, to so young a person, to be the object of so much interest," he wrote, "to receive so much public applause, and to possess so great and happy a talent for holding and swaying the minds of large audiences."

But if the pressure made her anxious, Dickinson didn't let on. She spent a summer tweaking her lectures and then went back on the road. Her work had come to the attention of prominent Republican politicians, who hired her as a paid speaker and sent her on a tour of New Hampshire, Maine, and Connecticut. Elections were imminent, and those who believed in her talents greeted her like a voice from the heavens. An editor at the *Hartford Press* in Connecticut heralded her arrival, writing that she had been "sent from on high to save the state."

She impressed her audiences. She baffled the media. Was Dickinson beautiful or plain? Did she have actual ideas to offer, or was it her charm that turned out crowds to see her speak? Her gender became an obsession: Was she feminine, or did her rhetorical prowess make her seem, as *The Philadelphia Press* reported, almost "statesmanlike"? Was she a "perfect mistress of her art," or was she, as her biographer puts it, "a gender transgressor"?

When the Republican candidate for governor won in Connecticut in 1863, Dickinson was credited for his triumph. Her boosters were ecstatic. The abolitionist Wendell Phillips, who had become a mentor, was said to have likened Dickinson to none other than David himself for defeating the "Goliath of Connecticut Copperheads," as the faction of Democrats in the Union were known. Others reached for that irresistible comparison—Joan of Arc. Outlets that sided with Democrats called her a "spiritual medium," a "political witch," and a "parrot"—the easiest insult with which to undermine girls whom critics would rather dismiss than reckon with. (Recall: Republicans favored abolition and sided with Lincoln; Democrats opposed him.)

The press was split, but Dickinson was rewarded for her contributions to Republicans. At twenty-one, she received a hand-delivered invitation from two prominent officials—a congressman and one of Abraham Lincoln's secretaries—offering her the chance to speak to senators, cabinet members, and Supreme Court justices in the House of Representatives; the letter bore almost one hundred congressional signatures. When she made the trip in 1864, Vice President Hannibal Hamlin himself escorted her to the rostrum.

The moment was a first. No woman had ever addressed the chamber.

She made the most of it. In the *Washington Chronicle*, a reporter described a "red-lipped, slim-waisted girl, with curls cut short, as if for school . . . holding spellbound in the capital of the nation for an hour and ten minutes, two thousand politicians, statesmen and soldiers." President Lincoln walked into the hall in the middle of her speech, finding Dickinson castigating the policies he'd laid out the previous month in an effort to offer an olive branch to the Confederacy. Did she notice him and decide to continue her critique? Or was she so inflamed with her own disdain for men who would entertain such a contemptible compromise that she didn't see Lincoln, sitting with his head bowed before her?

In *The Independent*, a newspaper aimed at radical Republicans, the speech was deemed a triumph. The review concluded that while Lincoln hadn't looked up to meet Dickinson's gaze, he had paid close attention while she spoke. She had ended her speech with an endorsement of the president, who must have at least seemed to her better than the alternatives. When she did, the paper noted that the "careworn face of the President dropped lower still."

The guts! Dickinson was a slender, brown-haired woman staring down a president whom she could not vote to elect. Young and not rich, she was dependent on the continued support of her Republican boosters. The speech was nervy. It also—like any canny confrontation—elevated her brand. She was cheered and reviled. She was the toast of some towns and a clown in others. One newspaper claims that she appealed "to the same love of the marvelous and monstrous which Barnum has made his fortune in exhibiting," while another accused her of masterminding a covert effort to turn the United States into what the writer called a "Gynaekokracy, which manifests itself in the absurd endeavors of women to usurp the places and execute the functions of the male sex."

Circus animal? Devious woman? What's the difference?

She was not the sole female orator, but she was the lone "girl orator," as Garrison had christened her. In the press, that status turned Dickinson into a media fixation. Dickinson was a sensation and a test case. She was an omen. How much could be extracted from her? And for how long? Her old friend Wendell Phillips later identified what made Dickinson so valuable to the cause: "She was the young elephant sent forth to try the bridges to see if they were safe for older ones to cross."

IN EACH GENERATION, girls who are committed to their activism see how far it can be pushed, whatever "it" is. Their platforms can help them advocate for a cause, but part of their power is their knack for upsetting convention. Youth lets them disrupt the status quo. Youth mesmerizes.

The real Joan of Arc—Dickinson's namesake—was seventeen when she roused the French to beat back the British in 1429. She was burned alive at the stake in 1431. She was accused of being a witch and a heretic. She was charged with dressing in men's clothes—a decision she defended. The scholar Françoise Meltzer writes that the tunic and hose she wore on the battlefield were meant to protect her from rape. The trial and execution were political, but the clothes were a genuine reflection of her chosen role. In refusing to wear women's dress, she rejected a rite of girlhood. She paid for it. So did the girls who took after her.

Dickinson embraced her sobriquet as America's Joan of Arc and invoked it in her speeches, but she fell out of favor as a lecturer in her thirties. Economic forces were a factor. The speaking circuit declined after the Panic of 1873. Her age became a drawback as well. Furious women were less captivating than incandescent girls. Without speaking opportunities, Dickinson started to write more. In 1876, she premiered her play *A Crown of Thorns* and cast herself in the part of the doomed Anne Boleyn. Later, she performed in drag as Hamlet. Both performances were met with scathing reviews. In 1893, the editors of a book trumpeting biographies of 1,470 "leading American women" include Dickinson, but write of her attempts at acting that "the stage and the dramatic platform were not suited to her."

There's no reason to doubt her critics. Her writing might have been woeful. Perhaps she was a terrible actress. If Dickinson's furious oration is an indication, she wasn't the kind of person who could lose herself in a character. It's also true that even if her performances had been stellar, the themes she tackled in her work were becoming more and more out of step with the emerging trends of her era. One historian notes that "female spectacles" were growing popular, encouraging "overwrought emotionalism" from women actors. Perhaps with women fighting for access to the ballot box and waging a war on alcohol, there was less appetite for moralizers. Dickinson had defied expectations as a girl. But audiences didn't want that posture in a woman. Better the ridiculous, the romantic—the punch line. Dickinson became one too.

In 1888, Dickinson returned to the stump to campaign for the Republican Benjamin Harrison in his race against President Grover Cleveland. Her speeches seemed to have gone over well, but Democrats launched a counteroffensive against her. One paper called her insane. Another made it a point to describe her short hair and "somewhat muscular appearance," reviving those old gendered criticisms and hinting at the rumors that she'd had relationships with both men and women. But it was Dickinson's own lectures that earned the most negative press. The zealousness that had set her apart as a girl now made her an outcast. In Bath, New York, a local publisher praised her speech but bemoaned her vehemence. She was just too much—too retributive, too furious. "You want to sit down on her hard," he observed, sounding less like a dispassionate journalist than a perverse disciplinarian. The adoption of male habits—dress and oration—was a mark against this Joan too.

Dickinson didn't take the turn in her fortunes well. She sued the Republican National Committee, claiming that its officials had promised to give her what amounted to a bonus if their candidate prevailed in the election, which he had. She drank more and suffered what her sister identified as a nervous breakdown. Then her mother died, and her behavior grew more erratic. Close friends questioned her judgment. Some went so far as to echo the newspapers, wondering whether she was still lucid. The suffragist Susan B. Anthony, who had been Dickinson's friend and who some speculate was at one point a romantic interest, said, "[T]hought *centred* on *one's self* is sure to bring that one to grief sooner or later, & with poor Anna it has been sooner."

Dickinson embarked on a series of lawsuits in a misguided effort to revive her career and restore her good name (not to mention the contents of her bank account). None panned out.

In 1891, after weeks of mounting nerves, drinking, and suspecting those closest to her of conspiring to humiliate her, Dickinson had a showdown with her sister, Susan, which resulted in Susan having her committed to the Danville State Hospital for the Insane. When she was released, she sued both the outlets who had reported on her mental state and the people who had committed her. She never spoke to her sister again. In 1898, she won two out of three libel suits, but even the vindication didn't leave her with much disposable income. She died in 1932.

Her elders in the movement fared better. Lucretia Mott spent the rest of her life advocating for universal suffrage and helped incorporate Swarthmore College, which became one of the first coed colleges in the United States. The Grimké sisters were criticized as ever but remained ardent activists until the end of their lives. Sojourner Truth lived to be eighty-six. When she died, Frederick Douglass eulogized her. A thousand people attended her funeral.

The women orators survived. The girl orator who grew into womanhood never found her footing.

Dickinson lived out much of her adult life in Goshen, New York. She moved in with friends, the married couple George and Sallie Ackley. It was said that she and Sallie were lovers. In town, two identical plaques mark her gravesite and the home where Dickinson resided until her death, heralding the woman who was once "America's Civil War Joan of Arc." The signs include a few sentences about her life and work. Both cite a quote from Dickinson herself: "My head and heart, soul and brain, were all on fire with the words I must speak."

3

SEE ME

———

A GIRL'S BATTLE FOR
WOMEN'S SUFFRAGE

n 1912, Mabel Ping-Hua Lee led seventeen thousand people up
Fifth Avenue on horseback. Lee couldn't have been older than seventeen, but she didn't fade into the cavalcade. She was a Chinese
girl in a sea of white women. Her presence made its point. The march
was one of the most robust demonstrations of public support for the
women's vote to date. Lee was still a child. The movement to secure
women's suffrage had reached middle age.

SIX DECADES BEFORE Lee trotted up the bluest-blooded vein in Manhattan, activists assembled to hold the first convention for women's
rights in Seneca Falls. In 1848, in upstate New York, three hundred
women and men gathered, and one hundred of the participants—
sixty-eight of whom were women—signed a Declaration of Sentiments, modeled on the Declaration of Independence. "We hold these

truths to be self-evident," the document read, "that all men and women are created equal." It went on to outline the exclusions and barriers that women faced in public life, from political representation to access to education and credit, and called for such obstructions to be torn down.

Several boldface names were present at the meeting. Lucretia Mott had arrived with her husband and sister. Elizabeth Cady Stanton had come with her son. Frederick Douglass was the lone Black person in the crowd. Just one attendee would live to see actual women vote in an actual federal election. Charlotte Woodward, later Charlotte Woodward Peirce, was eighteen when she corralled a group of friends to travel with her to the convention. She had been raised in the area, but the excursion was an exhilarating departure from her usual routine. Like most girls who lived at home, she was consumed with constant and unremitting household labor. She did chores. She cleaned and cooked. She also had a part-time job stitching precut gloves and delivering them to a manufacturer in town to sell. Her parents relied on that income, but wouldn't have dreamed of sending her to work outside their home to earn it.

"We worked . . . in the seclusion of our bedchambers," Peirce recalled in an interview in 1920 on the eve of that first presidential election in which women had the federal right to vote. Her parents—and parents like them—clung to the fiction that the world was indeed built on the wages that men earned to support their families. Peirce loathed the posturing, and she couldn't stand the men who spent their afternoons in stores and bars while depending on the salaries that their wives and daughters earned in secret.

Such undeserved self-regard infuriated her. It also inspired her ideals. Most women, she later said, "accepted this condition . . . as normal and God-ordained," but she found a sacred few who shared her outrage—women whose souls were "beating their wings in rebellion." Peirce told her interviewer that she too "rebelled, although silently, all the hours I sat and sewed gloves for a miserable pittance which, after it was earned, could never be mine."

It wasn't leisure Peirce was after, but independence. Congress did not grant her some fraction of it until she was in her nineties. Peirce lived the movement. She stood at Seneca Falls as a girl. She died in 1924, a voter. But progress was not so linear or neat as the biographical bookends make it seem.

The movement for suffrage proceeded in fits and starts. It detoured, doubled back. In 1861, the outbreak of the Civil War put organizing efforts on ice. The annual National Women's Rights Convention was halted between 1861 and 1865. When it was at last rescheduled for 1866, it was impossible to miss how much time had passed. The pause was etched on the faces of its attendees. Lucretia Mott was in her seventies, an elder stateswoman. Several of her contemporaries had not been able to make the trip as the trek would have been too taxing.

At the convention in New York, Mott acknowledged an inevitable generational transition. She must have known her actuarial tables. Change might not happen fast enough for her to live to see it.

"It is no loss, but the proper order of things, that the mothers should depart and give place to the children," Mott said, resigned and stalwart. "Young women of America, I want you to make yourselves acquainted with the history of the women's rights movement."

YOUNG WOMEN OF AMERICA encountered a history that was not all uplifting. The movement had been built to advocate for justice, but several of its leaders had been known to collude with avowed racists. The movement owed a tremendous debt to abolition, which had incubated conversations about what it meant to be equal, and demonstrated in practical terms what effective organizing could achieve. Even so, women's rights activists learned to use tactics borrowed from anti-abolition forces when such strategies served their own aims.

Fissures between Black men and white women deepened after the Civil War. It was clear to both sides that the United States would give Black men the vote before allowing women to participate in federal elections. When white women like Stanton expressed their shock over that development, it was often tinged with disgust. Contemporaries would not have put it like this in 1870, but we can: The racism jumps out.

Alliances and entire organizations splintered. Some Black women lost their political homes in two movements. Several white leaders allied themselves with virulent white supremacists and stoked racial divides in the hopes of securing the vote for white women. When some took their bid on tour in the South, innuendo was made explicit: Enfranchise white women to cancel out the new votes of Black men.

The next generation of activists that Mott had wanted to encourage did rise to the occasion. Their arrival wasn't an instant fix to entrenched movement problems, but it did mean fresh perspectives for the cause. Some organizers could see better than their predecessors that racist white men were not the people likeliest to support their true liberation. Several more had practical ideas about how to bring it about.

Between 1890 and 1896, referendums on the women's vote started to gain traction at the state level, with four states moving to enfranchise women. Soon after, two recent Radcliffe College graduates, Inez Haynes Irwin and Maud Wood Park, founded the College Equal Suffrage League (CESL), which aimed to secure the vote for women in California after a robust effort had been defeated in 1896. CESL reorganized as a national organization a decade later, this time with more students at the forefront.

The historian Ellen Carol DuBois chronicles their operation in *Suffrage: Women's Long Battle for the Vote*, distinguishing the so-called new women from earlier activists. These organizers shrugged off "the rules of female respectability" and relished the chance to make their case in public.

Their tactics were unorthodox and energetic. Young women "went for the emotions," DuBois writes, stoking "excitement, attraction, desire." Activists preached on street corners. Students and recent grads "treated their audiences as consumers, and their job was to sell their product." No more debating over rights and liberties. This was advertising.

Persuasion worked. In time, organizers defanged the opposition. Over a decade after that first referendum had been defeated, California became the sixth state to grant women the ballot, joining Wyoming, Colorado, Idaho, Utah, and Washington. "The agony is over," declared a suffrage paper in Iowa. "The victory is ours in California."

Elsewhere, activists were eager to replicate the success. Around the same time that the campaign for the California referendum was gaining steam, working women and girls—tired of their marginalization in unions that presumed their jobs were a diversion to be abandoned after finding a husband—had started to form their own trade groups in New York and Boston. Their unions—like the associations of Lowell mill girls before them—became incubators for ideas about labor and independence. Suffragists flocked to them.

In November 1909, shirtwaist workers went on strike in New York just before the Christmas rush. The previous summer, discontent with factory conditions had started to grow. Wages were low. Hours seemed endless. That fall, the ire culminated in a contentious meeting held at Cooper Union. A parade of men spoke to oppose a general strike. Having heard them out, the Jewish immigrant Clara Lemlich stood to address the room. She was twenty-three and a seasoned labor activist. She was tired of waiting her turn. "I have listened to all the speakers, and I have no further patience for talk," she said. "I am one who feels and suffers from the things pictured. I move we go on a general strike!"

The crowd roared its approval. Local unions, including the Women's Trade Union League, expected four or five thousand Jewish women to heed her call. Triple that number turned out. The strike kicked off with twenty thousand women and girls marching in the streets.

It was an inspiring showing. And it was met with brutal force. Strikers were arrested. Bosses hauled in out-of-state labor to break up picket lines. Somehow resolve held. Perhaps chronic underestimation fueled the demonstrators. Perhaps the bonds between them were more potent than their adversaries realized. One union leader expressed particular awe: "An equal number of men never would hold together under what these girls are enduring."

The strike was not devised as a suffrage recruitment event, but activists weren't about to overlook the fact that tens of thousands of riled-up women and girls had demonstrated a willingness to embrace confrontation. Rich suffragists like the socialite and activist Alva Belmont—who had once been married to William Kissam Vanderbilt and was later the widow of Oliver H. P. Belmont—poured dollars into the strike and drew an explicit line from the abuse of women at work to their fundamental disenfranchisement as citizens. She framed her support for the effort as an obligation of sisterhood.

"Women the world over need protection and it is only through the united efforts of women that they will get it," she told the press. After a visit to the Jefferson Market Courthouse in New York, where strikers had been tried and convicted, Belmont declared that what she had seen had left her convinced: Suffrage was essential. How else were women ever going to be able to fight their mistreatment?

The New York Times—no great fan of either the strike or the prospect of women voters—saw the evident links between the issues too. The paper grumbled about a thrumming undercurrent in the shirtwaist workers' bid for improved wages and conditions. It wasn't just about labor reform, the paper wrote. "There was no doubt that many of the women in the union were in favor of woman suffrage."

In December, the strike spread to Philadelphia. College students collected funds to support activists, raising several hundred dollars for the shirtwaist workers. With the action gripping two major cities, New York manufacturers struggled to import strikebreakers. Production halted.

After New Year's 1910, a mass gathering was convened at Carnegie Hall to encourage the workers and boost morale after weeks of bitter campaigning. Leaders had three hundred women and girls who'd been arrested for their participation in the strike sit facing the audience. Each wore a sash describing how the court had sentenced her. Rose Perr, a teenager, recounted her arrest to the captivated crowd, an account that culminated in her recollections of the week she was forced to spend in a workhouse.

When the strike did unravel, it fell apart for the usual reasons. Bosses could afford to hold out longer than workers. The unions were short on funding. Bills for participants added up—rent and food at the bare minimum. Shops came to the table and made their modest compromises. The shirtwaist workers were back at their posts within a few months.

Young women, however, could see that the exercise had not been a total wash. Organizers had secured real improvements in their treatment and hours as a condition for their return to work—a partial triumph. Union recognition remained out of reach—a bitter disappointment.

But the strike did introduce tens of thousands of women to the idea of suffrage. Lemlich herself came to see how the issues of labor and enfranchisement were intertwined and in fact irreducible. She didn't view suffrage as a recreational pursuit for rich ladies, as some had claimed it to be. She understood what the vote could do and what it could have done for her. When the strikers protested their abuse in the care of the police and the courts, Lemlich huffed that elected officials might not have been so quick to dismiss them if leaders knew that "we girls have a vote."

THE EFFORT TO win women the vote in New York drew on the organizing expertise of middle-aged and older women. Beneath the banners and the demonstrations was a machine of activists, socialites, socialite-activists, well-off widows, working women, labor organizers, and political bosses. Harriot Stanton Blatch, head of the Women's Political Union and daughter of Elizabeth Cady Stanton, was in her fifties when the campaign in her state kicked into gear. Leonora O'Reilly, the garment worker who became one of New York's most effective working-class leaders, was in her forties.

But the speeches of girls like Rose Perr and their marches were not peripheral to the cause. Leaders knew that sweet girls could help brand the movement, and their attractive faces—their convincing and innocent and beseeching faces—were not beside the point. If the movement was going to persuade people, optics were not some superficial extra. Optics were the whole game.

Blatch had seen their impact in New York. The strike had demonstrated collective resolve. The lethal Triangle Shirtwaist fire showed how unprotected workers remained, girls included. And still, state government refused to print a referendum on the ballot. The visuals had stoked the public's emotions. Now it needed to inspire a conversion.

Blatch decided she needed a spectacle. Not just arresting photos, but something awe-inspiring. Blatch had seen the kind of outré tactics that suffragettes in England relied on. She seems to have come to their same conclusion—the one at which activists in California had also arrived. The movement needed an even greater public presence. It needed an out-in-the-open mobilization effort. It needed to be more shameless. It had better make a scene. Who else but girls could pull it off?

Blatch had organized parades before, but this march—scheduled for 1912—would eclipse previous events, in terms of both its size and its ambitions. So she focused on the aspect of the demonstration that she knew would be most consequential. She centered her attentions on controlling the visual impact that her marchers would make. She outlined how much space she wanted between the columns of participants, demanded that marchers walk with their heads up and their gazes fixed on the horizon, and insisted that no one leave before the parade's prescribed end. Picture the photos: She didn't want her ranks to thin as the march wore on.

In the months leading up to the event, Blatch obsessed over the details. Local department stores carried parade-specific hats sold for just over a quarter—a precursor to the pink knit hats of the post-2016 era. Posters encouraged participants to wear white. It helped that Blatch had her pick of radiant working women and girls who could be dispatched into the streets to spread the word. It did not help that Jewish women

workers demanded the parade start after sundown to accommodate observers of the Sabbath. Blatch balked. She knew photos wouldn't turn
out as well after dark and that a later start could mean limited press in
the weekend papers. In a nod to the number of Jewish women involved
in the movement, the parade did kick off an hour later than Blatch had
planned. But she prevailed. The event started almost two hours before
sunset.

Even suffrage skeptics had to concede that public demonstrations
were one of the better tactics available to organizers. In 1911, a reporter with *The New York Times* admitted that he hoped the women
would fail in their bid for the vote. But he conceded that a well-
planned parade or public protest had its virtues: "It will indicate the
courage of the paraders, the strength of their conviction, and their
determination to win."

These marches were not for the true believers. The equivocat-
ing masses were the people who needed them. Women would never
get their constitutional amendment if their strategies were limited to
"reading papers at women's clubs and passing resolutions," as the *Times*
reporter wrote. He considered the kind of social and cultural mechanisms that could drive people—in this case, men—to change their
minds.

"No cause," he wrote, "can be won without efforts of this strenuous
and showy sort."

"The enemy must be converted through his eyes," Blatch said, evi-
dently concurring. "He must see uniformity of dress. He must realize
without actually noting it item by item, the discipline of the individual, of the group, of the whole from start to finish."

The "enemy" had to be transfixed. So Blatch enlisted the people
whose charm has forever been used to placate and sweeten and sell.
She wanted girls. She got them.

. . .

MABEL PING-HUA LEE blended in with her peers at the parade, just as Blatch had intended. She wore the same three-cornered hat and had it knotted with the same colored ribbons. She was "clad"—in the words of one newspaper commentator—just "like the rich and fashionable suffragettes around her, in a tight fitting black broadcloth habit." But compared with the white activists who were also leading the march, she did stand out. There were not a lot of Chinese girls on the front lines of the American battle for women's suffrage.

In the months before Blatch's parade, rumors spread that China had extended the vote to its women. The chattering classes in New York were horrified. For white women who were desperate to vote and who lived in a nation founded on the supposed ideals of freedom, it was a bitter pill. For those who harbored anti-Chinese sentiments, it was humiliating. With the Page Act of 1875 and the Chinese Exclusion Act of 1882, the United States had barred most Chinese people from crossing its borders. Implicit in the bills was the racist conviction that their mere presence posed a threat. News of the enfranchisement of women in China complicated the narrative. How was it possible America had failed to extend to its women a right that that nation had offered theirs?

Activists raced to capitalize on the scandal. In cities like New York and Boston and Cincinnati, advocates for women's suffrage joined up with Chinese activists to get the word out, contrasting American inaction on the issue with Chinese progress. Prejudices ran so deep that even the fact of their meeting drew attention. In *The Oregonian,* in April 1912, a writer crammed the newsiest bit of the article into its five-word headline: "Chinese Women Dine with White."

In New York, three prominent white suffragists, including Alva Belmont, called for a similar summit. The women invited a handful of activists and Chinese leaders to discuss opportunities for collaboration. Lee and her parents, a minister and a teacher who'd been permitted to settle in the United States thanks to narrow exemptions to the nativist laws, attended. Mabel was given the floor.

She was a well-rehearsed public speaker. The recent revolution in China had driven scores of Chinese American students in the United States—girls in particular—to get involved in local politics. Chinese nationalist leaders preached an ethos of self-improvement, which meant urging girls to pursue education, develop experience and expertise, and then pledge to give back to China. Lee had become a fixture at local events, with impeccable credentials to match her rousing rhetoric. She had graduated from the famed Erasmus Hall High School, where she was the lone Chinese student in her class. She was headed for Barnard, where she would enroll in the fall of 1913.

But not all the women who had met to discuss the future of suffrage knew that, which must have made Lee's remarks much more jarring. Had some expected a pat on the back for their belated attempt at inclusion? Had some hoped to encounter a modest, grateful good girl? She didn't give them the satisfaction.

"All women are recognized in New York, excepting Chinese women," Lee said. Educational institutions were closed to them. Social hubs and recreational centers excluded them. Their marginalization was deliberate. Lee couldn't stand it. She invoked her proverbial Chinese sister and demanded an answer: "How can she learn!" Hers was not a private call to account. It wasn't a request. It was a barn burner.

We can't know whether the white women in attendance felt chastened. We do know that parade organizers took notice. Lee, who would later become the first Chinese woman to earn a doctorate from Columbia, was invited to ride in the march.

Had her remarks moved her audience to revisit its biases? Had it motivated them to redouble their efforts to work with and elevate the voices of women like her? Or was it a simpler calculation: In the fact of her being, Lee served as a taunt. Here was a girl whom China would allow to grow up and vote. How would America respond?

Newspaper articles profiled Chinese women who had come to support suffrage stateside. Some stories took credit for the supposed American roots of the recent Chinese revolution. Others expressed a newfound interest in the lives of Chinese students in the United States. Several marveled over the sudden reversal in the fortunes of Chinese women. Writers obsessed over the practice of foot-binding that rendered some women immobile. Reporters scrutinized their clothes. These women—these women!—would now be permitted to vote?

With a month to go before the march, *The New York Times* asked Lee to comment on the shift—how "these fair representatives of an old conservative nation" had become the kind of women who wanted to ride on horseback up the streets of Manhattan. Lee answered that their "great awakening" was a function of just how long Chinese women had been held back. "Is that not natural?" she said. "The accumulated need of centuries is bursting out. This is our recompense."

That "accumulated need" did burst out on the morning of the march. *The New York Times* blared a reminder: "Chinese Women Will Ride." The paper also made sure to mention that some parade participants would have to follow the marchers in cars because their feet had been bound. Lee's mother, Lai Beck, was one such woman. The paper couldn't help but sniff: Despite their historically poor treatment, "their men have enfranchised them." So much ado about the state of women in China. So little about the treatment of the Chinese in the United States.

Mainstream papers did not seem to see the contradictions in their coverage—not in how their stories fixated on the cause of Chinese suffrage but ignored the routine discrimination against Chinese immigrants in America, and not in how the organizing of disenfranchised girls like Lee was fetishized, but the large-scale activism of Black women was for the most part ignored.

Black women lined up to march in New York in 1912 and in Washington, D.C., in 1913, when Alice Paul planned her famed parade for the women's vote. Both times white leaders sidelined them. In 1912, white women were the face of the operation, with Lee serving as a notable and purposeful exception. To placate Southerners in 1913, Paul and other leaders allowed states to decide whether to integrate their delegations. In several, this meant that Black women were made to stand behind hordes of white participants. The journalist and activist Ida B. Wells refused to be minimized. She marched with the white delegation from her home state of Illinois.

In the end, ten thousand people participated in the parade in 1912, per *The New York Times*. The *New York Herald* put the crowd closer to seventeen thousand, with at least four times that number in onlookers. It would take almost a decade for women to win their constitutional amendment, but each parade and demonstration and bill dented the opposition. That was the plan. *Optics.*

Several women who marched in the procession held up a banner emblazoned with a mother's battle song: "We prepare children for the world. We ask to prepare the world for our children."

The world was not prepared for their children.

WHAT HAD BLATCH'S obsessive focus on her girls—including Lee—netted? One reporter considered the turnout and concluded that there might no longer be a single person in New York "who does not now know the meaning of the word 'suffragette.'"

The parade had elevated Lee both on horseback and in the public consciousness. She was adored—at once famous and beloved, and foreign and unknown. Not unlike a child star, Lee was well spoken and charismatic, the picture of female promise, but not quite familiar. She captivated audiences. She spoke immaculate English. She retained a little magic. In 1914, an attendee at a conference where she had been asked to speak remarked that audiences left "Mabelized" from her talks.

Suffragists in New York needed such charms—or at least needed a fresh voice that could make the case for suffrage sound somehow new while stoking that old competitive patriotism too. Even as the national push to pass a constitutional amendment to enfranchise women was heating up, New York's activists remained committed to having their state pass suffrage at the local level. It would be the first state east of Mississippi to do so. Lee could boost their chances.

Lee joined the battle to expand the vote in New York at the same time as she started her studies at Barnard. The school proved to be a more hospitable environment to someone like her than most. It didn't accept Black students until 1925, but it did admit Catholic and Jewish applicants far earlier than similar institutions and made it a point to educate the daughters of both the elite and the working class. Lee attended lectures and debates and speeches. She was invited to events with activists. Week after week, she was introduced to the latest feminist ideas and mingled with the people advancing them. She was a student—part of a generation that put an increasing emphasis on education.

Lee settled in. She was part of a generation that seemed resolved to continue its education. Between 1919 and 1922 alone, the number of students in universities doubled. Soldiers who had just returned from war in Europe drove the trend. But a determined few of the new pupils were girls. And though Lee attended Barnard before the war broke out, she was representative of the imminent boom. She was ambitious. She was determined. She was one of four Chinese students in her entire school. That all were active on women's issues must speak to both the kind of students that Barnard drew and the preoccupations of Chinese women of the era. Alice Huie Lee was American born but had grown up in Chinatown; she became captain of her class swim team and knew Mabel from the Daughters of China Club downtown. Anna Kong made a splash at the Young Women's Christian Association (YWCA) when she delivered a speech entitled "Oriental Girls." The YWCA appealed to Lee too. She became involved in the organization and started writing more. One of her pieces was titled "China's Submerged Half." It echoed the comments she'd made to the reporter at *The New York Times*. China's women were emerging "with a vengeance." She urged on their efforts and called for equal opportunities for girls. The "welfare of China," she wrote, and even its "existence as an independent nation," depended on its swift administration of overdue "justice to its womankind." She invoked President Abraham Lincoln as she concluded: If the Union "could not endure half free, half slave, how can China maintain her position among independent nations half free and taught, half shackled?"

While Lee studied, she kept a hand in the activities of New York activists. When leaders redoubled their efforts to get an amendment to the state constitution approved in 1915, Lee was a frequent presence at events, often at the behest of Mary Beard, the historian and feminist activist. But the more time Lee spent at Barnard and with students at Columbia, the more she intensified her commitment to furthering the advancement of Chinese women above all. She was a leader at the Columbia Chinese Students Club, a chapter of the

Chinese Students' Alliance. She wrote articles for its magazine and spoke at its conferences. In 1917, she ran for president of the national organization and lost. In the final vote count, the incumbent, T. V. Soong, came out ahead with a single vote. Lee wanted a recount. She had come so close. But Soong smeared her and was declared the winner. The election ended as countless have: with a woman back in her place and a man back in leadership. New York enfranchised its women that November.

Before the election, Lee had served as one of the organization's secretaries. After the race was called for Soong, she went back to the executive and education boards but didn't take another stab at the top job. She was in her twenties now, with a deeper and more sophisticated understanding of feminism and her own values. The men she knew climbed professional ladders. She did not have another obvious rung to reach for.

IN ONE OF THE EDITORIALS she wrote about women's rights, Lee addressed the insidious idea that "woman has gone so far, she can go no further." The notion implied that women had reached their full potential. It had all been realized! She could see how the women in her generation had been pioneers. But there were whole territories that remained unexplored and still out of reach. At Barnard, she took classes with women who had to drop out of graduate school after getting married or pregnant. Women were fired or forced out, considered unsuitable for work once motherhood claimed them. Their career possibilities were meager. What sense did it make to stop pushing now— to accept the progress made so far as total? There was more she wanted to do.

Two weeks after the United States declared war in Europe in 1917, Lee found out she'd been accepted into a PhD program at Columbia, along with three other women. The college would not admit women until 1983, but a select few had started to enroll in its graduate programs. Unlike most women, who chose to focus on the humanities, Lee pursued coursework in political science and economics. She graduated in 1921, becoming the first woman to receive a PhD from Columbia. Her dissertation was close to 650 pages and focused on the effects of agriculture on economics in China. To travel to Europe and China to continue her research, she had to seek permission from the Chinese Department of the Immigration Service—despite having lived in the United States for most of her life.

Permission was granted. She arrived in China, encountering a nation under construction, in which several people she knew held prominent positions in government. She returned to New York brimming with plans to start a business of her own. But soon after, her father died and the Depression settled in. She gave up on the business and instead took up a position in her father's old church. Her peers were horrified. All that education and fortitude just to help run a small mission in Chinatown? A friend wrote to her, reminding her that she had once intended to found a settlement house in the tradition of the great reformers Jane Addams and Lillian Wald. He pressed her to dedicate herself to something befitting her capacious talents. Lee must have shrugged him off. She remained with the church. She died in 1965.

The First Chinese Baptist Church in New York is still lined with photos of Lee and her parents. Was this the life Lee had dreamed of? She swore to friends who inquired that she was content. She could have moved back to China, although perhaps the violence between China and Japan and then the start of World War II kept her stateside. She could have tried to teach in America. Teaching would have been one of the few jobs open to a woman with her credentials. Did she choose not to? Did she feel bound to honor her father? Did she ever find a place—in all her travels and studies—where a woman like her could have what she knew she was entitled to? True participation? Equal standing with men? Lee never married. She also never voted.

In 1919, Congress passed the Nineteenth Amendment to the United States Constitution. It was ratified in 1920, although the full enfranchisement of Black women and other minorities would not be realized for decades. Suffrage had depended on girls like Lee, who could lend the movement their faces, their energies, and their deep ties to communities to which leadership needed access. What did suffrage give them in return?

Lee was a devoted feminist and an immense intellect. But she lacked options. She wasn't a citizen. The United States did not repeal the Chinese Exclusion Act until 1943. Lee had two degrees in an era in which women often had zero. She had no job prospects.

No one can know the counterfactual: what she might have done if the stock market hadn't crashed and her father hadn't died and if she'd been born into a different time and if she'd been white.

Can we presume her unhappiness? What more do we want from her? Here is one more thing we do not know: How often did Lee march into rooms—the lone Chinese woman—and strategize with activists who relied on her but kept her and her people at a distance?

4

BAD GIRLS

TROUBLEMAKERS AND THE
CIVIL RIGHTS MOVEMENT

You know about the good girl: In September 1950, Oliver Brown walked his daughter Linda four blocks from their home to the local school for white children in Topeka, Kansas. He wanted to enroll her, but was informed Linda would not be allowed to attend. Sumner didn't accept Black children. Instead, Linda would have to go to Monroe Elementary, which would mean leaving her house almost an hour and a half before the start of classes if she wanted to be on time. The Browns sued, and the verdict came down in 1954. The Supreme Court ruled that racial segregation violated the equal protection clause, and that schools—not just in Kansas but nationwide—would have to be desegregated.

Linda Brown is the girl we think of when we think of *Brown v. Board of Education*. It's her narrative of waiting outside the principal's office while her father tried in vain to secure her place in a school he knew would reject them both that has resonated with people for decades. It's her last name on the case.

But there was another girl—an older girl—whose fate was adjudicated in *Brown*. She was behind the sole school desegregation case that students themselves initiated. The case that we call *Brown v. Board of Education* was in fact a collection of five disputes, with those four other cases—which originated in Delaware, South Carolina, Virginia, and Washington, D.C.—subsumed into *Brown*. All posed the same existential question. When Chief Justice Earl Warren handed down the unanimous opinion, he answered: The status quo would not stand.

It's no surprise the best-known civil rights case of the modern era concerned children. School is where the war for a more equal America has been waged. It's the battleground where the front lines are drawn and redrawn. It's where progress can be rolled back. School is our gauntlet.

All this time later, the reactions from people who supported the landmark decision still seem alive with a sense of promise. Crackling, vital. The Black press was ecstatic. Mainstream liberal outlets approved. When the acclaimed novelist Ralph Ellison heard the bulletin come over the radio, he shook with emotion and cried. "What a wonderful world of possibilities are unfolded for the children!" he wrote.

He centered it on them. That was the other quiet revolution in the *Brown* opinion, which Justin Driver, the Yale Law School professor who covered *Brown* in his book about the relationship between education and the Supreme Court, names. With one crucial sentence, Warren reframed the constitutional offense at the heart of the legal quagmire. "In each of the cases," he writes, "minors of the Negro race, through their legal representatives, seek the aid of the courts."

It wasn't parents, in other words, whose interests would be served in this decision. The law had to be responsive to the needs of children. "Warren's phrasing renders students the protagonists in this legal drama," Driver explains. He "consigns parents to a supporting role."

Students have forever concurred, although perhaps some in this case might have split with Driver over the idea that it was even up to Warren to decide who should be cast in which part. In the world of law, fine. But out on the streets, children had not waited to be given their parts.

No one had to tap them on the shoulder. Girls took their places.

BARBARA JOHNS WAS THE ELDEST of five brothers and sisters, so it was expected that she would set an example. She had learned as a child to pick tobacco on her grandmother's land in Farmville, Virginia, and she did the work without complaint. One of her responsibilities was tearing off the shoots that grew out of the leaves and threatened to slow their development. She primed the plants to flourish. It must have been tedious work for a girl who had been uprooted from New York and now lived an hour southwest of Richmond. But her father had served in World War II and returned unharmed. She made her peace with the farm.

Johns's parents, Robert and Violet Johns, had also grown up in Virginia. When Johns was sent back, she lived with her maternal grandmother. But her father's relatives were the people who helped shape her awareness of stark racial inequities in America. Her paternal grandmother was fearless; Johns remembered her as not in "the slightest bit subservient to whites." Her uncle, Vernon Johns, was even more outspoken.

Vernon Johns was a pastor and an ardent activist. He identified what he called the "insane hatred between races" as the "nastiest and deadliest problem before the world." He railed against white Christians who perpetuated hatred and even lethal violence against Black people while feeling "at peace with their ritual-loving God." Later, he would accept a job as the minister of the Dexter Avenue Baptist Church. His hot-tempered sermons received a mixed reception, but he did leave a lasting impression on the man who would succeed him as the leader of the Alabama congregation—Martin Luther King, Jr.

When people told Johns she took after him, it wasn't supposed to be a compliment. Still, Vernon's example did affect her. Johns's father operated a local mill and store with Vernon in town. Johns's sister, Joan Cobbs, remembered sitting with her there when a white man came in and called over to their father, greeting him as "Uncle Robert." It was a condescending habit of the South—white people referring to Black strangers as "aunt" or "uncle."

"Barbara took umbrage to that," Cobbs recalled. It was just like her sister: to speak up even when it was ill advised. She couldn't be quiet "when she saw something about a situation she didn't like." Cobbs could still remember her outburst: "Why are you calling him 'uncle'?" Johns demanded. "He's no kin to you."

The man looked incredulous. Johns didn't blink.

When she first moved to Farmville, Johns was educated in a wooden schoolhouse in which seven grades received instruction in the same cacophonous classroom. Older students in the area attended Robert R. Moton High School, which consisted of several tar-paper shacks that the all-white school district had been promising to replace. In the winter, Barbara and Joan had to sit in coats and boots to keep warm. When it rained, students would race around the room, putting out pails to catch the water. Their textbooks were tattered, out-of-date castoffs from the local white school. It didn't shock Johns that Black students would have less than white students in Virginia. But it gnawed at her that Moton was even shabbier than other Black schools in the state. She knew, because she had visited them when their sports and debate teams competed. The standards were low across the board. At Moton, the standards were subterranean.

She was fifteen when she decided that she could not tolerate her circumstances. She couldn't stand the white school district leadership, who could not be bothered to do the bare minimum. She offered no more latitude to the Black parents who preached patience. In the fall of 1950, Johns approached Inez Davenport—a music teacher and the girlfriend of Moton's well-liked principal—to air her grievances. The Greensboro lunch counter sit-ins were almost a full decade off.

"I told her how sick and tired I was of the inadequate buildings and facilities," Johns later said. She wanted something done to fix it. If she expected commiseration, she didn't get it. Davenport threw the question back at Johns. That prompt proved effective. "Soon," Johns said, "the little wheels began turning."

Johns handpicked four student leaders and organized a meeting in the spot where all the best dubious high school plans are laid: the athletic field's bleachers. One later remembered her pitch: Their parents had asked the children of Farmville to listen and wait. But Johns invoked Scripture—"a little child shall lead them."

For what it's worth, Johns did believe that Moton's principal wanted his students to have what was owed to them. But when she had tried to raise her concerns with him and was brushed off, she decided to take matters into her own hands. "We knew we had to do it ourselves," Johns said, "and that if we had asked for adult help before taking the first step, we would have been turned down." Better to get out ahead. Better to lead and let the others catch up.

For months, Johns plotted. The scheme was simple, but it needed to be implemented with precision. She chose a date in April 1951. At the appointed hour that morning, the principal received a call telling him that two of his students had been detained at the bus station and needed his help. He set out for them, and Johns swooped in. She dispatched her fellow organizers to each classroom with a note bearing the principal's forged signature. It instructed teachers to send their students to meet in the auditorium at eleven a.m.

Once the room was full (and with a cinematic flourish for good measure), Johns had the stage curtains parted at the front of the room. She stood behind the podium and wasted no time getting down to business. First, she dismissed the teachers. When some protested, Barbara Rose Johns—the same quiet and gracious girl who had once been a member of a club called New Homemakers of America—took off a shoe and thwacked it on a bench.

"Out," she shouted.

Then Johns made her pitch. She called for a student strike and whipped out posters lettered with phrases like "We Want a New School or None at All." Her sister, Joan—seated three rows from the front—was so shocked she almost slid off her chair. After Johns laid out her plans, someone stood to ask what kind of punishment protesters could expect to face for leaving school. Johns told her classmates Farmville's jail wasn't big enough to hold them all.

With that, she led hundreds of students out of the auditorium and into the streets. Later that afternoon, Johns mailed a letter to the Richmond NAACP, in which she requested legal help in demanding new school facilities for Moton. The strike was not a furious adolescent outburst, but a calculated preemptive blow. She would need backup. The steering committee that Johns had assembled was coed, but the letter was not. Two girls signed it: Johns and an even unlikelier rule breaker—Moton's student council president, Carrie Stokes.

Johns didn't know it, but her overture reached an organization that had resolved to fight for desegregation alone, not just a marginal improvement in the conditions of Black children's education. Three representatives from the NAACP came to Farmville to level with the strikers. Change seldom came first to rural parts of the South. The district could retaliate against them. It could scrap provisional plans for the school it had been promising to build or even throw the students in jail as truants. But the girls weren't shaken.

"[T]hese kids turned out to be so well organized and their morale was so high, we just didn't have the heart to tell 'em to break it up," one of the NAACP officials said. The team changed course. It laid out the case for going for broke. Desegregation, now. In Farmville.

Johns was elated. "It seemed like reaching for the moon," she said.

The principal, a man named M. Boyd Jones, was less enthused. Jones circulated his own letter a week into the strike and urged the students to stop the protest. The flare-up was costing them valuable time in school and affecting their education. He worried it was giving "the wrong impression" to white leaders in the school district. The historian Richard Kluger cites some evidence that indicates Jones was supportive of his kids. He hadn't wanted to send the letter. But he had a superintendent to answer to—a boss. Johns did not.

Students could not dismantle Jim Crow alone. Adults—with their paperwork and their courtrooms and their well-developed frontal lobes—would prove essential. But Johns anticipated the order of operations: student action first, support from the powers that be second. Not all parents liked it, but several understood. A week after the representatives from the NAACP explained what it might look like to push for desegregation, another mass meeting was held—this time with parents in attendance. One father said that he wished he'd known in advance what the high schoolers were up to. Lester Banks, who served as the NAACP's main organizer in the state of Virginia, had remained in Farmville to be present at the gathering. He responded that as a parent, he felt the same. It would have been nice to know. But as a movement person, he had to be glad word hadn't gotten out. If the parents had known, he went on, "there wouldn't have been a strike."

The meetings continued. A little belated talk, following Johns's action. After Principal Jones's letter went out, one more confab was held to decide what to do next. Johns spoke, and a handful of speakers who were opposed to further upheaval followed her. One of Moton's former principals cautioned that further antagonism could alienate the school district. But Johns refused to grant her critics the last word. She called for her audience to resist intimidation. Her grandmother—whom Barbara called Ma Croner—was there too. And she was terrified for her granddaughter.

When she was a child, Ma Croner had liked to take walks in the woods to deliver her own impassioned speeches about the discrimination she endured. She gave up the ritual when she married. A futile habit of girlhood. But when she heard Johns speaking, the memories rushed back to her. "It came to me that it was my grandchild who was carrying on the speaking," she said. "I felt that God had instilled in her what I was trying to do."

The stories we tell about teenage protest tend to flatten the relationship between generations. It has to be either that children are put up to their actions, with adults goading them into serving as photogenic representatives for the cause, or that children rebel, flouting their parents' rules in an expression of generational animus. But the proposition is oversimplified.

Barbara Johns didn't berate the men and women who had come

to hear her at the meeting. She hadn't broken with her parents and grandparents, but had built on the foundation of their convictions. When she took the floor, she didn't lambast her audience. She compelled the crowd to stand with her.

Johns won the hour. The parents of Farmville took their children's lead.

Less than a month later, the NAACP filed suit at the federal courthouse in Richmond, Virginia, representing 117 Moton students. The first on the list of plaintiffs was not Barbara Johns but a ninth grader named Dorothy E. Davis, who gave the case its name: *Davis v. County School Board of Prince Edward County.*

In his opinion in *Brown*, Earl Warren cited the research of social scientists Kenneth and Mamie Clark. The two had been called as expert witnesses in *Briggs v. Elliott*, another one of the five cases that were later combined into *Brown*. Their testimonies touched on a number of their studies, but the most famous was the "doll test." The experiment gathered Black children between the ages of three and seven and had them introduced to four identical dolls—two brown, two white. The Clarks asked participants to choose which doll was "nice" and which one looked most like them. "Give me the doll that looks bad," read another prompt. Most Black children, the Clarks found, "indicated an unmistakable preference for the white doll and a rejection of the brown doll."

The Clarks' work had a profound effect on Warren, who noted in his decision that legal separation of Black children from white could make them feel so inferior as to "affect their hearts and minds" to a degree that would perhaps never be undone. That finding was foundational to Warren's decision, but it doesn't capture the full scope of the couple's research. In parsing the effects of the American institution of racism, Kenneth Clark found that segregation did more than harm Black students. It stunted the development of white children too. Integration, he felt, wasn't just a prize for Black children and a phenomenon that white children would have to tolerate. He rejected the idea that fairness was a reward and that integration was something to be humored. It was a position that Johns shared. She didn't want integration bestowed on her as an honor. She wanted it to be accorded to her as a right. She didn't want to be "good." She wanted justice.

After Johns led 450 students in the walkout she had masterminded, she told Ma Croner what she had done. Her grandmother was taken aback. "I said to her, 'You reckon you done the right thing?'" she remembered. Johns said she believed she had. She said to her grandmother, "Stick with us."

The Supreme Court handed down its ruling in *Brown v. Board of Education* in 1954. Years had passed since Johns's walkout. The decision explicated the law, but it could not reach into the minds of resistant white parents and convince them to accept it. Across the South, their horror was as immediate as Black parents' euphoria had been.

On both sides of the issue, children came to represent the stakes.

Linda Brown and Barbara Johns were potent representatives for the cause of civil rights. In 1957, Elizabeth Eckford—one of the nine students to integrate Central High in Little Rock, Arkansas—became another. She wore a pristine white-and-gingham skirt in the iconic photo that came to encapsulate so much of the project of integration. Eckford has the face from the textbooks—staring ahead, mouth fixed in a line. Photos of her humiliation forced even President Dwight D. Eisenhower's hand. He federalized the Arkansas National Guard to protect Eckford and the other Black students. The Little Rock Nine muscled through the academic calendar. And the segregationists got to work.

White girls were their weapon, with the howling mass of them standing behind Eckford in that famous photo as just one example. A pamphlet circulated in response to *Brown* alleged that a white girl had been gang-raped in her high school's boiler room and had identified thirty Black male students as the culprits. A father called on other white fathers who wanted "to have white grandchildren" to oppose the decision.

The pressure worked. With no explicit plans for implementation spelled out in *Brown,* and no desire on the part of most white Southerners to consider how the principles that had informed the decision could transform other parts of their social and commercial lives, institutions—schools, churches, bus stations—remained segregated.

The law on its own was just a pile of words. It needed a movement behind it. The issue had to be forced. Girls would have to force it.

THERE WAS NO ONE RACIST INSULT that drove Claudette Colvin to refuse to give up her seat on a segregated bus in March 1955, nine months before Rosa Parks became an icon of the movement for her own act of civil disobedience. It was a series of indignities, stretching back as far as she could remember. When she would later describe that moment and the arrest that followed, she made it sound like neither a spontaneous act of rebellion nor a premeditated stand. It was something else. Closer to fate. It wasn't a choice. It was like divine intervention.

"I just couldn't move," she told a reporter. "History had me glued to the seat."

Colvin was born Claudette Austin in Birmingham, Alabama. Her father bolted when she was an infant. She and her sister, Delphine, moved in with their great-aunt and great-uncle as children. For the girls, the couple became parents, and the two took their last name.

The Colvins, the "quartet," as Claudette called them, lived in a town called Pine Level. It was sedate—just a school, a church, and a general store. But she was "at home in all of it," as she later put it. She knew its trails and quirks. She spent one summer cataloguing its insects. Older women in the neighborhood were like second mothers to her, taking her in for dinner and letting her sleep over. When she and her best friend went off exploring, the two were fearless. "A 'No Trespassing' sign meant nothing at all to us," she once said.

That freedom fed her interest in the world around her. She had questions. About stars and the cosmos. About Japan—how far was she from it? She believed in God. She wondered how he'd made Earth so fast.

The one riddle she could never quite solve was how, as she once phrased it to biographer Phillip Hoose, "the white man came to dominate us." She had heard as a child the biblical teaching that the curse of Ham had condemned Black people to lives of toil and pain. That explanation did not sit well with her. Colvin informed her pastor that she didn't "want to serve a God that would have a cursed race." If Reverend H. H. Johnson was surprised to hear a child question white Christian dogma, he didn't show it. Colvin remembered him looking back at her, proud.

When Colvin was still in grade school, her mother inherited a house in Montgomery and the quartet moved. Their new home was perched on a hill on the northeast side—far from the wide-open sprawl of Pine Level. The area lacked Colvin's beloved woods, but it made up for that with more cosmopolitan pleasures. It had restaurants, lunch counters, and a real, bustling downtown.

Colvin grew up in an Alabama so racist that even basic errands could turn into almost ritualized humiliation. Simple trips to shop for groceries were crosshatched with trip wires. One misstep could mean a brutalizing experience. Black people couldn't sit in restaurants. Black customers weren't allowed to use fitting rooms, so Colvin's mother traced her foot on brown paper to estimate her size when she needed new shoes. Black women who wanted to see how hats looked had to pull hose over their heads, lest their hair "contaminate" the pristine fabric.

Colvin remembered cruel encounters. She arrived at a local optometrist's office when it opened, but was told to come back later. He couldn't risk it. "He knew no white patient would ever sit in a chair that he'd seen a Black sit in," she said. She went shopping and saw a hat she liked in a store downtown. But when she asked the white saleswoman to show it to her, the woman pointed Colvin to other hats instead. What did the woman think? That Colvin couldn't afford it? That she was too unsophisticated to know what kind of hat would suit her?

Racism was destructive and evil, but it could also be exasperating. "For some reason she didn't want me to have the hat I wanted," Colvin said. "I got madder and madder." She informed the saleswoman that she wanted the hat she'd chosen because, unlike her, Colvin didn't have such enormous ears. Her mother put a hand over Colvin's mouth and swept her out of the store.

Colvin didn't set out to make trouble, let alone to get arrested. But she wasn't keen on submitting to a set of unwritten rules that emphasized her second-class citizenship. She didn't want to take on an active role in her own debasement. Neither did her friends. It seemed to her generation that older Black people gave white people a pass. "Older black people were . . . respectful to the white people," Colvin said. Her elders didn't acknowledge the pain, choosing instead to bottle up their resentments. Their anger had no good outlet.

Colvin could get mad too. Her rage would find its target.

. . .

DURING THE HEIGHT of the civil rights movement, activists traveled across the Deep South to organize Black voters. But the earliest recruits to the cause in town after town tended to be people who could not cast a ballot. True believers introduced themselves to organizers on ball fields and in school parking lots. Most of them were children. A disproportionate number of them were girls.

In her account of the women of the civil rights movement, the writer Lynne Olson explores the gendered experience of Jim Crow. Women and girls were often victims of sexual violence and harassment. But Black men faced particular risks. The omnipresent threat of lethal force meant that even a slight show of independence or "insubordination" could cost Black men their lives. Olson writes that the circumstances in part explain the overrepresentation of women and girls in the movement. If someone were going to speak up on the street or in a school or on a bus, as Colvin did, and live to tell the tale, chances were it would be a girl.

The research supports her speculation. In 1949, scholars published a paper that concluded that Black girls experienced less frequent "aggression" and "discrimination" from white people and talked back to their tormentors more often. But the research also underscored fundamental common ground between the sexes. Black children—no matter their class position or gender—all ranked "indifference" as one of the unlikeliest responses to encounter with racism. Their generation would not be quiet.

Several factors contributed to that conviction. Peer culture and the development of mass media illuminated a world outside of the Jim Crow South. Ideas about the nature of childhood had started to evolve. Wasn't it a universal experience? Didn't Black children deserve it too?

And then there was the simple matter of the historical timeline. Colvin's peers remembered World War II. Barbara Johns's father had served in the war. Colvin felt its impact on the farm at Pine Level. "Whenever one of our hens would lay a bad egg," she recalled, "we'd mark it with an 'H'—for Hitler."

Black children as well as white understood what their teachers told them—that the United States had entered the war to beat back fascism in Europe. The contradictions in that effort were obvious to those who experienced vicious racism in the supposed land of the free. America trumpeted equal rights even as its laws sanctioned discrimination. In 1943, at an NAACP conference, student members issued a declaration that connected the struggle at home with the one abroad: "We Negro youth of America, living in a democracy, would be traitors to our country and its principles if we ever ceased in our fight for absolute and complete freedom."

OVER THE SUMMER OF 1952, Colvin's sister, Delphine, came down with polio. She was rushed to the hospital, where Colvin was barred from visiting her. She died within a matter of weeks—just before Colvin was due to enroll in Booker T. Washington High School. The loss made Colvin sensitive. But even if she hadn't been mourning her sister, she might have found her new social environment exhausting. Lighter skin and straightened hair were prized. Colvin's dark skin and curls were scorned.

"For some reason we seemed to hate ourselves," she said later. "We students put down our hair texture and skin color all the time."

In November, one of Colvin's neighbors and classmates was arrested. Jeremiah Reeves was sixteen when he was accused of raping a white housewife. Martin Luther King, Jr., who would become the full-time pastor at the church on Dexter Avenue in 1954, wrote that Reeves had been compelled to confess to a crime that he hadn't committed. But the prospect of a false confession made no difference. He was sentenced to death. For students at Booker T. Washington, the case was a devastating call to action. Colvin went to her first-ever demonstration to protest his treatment. She wrote letters and went to rallies. The NAACP took up the case. It was the first time she had heard of the organization.

The verdict, which was reaffirmed when Reeves was retried, shattered Colvin. She knew racism was immoral. Now she knew it to be lethal. Later, similar shockwaves rippled out when Emmett Till was tortured and murdered in 1955. Then too, his peers reacted with a unique and knowing horror—it could have been them. One Mississippi native remembered how distant she felt from even her own mother in the weeks and months after Till was found dead. She had lost patience with the adults she knew who tiptoed around white men, deferential. What good had placating them done?

The Reeves case galvanized the neighborhood, and Colvin in particular started to formulate new ideas about racism and American culture. One of her teachers asked her to write a paper describing how she saw herself. She wrote that she felt clean and could not understand the laws that kept her out of the downtown fitting rooms. She refused to hate her natural hair. Was it so awful?

"I wrote I was an American," Colvin said. She counted too.

The teacher read Colvin's paper in front of the whole class. It had impressed her. Colvin's classmates were horrified. "Everybody said, 'Oh, Claudette! You're crazy,'" Colvin recalled. "And my closest friend said, 'Claudette, would you really come to school with your hair kinky?'"

Colvin felt dared. She went home and washed her hair. She returned to school with it set in braids. Her classmates were appalled. Her boyfriend broke up with her. Colvin was undeterred.

"I kept wearing it like that, and they kept me out of school plays," she said. "Everybody at school had heard about my braids. I wore them until I proved to them that I wasn't crazy. I had to convince them that I wasn't crazy."

The hair debacle has come up in multiple interviews with Colvin—some of them conducted decades apart. Reading them, it almost seems like a detour. The stream-of-consciousness memories of a girl recounting a pivotal period in her own adolescence: Delphine's death. The Reeves case. Her hair. Her protest.

In the list, the hair should be the obvious outlier. But is hair ever a matter of minor consequence to a high school student? In her recollections, Colvin dwells on it. She situates it in the timeline—Delphine, Reeves, the hair, her classmates' reactions, the breakup, her sense that Alabama needed to change and that she could help change it. Put like that—put as Colvin put it—the hair was not incidental. The hats were not incidental. Shopping was not beside the point. Girlhood could be restrictive and limiting, but its rites could be determinative too.

High school resumed with its attendant dramas. In the winter of 1955, when Colvin was a junior, two of her favorite teachers co-led a week on Black history. The unit presented a rare chance to learn about Black culture at a time when the entire set of reference books to which Colvin had access included a total of two entries on Black people. (Both were men.)

Colvin later tried to find the words to describe how the experience had motivated her. She once more invoked hair. "I was done talking about 'good hair' and 'good skin' but not addressing our grievances," she said. "I was tired of hoping for justice."

In March, with memories of her teachers' lessons fresh in her mind, Colvin and a few friends boarded the Highland Gardens bus at the corner of Dexter Avenue and Bainbridge Street. It was the middle of the school week, and Colvin had been dismissed earlier than usual because of a staff meeting for teachers. There were no white riders on board, which meant Colvin could avoid one of the more degrading rituals of public transport in Jim Crow–era Alabama: She didn't have to disembark after her fare was paid and reboard from the back of the bus. Instead, she handed the driver her student voucher and walked down the center aisle. She slid into a seat and piled her textbooks on her lap. The bus was headed downtown and it soon collected white workers, who filled their designated seats at the front and crowded into the aisle.

The bus driver called back to the schoolgirls as one white woman hovered around Colvin. He needed their seats. Three of them moved back. Colvin remained. The driver repeated himself. Get up. But Colvin said nothing. She didn't move. Hadn't she paid her fare? Wasn't she entitled to her seat?

People on the bus—Black and white—started staring and talking. She had to get up, said one girl. But another waved her off: "She doesn't have to. Only one thing you have to do is stay black and die."

The bus was now clogged with people. The driver warned Colvin: He'd call the police if she didn't make room. At the intersection of Bibb and Commerce streets, two men in uniform climbed aboard with their squad car idling outside. "Who is it?" one asked. The driver pointed to Colvin. The police knocked her books down. She was dragged off the bus and kicked. The police handcuffed her and took her to jail.

The cops called her a "Black bitch" and a "whore." The police report filed with her fingerprints described the scene in words that ring with momentousness now: "An unidentified colored female that was sitting in this disputed seat moved to the rear when we asked her to, but Claudette Colvin, age 15, colored female, refused."

She was led to a cell, and when the door shut behind her, she heard the lock fall into place. "It was the worst sound I ever heard," she said. "It sounded final. It said I was trapped."

Colvin had not been permitted to make a phone call, but the classmates who'd been on the bus with her rushed home to tell her mother what had happened. The Colvins' pastor drove her to the police station and he bailed Colvin out. Back at the house, friends and neighbors started gathering, fussing over Colvin when she got home. "I had been talking about getting our rights ever since Jeremiah Reeves was arrested, and now they knew I was serious," Colvin recalled. In another interview, she explained her state of mind: "I was just angry. Like a teenager might be. I was just downright angry."

Word of the arrest spread fast. Most people in town were incensed on her behalf. A few were impressed. When the widow of a prominent Black dentist in town heard the news, she beamed. "Bless her heart," the woman said, "she fought like a little tigress." Several more wanted to get to work. The members of an organization called the Women's Political Council had been hoping to mount a real effort to take down segregation in Alabama, and its leaders had waited almost a decade for a suitable flash point. Now here was a fracas.

Leaders and activists like Virginia Durr and Rosa Parks, who helmed the local NAACP Youth Council, floated a protest. The lawyer Fred Gray—one of just two Black lawyers in the area—said he was prepared to file a civil lawsuit on Colvin's behalf. He'd grown up in Montgomery and had always planned to return after law school to take aim at his hometown's racist policies. Jo Ann Robinson— president of the Women's Political Council and an English professor at Alabama State College—volunteered to fundraise for the cause.

Letters poured in, applauding Colvin. "The wonderful thing which you have just done makes me feel like a craven coward," one man wrote to Colvin in a letter of support. "How encouraging it would be if more adults had your courage, self-respect and integrity." Some criticized her, but Colvin came to feel that the teachers and parents who tut-tutted felt more judged than judgmental. "I think they knew they should have done what I did long before," Colvin said. "They were em-barrassed that it took a teenager to do it."

After Colvin was charged with violating the state law that man-dated segregation and disorderly conduct, E. D. Nixon, the president of the Montgomery chapter of the NAACP, offered to put her in touch with Parks while her case was still pending. He wanted Colvin to have a mentor. When the two were introduced, Parks could not hold back her surprise. "I was looking for some big old burly overgrown teenager who sassed white people out," she told Colvin. "But no, they pulled a little girl off the bus."

Little girl, indeed. At the time of her arrest, Colvin was underage. She lived at home. The *Alabama Journal* described her as "a bespec-tacled, studious looking high school student" and remarked that she accepted the terms of her "indefinite" probation while she awaited a court date "with the same cool aloofness she had maintained through-out her 2½-hour hearing." She was the picture of adolescence.

But childhood is a social determination. And while we have our legal cutoff points to mark its end, the definitions of "child" and "adult" have never been fixed. That slack explains how a white teen-ager accused of rape can plead juvenile indiscretion and hope for le-nience, but a Black one accused of insulting a white woman can be tortured to death. It explains how one minute Colvin was a girl and the next she was not.

The timeline is a matter of dispute, but what we do know is that at some point, Nixon announced that Colvin would not be serving as the test case the movement had been waiting for, and within a few months, she was pregnant.

"Doubts crept in," wrote Phillip Hoose, who collaborated with Colvin on the book *Claudette Colvin: Twice Toward Justice.* "A swarm of adjectives began to buzz around Claudette Colvin, words like 'emotional' and 'uncontrollable' and 'profane.'" She didn't have the right pedigree. She didn't have the right parents. Nixon believed that to take on the buses in Alabama, he needed a plaintiff he was sure could win. That meant not just making a careful legal case, but also staging a precise kind of public relations campaign. Colvin did not fit the profile.

Once it became clear that Colvin was pregnant, even Parks agreed that the movement would have to look elsewhere. "If the white press got ahold of that information, they would have [had] a field day," she said. "They'd call her a bad girl, and her case wouldn't have a chance."

Would Colvin still be presumed innocent? Was she still the little girl whom Parks had cheered for? She was a student, but stamped with sex. It threatened to stain the entire effort.

The civil suit was dropped. Fred Gray did defend Colvin in court, where she was found guilty and placed on indefinite probation. In her memoir, Jo Ann Robinson writes that Colvin had been calm during the trial. But when the verdict was read, her "agonized sobs penetrated the atmosphere of the courthouse." Colvin hadn't even turned sixteen.

Colvin's trauma was a public spectacle, but in private, she harbored even deeper pain. She never named the man who'd gotten her pregnant. He was married but told her he was separated from his wife. He was much older than she was. "Nowadays, you'd call it statutory rape, but back then it was just the kind of thing that happened," Colvin said in an interview with *The Guardian* in 2000. "When I told my mother I was pregnant, I thought she was going to have a heart attack. If I had told my father who did it, he would have killed him."

After the trial, a few Black riders refused the buses in a show of support for Colvin. But with no organizing apparatus backing them up, the ad hoc protest fizzled. At school, her classmates avoided her. She hadn't won her case. She'd gotten pregnant. For teenagers, is there a more toxic combination than "loser" and "slut"?

People whispered behind her back. A few mocked her stand, imitating how she'd cried out on the bus: "It's my constitutional right! It's my constitutional right!" She was no longer the girl who had inspired grown men. She was a woman who had come unglued.

"I cried a lot, and people saw," Colvin told her biographer. People called her emotional, overwrought. "Well, who wouldn't be emotional after something like that?" she wanted to know. Who wouldn't have cried?

Movement leaders who had swept into Colvin's orbit hustled out just as fast. Parks was a notable exception. She still invited Colvin to participate in the NAACP Youth Council. The message from adults was otherwise clear: Someone else would represent their discontent. Someone who looked the part.

The bad news: The next person to get arrested on a segregated bus also did not look the part. She was another Black girl. In the fall of 1955, Mary Louise Smith, then eighteen, was told to hand over her seat. Smith declined. She told the driver that she had no less "privilege to sit" than a white woman did. The police were called and Smith was arrested. The incident reached the well-sourced Nixon. He did want a protest, but this girl was no more suitable than Colvin had been. He'd heard her father was a drunk and that she lived in a shack in a destitute neighborhood. He had a practical and more concrete concern as well. Smith's father had paid her fine, which complicated a potential appeal. Smith later contested Nixon's characterizations. Her father was not an alcoholic, although he was a single parent. She lived in a frame house in a working-class neighborhood. It didn't matter. She too was passed over.

At the Women's Political Council, the mood was impatient. Robinson had drafted a memo to announce a mass plan of action soon after Colvin was arrested. It was finished and finalized, save for a blank spot where she planned to fill in the date when the protest should start. She had written the memo in March, and now it was October. She didn't want to lose even more momentum. Two girls had stood up. Two girls had been dismissed. Someone else would have to follow their lead.

LOST LEADERS

—

THE MOVEMENT'S INVISIBLE GIRLS

T wo months after Smith was arrested, Rosa Parks boarded a bus to head home. It was three weeks before Christmas. The driver asked her to stand as white riders filed into their rows. Parks said no. The wheels turned. Fate clicked into place.

When the driver told her he was going to call the cops, Parks would have known the risks. She was a committed and plugged-in activist. She knew people who had lost their jobs or were harassed for even minor acts of protest. People had been killed for no more than this—this kind of insubordination. But while she waited for police to arrive, she wasn't thinking about what would come next. She was instead meditating on the same issue that had been bothering her for months. She was thinking about how the adults she knew had failed their children. Perhaps she was thinking about how the adults she knew failed one in particular.

Parks was arrested and spent a few hours in jail. It was all the time the Women's Political Council needed. Jo Ann Robinson whipped out her memo. How long must it have taken her to update the date on the announcement? A minute? Two? The protest would start on December 5.

Calls for mass action had been growing louder since Colvin's arrest nine months earlier. Her degradation put the humiliations of others in sharper focus. Parks's arrest was the last straw. The council called for Black residents to remain off the buses beginning later that same week. Leaflets were stacked in piles, and distribution routes were mapped out. Robinson knew that the information had to get out fast. So, fine, she went a little overboard: She made thirty-five thousand copies of her flyer.

On December 5—the date of Parks's trial—Parks's friend Johnnie Carr woke up and looked out her window to see the sidewalks crowded with Black women walking to work. At the courthouse downtown, hundreds more turned out to show their support for Parks. Kids skipped school to cram into the plaza outside. When Parks arrived, one of the girls shouted so loud that Parks could hear her over the din: "They've messed with the wrong one now."

The action started and did not stop. People walked miles. When it was late, when it rained, when their legs ached. People were fired, and Black women who worked as maids or cooks for white people demonstrated particular resilience. Participants were harassed and threatened. Homes and cars were vandalized. The protest was nonviolent. The response was not so principled.

One month turned to two, which became four. Buses whizzed past the Black protesters, picking up and dropping off white people. In the meantime, leaders had to come to a consensus about what its precise aim would be. Desegregation seemed inconceivable. More modest proposals were suggested. One would have allowed Black riders to remain in their seats in *their own section* at the back of the bus even when white people ran out of space in theirs. Another advocated for hiring more Black drivers to serve bus routes in Black neighborhoods. But Fred Gray, who had represented Colvin in court ten months earlier, waved off the compromises. He wanted to force a reckoning on the practice of segregation, not just on the minutiae of its implementation. It was the same approach he had intended to pursue with Colvin in the civil case that never was. Now he could take another crack at it. Parks was the ideal figurehead for a mass demonstration, but as before, the civil case still needed a plaintiff. She was less well suited to that cause. Parks had her own trial in state court to contend with. Meanwhile, Gray hoped to file a federal case, representing Black bus riders who could prove that race-based discrimination had been a factor in their mistreatment. He canvassed for volunteers. He didn't find them. Who could blame people for not wanting to step forward? Participation could mean severe consequences. Gray spoke to office workers and men who labored downtown. He went to see a group of ministers, hoping a reverend would join the cause. No one did.

He should have known who would show up. Women came forward. Five became four when one dropped out. Two of them were teenage girls: Smith and Colvin.

PARKS HAS BEEN CANONIZED in popular culture as an exhausted older woman. In the picture books published decades later, she is depicted less as a radical activist than as a seamstress too tired to stand after hours on her feet. Her fierce organizing—her role in the NAACP and her ties to the likes of Robinson and Nixon—seldom made an appearance. Her relationship with Colvin is almost never mentioned.

That dominant narrative works to set her apart from the movement. It focuses on the individual actions of one woman and makes them seem spontaneous. But Rosa Parks had been committed to ending segregation and to bringing about justice for Black women well before she refused to give up her seat on that bus.

Like Johns and Colvin, Parks had been a defiant child. Her teachers instilled in her a deep confidence—not based on looks or smarts, but grounded in the fundamental conviction that she had a basic human right to be respected. She learned to demand it. In the memoir she later published, she writes about a white child in her neighborhood who had threatened to hit her. Parks remembered that she didn't run or seethe in private. She told him that if he dared, she would smash his head in with a brick.

Parks first got involved with the NAACP in 1942, when she was in her late twenties—the start of over a decade of organizing leading up to her fateful bus ride. She became the adviser to and leader of the local NAACP Youth Council in 1949. The group gave her a place to build genuine relationships with children, despite having none of her own. "We just kind of fell in love with her," said Doris Crenshaw, who served as vice president of the council under Parks. "I had a feeling that I could help alleviate all of the injustices that were going on, and I wanted to be part of that." Colvin, who joined at Parks's urging, would sometimes sleep over at her house after meetings.

Working with adolescents was a calling—one that Parks had recommitted to after taking part in a workshop at the Highlander Folk School in August 1955. The center, located in Appalachian Tennessee, was an interracial quasi–boot camp for labor and civil rights organizers. It revived Parks, who'd been despairing about the state of progress in the Jim Crow South. The workshop introduced her to a once-unfathomable future—one in which she might be able to live and work and learn and eat on an equal basis with white people.

Still, when her two-week session ended, and Parks was invited to answer the question that all participants did about what she would do with the skills she'd acquired once she returned home, she reverted to her usual skepticism. She was a realist about what she would have to work with in Alabama—bigoted white people, divided Black people, not at all the kind of place that sustained transformative action. Parks did not pledge herself to a particular plan or set benchmarks to evaluate her own success. But she did vow to redouble her efforts to reach the group she believed mattered most: children. Her peers were a lost cause. Young people could still be saved.

The beloved educator and activist Septima Clark—who mentored Parks at Highlander—remembered what she said next. When she went home to Alabama, "she promised to work with those kids." That generational divide—busted. Parks was a woman who put her faith in girls.

She did have a soft spot for adolescents—their resolve and their passions. She also knew their vulnerabilities. Parks and her childhood friend Johnnie Carr agonized over the fate of Black girls who'd been raped but whose white abusers would never be held to account. She went out looking for justice.

Parks spent part of the summer that she traveled to Highlander with Colvin. She had welcomed Colvin into the NAACP Youth Council in the hopes that it would be a forum for her to cultivate her activist streak. After Parks returned from Tennessee, she pushed Colvin more. When the council met at a local church, Parks urged Colvin to recount the details of her arrest on the bus. Colvin—attuned as girls are to their relative position in a crowd—noticed that her peers "seemed bored with it." The anecdote had been told and retold. What better evidence is there that Parks embraced her role as a mother of the movement? The kids were mortified.

The time that Parks spent working with the NAACP is not at the center of stories about Parks and activism. But stories from that summer and her time at the helm of the Youth Council paint a picture of a woman determined to understand and relate to the lives of teenagers. At council meetings, Parks would have listened to their gripes and their disappointments. She would have understood their motivations. It's not just that she had met Colvin a few times or had talked to her about her arrest once or twice. Parks spent so much time with Colvin in the lead-up to her own arrest that she knew how Colvin took her coffee. Parks could be reserved. She was introverted and quiet even at Highlander. But she came alive around her kids. Colvin remembered her passing around handouts, brimming with conviction: "We are going to break down the walls of segregation."

When Colvin's role in the movement was rediscovered and publicized decades later, no one could have intended for her readmission into the record to replace or diminish Parks's stand. But we are not so good at holding two truths at once. So the elevation of Colvin has sometimes meant at least a rhetorical demotion for Parks. It sounds like: You've heard about Rosa Parks. Meet the girl who did it first. The historian Jeanne Theoharis—Parks's biographer—takes issue with the narratives that frame the historical record as a winner-take-all competition. Lives do not line up on linear timelines. Stories and fates are intertwined.

Parks did not become an activist the moment she was arrested. Colvin did not cease to be one because her mentor refused to relinquish her seat on that bus.

Parks's season at the helm of the NAACP Youth Council is more than a neat biographical detail. Her work with students informed her own activism. She was committed to demonstrating that there was real power out there, available for someone determined to claim it. Wasn't that the point of Parks's insistence that Colvin relive her arrest "a million times," as Colvin had once complained? To show the children not just what was possible but what would have to be risked?

Picture Colvin, recounting the details to her stupefied peers. Now zoom out and see the woman in the corner who was listening too. If there was an adult in Alabama prepared to learn from the example of a girl, would it not have been Parks?

THE MONTHS AFTER PARKS'S arrest were a brutal time for Colvin. And the first weeks of December were a nadir. Because the flyers had not named Parks at first—other than to note that another "Negro woman" had been arrested on the buses—Colvin hadn't known who spurred the mass action.

When she found out it was Parks, she was torn. Colvin had wanted someone to do what she had. She had been desperate for it. In a sense, the fact that it was someone she knew made her own sidelining easier to take. "If she had been a total stranger, it . . . would have hurt me a little bit," Colvin later said. At least this: "We had the same ideas."

Still, when it happened, some part of her deflated. There had been a time when Colvin believed she would be "the centerpiece of the bus case," as she later put it. She wanted to appeal her case—that case, based on that arrest—to the Supreme Court. She wanted to lead the protest. She was denied the chance.

The odds had never been in her favor. Some questioned whether even the most poised teenager could have withstood the venom that a case like hers would unleash in Alabama. When she got pregnant, it was another bit of evidence that she didn't have the face—or the form—for the movement. At least Colvin knew Parks and liked her. It was a modest consolation.

While her neighbors walked in protest, Colvin watched. She'd been expelled from school for getting pregnant. Her shirts stretched over her stomach. She heard from Parks. She spent a lot of time alone. Around Christmas, she traveled to Birmingham on her own. She used the time to come to terms with her situation. She had been hurt and she hadn't deserved it. The hours she'd spent in jail still haunted her. But she would be a mother soon. It would serve no one if she fell apart, least of all her unborn child. She might not be a leader, but she didn't have to be shunned. When she returned home, she started attending the meetings and listening to speakers like King. She preferred the gatherings held on the other side of town, where fewer people recognized her.

It's odd how stories about Colvin focus on her arrest when her most tangible contribution to the movement came months later. *Browder v. Gayle*, as the case came to be called, was not some sideshow court case, and Colvin was not one of hundreds of plaintiffs. She was one of four. When she was asked to join it, she was sixteen. It was 1956, and the buses were losing tens of thousands of dollars a week as the protest stretched into its third month. Colvin was seven months pregnant—far from a picture-perfect plaintiff. But when Fred Gray came to the house and laid out his plans, she didn't hesitate. Her parents didn't either. The couple steeled themselves for the backlash and let her volunteer.

Browder gave Colvin another shot in court. She believed this time didn't have to end in tears. In choosing to be brave while "respectable" men cowered, Colvin fulfilled that old first wish—to tell people she wasn't going to just take it because of what she looked like or where she lived.

While she awaited her court date and counted down to her son's arrival, she tried to visualize what she wanted to accomplish. She wanted to channel Harriet Tubman. She rehearsed her lines. She pictured the courtroom as the Colosseum. "I had one last speech," she said. "I was going to make the most of it."

It was springtime when she testified. She was six weeks postpartum and still a minor. She should have been a month out from her high school graduation. Instead, she had an infant at home and pumped in the morning so breast milk would not leak through the front of her best blue dress on the stand. She was the final witness—saved for last because her account was seen as the most dramatic. The girl whose textbooks had been thrown from her lap. The girl who'd been carted off to jail because she sat on a bus after school.

When Colvin was questioned, government representatives didn't spend much time on the details of her arrest. She was asked instead about her politics. Who led this movement? Who had baited a bunch of women and girls into mounting such a harebrained crusade? Colvin and Smith might have seen themselves as independent people who were more than equipped to come to their own conclusions about fairness and justice. White officials recast them as pawns.

The questions were designed to get Colvin to point to King as the initiator of the convulsions in Alabama. The minister whose speeches had inspired Colvin after her return from Birmingham had been branded an outsider and an instigator in the local white press. He was the maestro. Colvin and Smith were the puppets. But the master plan didn't work. King would become an icon, and he did help mobilize the movement. But he wasn't the reason why Colvin remained in her seat on that bus. He wasn't responsible.

Colvin was under oath when she answered: "Our leader is just we ourself."

After both Smith and Colvin testified, the pair went to have lunch together—out of view of the hundred or so people who had packed the courtroom to hear them on the stand. With Jo Ann Robinson as chaperone, it was their first face-to-face interaction. Colvin reveled in the optics—a pair of teenage girls who'd been deemed so unsuitable, now the hope of the movement. It had fallen to them—the two troublemakers. Colvin was sixteen. Smith was nineteen. It was a gabfest.

"We sat there eating and comparing notes about what had happened to us," Colvin said. "I was proud that two teenaged girls had stood up."

Late in the afternoon, Colvin came home to find her son sleeping in his bassinet. She had been humiliated and ostracized, so marginalized in the movement that while her name was included on the handouts that the Women's Political Council distributed after Parks's arrest in December, it had been misspelled: "Claudette Colbert"—like the famous (and white) actress.

Now some of the same people who had overlooked her had shaken her hand. Before Colvin went to sleep that night, she whispered to her son, "I think I might have done us some good."

In June 1956, the decision came down. The three-judge federal court panel had ruled two to one in favor of the plaintiffs. Colvin heard about the outcome on the news. Despite how the movement had relied on her in court, no one had bothered to phone to let her know. If Colvin felt bitter, she didn't have much time to wallow in it. She had started to feel the financial strain of motherhood. Although she lived with her parents, which spared her the stress of finding and affording a place of her own, she had no real source of income. That desperation was part of the reason she had hoped some of the movement leaders would reach out to her in the aftermath of the *Browder* decision. Given her contributions to the cause and the personal peril in which she'd put herself to further their aims, she wondered whether someone would feel moved to help her. She wanted material support, but what she craved was acceptance. Instead, it was almost as if she'd been sacrificed for the cause.

The bad girl had served her purpose. The bad girl would not be embraced.

Colvin later admitted that she fantasized about someone offering to throw her a shower. It wouldn't have netted her much cash, but it might have shown her that the people who mattered most to her cared. "I didn't hear from . . . them after I left the courthouse," she said. "No one called after I testified." Not Parks. Not even Colvin's own legal team.

It must have seemed to Colvin as it does to most teenagers—that the adults had a plan and were unified in their decision to exclude her from it. But leadership—King, Nixon, Parks, Robinson—was more splintered than Colvin could have known. "There was all sorts of dissension," Theoharis explained. Colvin's heroes were at odds over credit and reputation and about progress and how best to achieve it. The fact that Black riders were still spurning the buses heightened the pressure on them. It's almost crueler, the truth of it: No one had made a choice about Colvin—about whether to contact her or include her or elevate her or abandon her. No one seemed to think about her at all.

The court decision in June can seem now like the consequential moment. It was the judgment that integrated the buses. It should be as known as *Brown*. But at the time, the consequences were less clear. Despite the favorable outcome, a pending appeal with the Supreme Court meant that white leaders could keep buses segregated for at least the short term. For six more months, Black residents kept walking.

In November 1956, the Supreme Court affirmed the June decision. It took an additional five weeks for federal marshals to serve written notices to local elected leadership in Alabama, demanding desegregation. It was not until the morning after that about half a dozen men and women, including King, boarded buses, paid their fares, and signaled the end of the protest. Colvin wasn't there to share in the photo op. Neither were the other women who had testified in *Browder*.

She didn't get the credit, but like countless women and girls who have expanded the bounds of what we think of as possible, Colvin did get her fair share of the blame. She couldn't hold down a job. Whenever someone figured out who she was—and word traveled fast—she'd be fired. She stuck to restaurant and cafeteria work, not wanting to spend too much time in white people's houses as a domestic worker. She knew the Ku Klux Klan was active in the area. It felt like too great a risk to be in such close quarters with people who might want to do her harm. At home on King Hill, her father sat with a shotgun near the door.

The threat of violence haunted not just Colvin but all the men and women who were visible in the movement. Law enforcement was uninterested in coming to their aid. More often, police and elected leaders were implicated. There was nothing for Colvin or the others to do but wait it out and hope for a combination of luck and quick thinking if the moment called for it. Colvin's mother had not interfered when Colvin said she wanted to join *Browder*, but she did tell Colvin to be quiet about her involvement in the cause, hoping to spare her this burden.

In an interview with *The New York Times*, Colvin still remembered what her mother had said to her after Parks was arrested: "Let Rosa be the one. White people aren't going to bother Rosa." She had lighter skin, for one. And people liked her better.

But white people did harass Parks. Like Colvin, she struggled to find work. Her husband and mother suffered too. Their situation was so untenable that, in 1957, Parks and her husband moved to Detroit to be closer to Rosa's brother and cousin. Parks accepted the first job she could get—as a hostess at a guesthouse for the Hampton Institute. The storied organizer and activist would be responsible for overseeing the dining room and housekeeping staff. She didn't mind the menial work, but the practicalities were less than ideal. Hampton was in Virginia. Desperate for income, she went. She did not return to Detroit until 1959, having been diagnosed with ulcers that would plague her for the rest of her life.

In a letter, Virginia Durr observed with considerable ire, "To be a heroine is fine, but it does not pay off." She was talking about her close friend Rosa Parks. She could have been talking about Colvin.

THERE IS A TEMPTATION in recounting the stories of the girls of the period—girls like Johns and Smith and Colvin—to make a great show of their fearlessness. Teenagers don't have a reputation for thinking through the consequences of their actions, and if the girls who helped spur the civil rights movement acted without thinking about potential repercussions, then we have a convenient explanation for what gave them the chutzpah to volunteer for a cause that most adults dared not touch. No worries, no risk-assessment capabilities—just impulse. It's a rationale that absolves. Worse, it turns acts of genuine daring into developmental inevitabilities.

The invented alibi fails to account for people like Parks and Robinson and King, who pushed for justice despite having an evident and keen understanding of what could happen to them as a result. King paid the ultimate price. Parks knew she could suffer for her involvement in the movement and she did.

But it's also dangerous. The idea that Black children are unable to feel pain or fear is a relic of the plantation. It persists with dire consequences. The "adultification" of Black girls has enabled centuries of violence—from Harriet Jacobs, who documented her abuse in *Incidents in the Life of a Slave Girl,* to Kaia Rolle, who was arrested and handcuffed at age six for throwing a tantrum in class in September 2019.

In the popular consciousness, that trope translates into depictions of Black children as either superhuman or deviant. Researchers have found that teachers use words like "loud," "defiant," and "precocious" to describe Black girls more often than applying those same terms to girls of other races. It's a trend that contributes to what educator and activist Monique W. Morris has identified as the excessive criminalization of Black girls and their overrepresentation in the juvenile justice population.

But the notion that students who organized and protested and spoke in public were fearless is above all ahistorical. The girls who participated in the civil rights movement made that plain in interviews and in their own records. Terror gripped them. It alienated them from their parents and peers. It wore them down.

Fear could be dealt with and sometimes even overcome—how else could Colvin have not just remained in her seat on that March afternoon, but testified on the stand fourteen months later? But it was ever present even as it was mastered. The secret was not to let it overwhelm the greater mission. It had to be used instead as evidence that the stakes were real. You were scared because the stakes were real.

In 1965, volunteers affiliated with the Student Nonviolent Coordinating Committee (SNCC) published a collection of poems and artwork. The poet Langston Hughes writes the foreword. The rest of it belonged to the students themselves. In one contribution, a poet, sixteen, declares that she would not let her fear prevent her from acting. She would not be dissuaded. "Here I have come and here I shall stay," she wrote. "And no amount of fear my determination can sway."

THANKS TO JOHNS and a generation of students like her, the walk-outs spread. We think of them as a phenomenon of the Jim Crow South. But Black and Latino students in the North and the Midwest and the West had hopes for themselves too. A de facto segregation ruled in education, even though no law on the books mandated it. Curricula were staid and out of date. Districts in poor neighborhoods lacked even basic resources. Girls like Johns had done it. Students from coast to coast planned walkouts too.

In 1968, in Los Angeles, several schools banded together to voice their opposition to a range of school policies—racist lesson plans, underresourced facilities, even dress codes. Just as threadbare accommodations had eaten Johns up, so too did inadequate classrooms and textbooks embolden a Chicana student named Paula Crisostomo. Growing up in East Los Angeles, a Chicano neighborhood, she didn't know quite what she was missing out on. It was in visiting schools in richer, better-resourced neighborhoods that she came to see the injustice. Crisostomo attended one of a handful of schools that spent that spring devising a massive strike. Wilson High School kicked it off on March 1. Then thousands of students at Garfield High School and Jefferson High School declined to go to class on March 5. On March 6, students at Lincoln and Roosevelt high schools walked out at the same time.

Brenda Holcomb, one of the strike leaders and a student at Jefferson, told the *Los Angeles Sentinel* that she and her peers turned to walkouts after exhausting other options. "Too often teachers and administrators shrugged off student complaints or branded students who differed with them as 'troublemakers,'" she said. The protest was how she and her peers could be heard. It took months for the walkouts to resolve; several students in East Los Angeles were arrested. The charges were later dropped, but there was no neat conclusion to the protests. More walkouts were held in Boston and New York throughout the 1960s and '70s, overlapping with other flavors of student protest. But the issues that drove girls like Crisostomo and Holcomb from their classrooms persisted and continued to fester. Perhaps that's one of the reasons why these demonstrations get even less attention in histories of the civil rights movement and the work it inspired: *Brown* had a clear-cut victor, even if the case has been undermined for decades. These student-led revolts had less obvious winners and losers.

Moctesuma Esparza, another organizer of the walkouts in Los Angeles, offered a different take: He came to believe that the demonstrations deserved to be remembered because the results were inconclusive. The protests left behind unfinished business. He and his fellow leaders had provided a "manual on how to organize . . . what the risks are, what has to be thought of, and what could happen, and what needs to be done."

Let it be an invitation. The work is incomplete.

BARBARA JOHNS WAS SENT to live with her beloved uncle Vernon after the walkout in Farmville. The uprooting, the move, what happened to her siblings who were left behind—for Joan Cobbs that period was at least as hard as what preceded it. Cobbs knew that Johns had done a "brave, courageous thing." But that didn't make the retribution easier to take. After the strike, white shop owners stopped accepting credit to help Black farmers bridge the gap between harvest seasons. The move affected Black families not just in Farmville but across the area. Cobbs's mother had to take a job in Washington, D.C., to bring in additional income. She lived with her sister during the week, not able to afford either an additional place or the long commute. "Things were hard," Cobbs said. "It was a difficult time."

It was much later that Cobbs was told that after word got out about what her sister had done, a farmer who knew Robert Johns well told him to get Barbara out of town. The man wanted to do him the favor of a warning. He might not get another. "He had heard the talk," Cobbs said of the farmer. It haunted Cobbs, thinking about what could have happened to her sister or to her parents and grandparents. "It could have been something that was tragic," she said.

Colvin left the South. She earned her GED and moved to New York in 1958. She was later hired as a nurse's aide at a Catholic hospital. She worked there for decades. She never returned to Alabama, and she made no attempt to get back in touch with the activists who'd moved on from her. The people who knew Colvin's past would sometimes mention it, amazed at how well known the Parks incident had become. Relatives noted that Parks was an icon of the movement, with Colvin relegated to a footnote or not mentioned at all.

"One day someone might mention you," Colvin remembered someone telling her. "They'll go through the court files and want to know who was Claudette Colvin." People have started to find out.

In a rare interview in 2009, Colvin said she had come to terms with her place in history—and with her heartache over how it had unfolded too. "I'm glad I did it," she said. "My generation was angry. And people just wanted a change."

Colvin's pivotal role in the movement is better known now than it was even a decade ago. A museum opened in Farmville to commemorate the student strike and Johns's leadership in it. Cobbs has healed from the trauma of that time; she said Johns has too. "I think some of the hurt and bitterness that I had from that time left—a lot of it, most of it," Cobbs said. She credited her faith and closure that has come with Johns's gradual recognition. When it was announced that the statue of Confederate general Robert E. Lee would come down in Charlottesville, Virginia, someone suggested to Cobbs that a monument to her sister take its place. "It's every kind of good adjective I can think of," Cobbs pronounced. "It's unbelievable."

There will be more books written about the students of the civil rights movement and more about its forgotten girls. We have recovered them and so it makes sense that we're so tempted to rewind the timeline—to start not with *Brown*, but with the girl who helped make *Brown* possible; not with Parks, but with the girl who preceded her.

But the correction of historical narratives isn't a matter of "find" and "replace." We don't just need to know the first. We need to know the arc. It's not just that girls did it when others wouldn't dare. It's that girls—in their flouting of convention—showed others what was possible.

Barbara Johns didn't organize the student strike anticipating a fight in the Supreme Court. She did it because she had come to understand that direct action—acting out—accomplished more than "behaving" and hoping for a reward.

Colvin could never have envisioned the months of disruption that would follow from her arrest—how it spurred Parks, how it sharpened the vision Nixon and Robinson and others had for what would come next.

We like our images of girls on the vanguard and alone. But their histories are better told—and their legacies better secured—when we contextualize them. Who helped them? Who fed them and calmed them and printed their flyers? Who abandoned them? And who learned from their example?

6

CLIQUES

——

FEMALE FRIENDSHIP
AND FREEDOM

n a piece for *The Nation* in 1960, the historian Howard Zinn observes a change happening among the polite Black girls who had done their parents proud and gone to elite schools like Spelman, a private liberal arts college for Black women in Atlanta.

He used to be able to spot one of them a mile off. He observes how she walked, talked, poured tea. How she went to church once a week. How she modeled good citizenship and class. Now something seemed to have set her loose.

"For the first time," he wrote, "the anger pent up in generations of quiet, well-bred" Black women was seeping out.

Spelman girls were "still 'nice,'" Zinn wrote, but not enough to keep them from protesting outside supermarkets and segregated lunch counters in Atlanta. Spelman girls were still well behaved: Just look at how groups of them marched off to jail in such neat lines.

Zinn saw a Spelman girl cross the lawn one afternoon to pin a notice to the bulletin board. She radiated decorum. He could see that she'd posted an invitation to her friends: "Young Ladies Who Can Picket Please Sign Below."

Zinn coined a new phrase. Oh, he could still tell a Spelman girl. How did he recognize her? "She's under arrest."

The start of the new decade seemed to usher in a new phase in the movement. The role that girls held in it shifted too. The intrepid Johns and Colvin had acted without waiting to see who could be rallied to the cause. Now in high schools and universities, teenagers were mobilizing in tandem. Science fairs, the cheerleading squad, sleepover parties—it had all been practice.

Friends did not let friends join the movement alone.

A FEW MONTHS before Zinn made his pronouncement, the brilliant and charismatic Diane Nash was sitting in her bedroom on the eve of her first sit-in, anguished. She had known it was coming. She had planned it. But the prospect of the demonstration now made her sick with nerves. In a sense, the timing was cosmic. It was the week of Valentine's Day and Nash was about to risk it all for love.

She was not an obvious rabble-rouser. Nash had grown up in Chicago. She was mesmerizing and beautiful, with thick hair and a wide, glimmering smile. The Chicago of her childhood was not at all immune to racism, but Nashville—where she moved to attend Fisk University in 1959—was an order of magnitude worse. Nash had never seen a segregated bathroom until Tennessee. She was used to eating lunch at department-store restaurants. Now she saw her Black peers taking their meals to the sidewalk. The South made no secret of segregation. Nash felt humiliated. Then she felt furious.

Within a matter of months, Nash became a frequent presence at a workshop that promised an education in nonviolence and civil disobedience. James Lawson, a minister, led it and radiated the kind of deep emotion that appealed to Nash. He had his tactical strategies, but he was never cold or calculating. He dispelled the idea that an activist had to exude untouchable bravado to succeed or to make a difference. The kind of organizing he wanted to do was grounded in love—a fact he emphasized to both his male and female disciples. Plans for a sit-in firmed up. Nash was elected a leader—point person for the action. The protest would be held at the site of her exclusion: the lunch counters downtown.

The journalist David Halberstam writes in his retrospective of the student movement that Nash felt "pure terror in her heart" on the eve of the protest. She would later become one of the most famous activists in her generation—so recognizable and charismatic that her face sold magazines at newsstands. But back then she wanted to disappear. She wondered whether she could still slink out, skip the sit-in. But she couldn't come up with an excuse that would extricate her "without causing great shame to herself and letting down these others," she said. Her friends were counting on her. She decided to get it over with.

Nash later said her fear never dissipated. Each action came with risks. She became better known, and the risks increased. The Nashville student leaders became examples for other students across the South and later nationwide, raising the stakes. Nash stopped dreaming about quitting, but that didn't mean she ever conquered her nerves. Week after week, Nash and the venerable John Lewis and others such as Gloria Johnson and James Bevel faced hordes of white crowds hurling not just racial slurs but cups of coffee and lit cigarettes. Nash steeled herself and continued. She and her friends "came to a realization of our own worth" under Lawson, as she put it. It seemed like something to fight for.

Within a few months, the Nashville activists had attracted enough attention to earn Nash an invitation to join a sit-in in Rock Hill, South Carolina. Nash was arrested. She was given the option of avoiding jail time if she paid a fine, which she declined to do. She would not validate the terms of her incarceration. Instead, she modeled what became a standard movement response: She would rather be behind bars. Nash was sentenced to one month in jail. Soon after she was released, she dropped out of college. She had been scared and she had faced her fears. It liberated her. "The Chaucer classes," she said, "became unbearable after Rock Hill."

The movement became her classroom. She learned with her friends.

A few months later, in the spring of 1961, thirteen of her peers, including Lewis, gathered for what some had christened "The Last Supper." Seven of them were Black. Six were white. All had decided to venture into the still-segregated South together, and so a farewell dinner was held at a Chinese restaurant in Washington, D.C. The Freedom Ride—the first one—would commence from there in the morning.

Its participants were almost all students. Their aim was to compel the South to implement the landmark Supreme Court decisions in *Morgan v. Virginia* and *Boynton v. Virginia.* The justices in the two cases ruled that interstate buses as well as their stations could not continue to be segregated based on race. The riders included John Lewis and Genevieve Hughes, who were both in their twenties and thus elders compared with the rest of the group. Joan Trumpauer—one of the white volunteers—was nineteen. So was William E. Harbour. Charles Person was eighteen.

The path the riders plotted functioned like Dante's *Inferno*—a descent. It would start in the relative quiet of the mid-Atlantic, then the group would burrow deeper into the South and into the heat.

James Farmer, a skilled organizer, had devised the progression. He was the cofounder of the Congress of Racial Equality (CORE), which had been established decades before to fight for integration through the Gandhian principle of nonviolence. Farmer had returned to the organization after an absence from its leadership with a point to prove. It was obvious to him that the South would never choose to hand over the rights to which Black citizens were entitled. He and other activists had to create the conditions that would force their hands. The rides could do that. He promised nonviolence. But had Gandhi ever come down on the matter of provocation? The rides were designed to "create a crisis so that the federal government would be compelled to enforce the law," Farmer said. It would not be a carpool.

Much to the surprise of the riders, the first stops of the trip proceeded without serious incident. Person was arrested in Charlottesville, Virginia, but the charges were dropped. The stop in Charlotte, North Carolina, went fine. In Rock Hill, South Carolina, Lewis was attacked and the press started to take notice. When the riders rolled into Atlanta, Georgia, a supportive crowd formed to greet them.

But the real test was not Virginia or South Carolina or even Georgia, and Farmer knew it. No one needed Virgil to tell them that hell was Alabama. It was a spring morning in 1961 when two buses set off from Atlanta, bound for Birmingham. Their departures were an hour apart and the riders were divided between them. The first bus didn't even make it to Birmingham. Its tires were slashed in Anniston, seventy miles up the road. Someone threw a firebomb. The activists—plus the passengers who just so happened to be on board—were forced out of the vehicle as it burst into flames. A mob of two hundred or so people had come armed with clubs and pipes. Some held the volunteers down while others punched and clawed at them. The riders escaped and reached hospitals, which refused to treat them. When rescue at last arrived, it took the form of Reverend Fred Shuttlesworth, who organized a caravan to drive the riders out of Anniston.

The people who'd been spread across the buses reconvened in Birmingham. No sooner were the groups reunited than another horde of furious white people attacked again. It was a miracle no one died. One rider needed fifty-three stitches. Others had broken bones and gulped down smoke. The media attention reached a fever pitch.

Would the ride continue? Its own leaders didn't think so. The riders still had two states to go after Alabama. Mississippi and Louisiana were supposed to be next, but no one knew how to get them there. No driver with the bus companies would let them board, knowing what awaited the vehicles that carried them. The federal government wanted the spectacle over with. While it has in general not been in the business of serving as a travel agent for private citizens, it asked activists to consider getting on a plane and avoiding buses altogether. The question of proceeding had turned existential. The mobs wanted blood. If the rides went forward, volunteers would have to accept the quite real chance that some wouldn't make it out alive. If the rides were halted, the Klan would learn from its triumph: Mob violence worked.

From her perch in Nashville, Diane Nash agonized over the fate of the trip. Lives were on the line and she knew it. But while others believed that meant the rides had to be stopped, Nash saw it as a mandate. With so much at stake, she had to find people who would finish the trip.

Who else but girls? Young women, fierce and resolute, stepped forward. Several of them, knowing what could lie ahead, wrote wills. Before the rides resumed Nash collected almost two dozen, sealed with instructions for the parents who would have to receive them. One of Nash's volunteers was Ruby Doris Smith, who had been jailed with Nash a few months earlier in Rock Hill. She was nineteen. She was old enough to risk her life to ride a bus.

The path back through Alabama did turn out to be a bloodbath. Less than a week after the riot that had welcomed the riders to the Deep South, the reconstituted group arrived in Montgomery, where volunteers were once more met with pipes and sticks. Lewis was beaten. A white activist named Susan Wilbur tried to escape into a taxi with some of the Black riders she knew. The driver threw her out of his cab. It was illegal for a Black taxi driver to have a white woman in his back seat.

When Wilbur and a friend tried to get into another car, the mob pulled them from their seats. Wilbur had grown up in Nashville. Her mother had raised her and her sister on her own after their father died of polio when Susan was a toddler. With her sister, Liz, she met civil rights activists in college and wanted in. Both she and Liz were interested in volunteering for the ride. "But we didn't want both me and Liz to go," she remembered. Their mother had lost a husband. Wilbur recalled the conversation with her sister. "We thought it wouldn't be fair to Mom," she said. She had two children. What if both were killed? Susan, nineteen, would go, and Liz would remain. Just in case.

Wilbur was staggering from the second car when she was knocked off her feet again. The force of the hit threw her into the street, and she landed in front of John Seigenthaler, a Justice Department official who had been sent to observe. Seigenthaler leapt out and shouted at Wilbur and her friend to get in his car. But just as he was waving them in, someone in the mob swung a lead pipe over his head and fractured his skull. Wilbur had never even seen someone throw a punch, let alone watched someone get their head cracked open. She ran, at first looking for help and then looking for a place to hide. She ended up in the car of a local policeman after some wandering. She was so dazed that she accepted his offer to drive her to the train station. She could still recall the chill in his voice when he told her that if she'd been his daughter, he'd have put a bullet through her forehead.

That night, over one thousand people gathered at the First Baptist Church to express their support for the ride while the mob crowded outside. The federal government had been reluctant to engage with the movement. Now the administration had no choice but to get involved. The attack on Seigenthaler meant one of their own had ended up on a stretcher. Diane Nash had come down to organize on the ground and was there when the call came in. The phone trilled. Martin Luther King, Jr. picked up.

Nash had turned twenty-three the morning after the violence in Anniston and Birmingham. She was not the same girl who had once been so shocked to encounter unfettered racism in the South. She was a tactician and a leader. She had revived the rides. But when the Justice Department phoned, it was King, with his closest allies around him, who was there to discuss their future. Nash wasn't even in the room.

The rides continued, over the objections of the administration. With Jackson, Mississippi, on the horizon, Doris Castle, seventeen, stepped forward and joined the effort. When James Farmer wished Castle luck on the road as she prepared to set off, she gaped at him. Wasn't he planning to come too? The presence of Castle, a petite high schooler, shamed him into action. He had his luggage loaded onto the bus at the last possible minute: "I'm going."

No sooner had the riders stepped off the bus in Mississippi than police arrived to arrest them. The group was charged with disturbing the peace. The swift corralling meant that the White House and the Justice Department didn't have to fret about more damning photos, but for all the relative calm on the streets, the jailhouse was vicious. The riders were beaten and crammed together in terrible conditions.

Smith was squeezed into a four-bunk room with twenty-three other women. They spent two weeks in local jails before being transferred to the fearsome Parchman Farm prison deep in the Mississippi Delta. The women were subjected to vaginal searches during intake. Filth caked the floors. The food was inedible. For the crime of singing freedom songs, their mattresses were confiscated. But somehow camaraderie survived. "There were a lot of little movements going into Parchman," explained one rider, "but one big one coming out."

That summer, riders kept coming down South, police kept throwing them in prison, and volunteers kept singing. Across Mississippi, high school girls picked up the tune.

ICIE TRAVIS EXPRESSED more than just the usual parental disapproval when she learned that her teenage daughter had volunteered to help with a voter registration drive in McComb, Mississippi. She was so worried that she banned Brenda from the effort.

With the riders sequestered in prison, a new batch of activists with the SNCC had arrived in the hill town on an audacious crusade: In an area with some of the harshest voting restrictions nationwide, the newcomers wanted to help Black people cast their ballots. The state laws in Mississippi were laced with arcane and sometimes ridiculous stipulations worded and implemented to stifle Black suffrage—not just the standard, racist poll tax but in one case an exhaustive application that included a section prompting would-be voters to interpret an excerpt of the state constitution. The local white registrar was responsible for evaluating their expositions. Surprise: He tended to find them deficient. The leader of the new corps of activists was a man from New York named Bob Moses. Brenda Travis was one of his first volunteers.

Her mother had warned her not to get involved with Moses or "that mess"—her words for what the movement was up to in Mc-Comb. But it made no difference to Brenda, who was sixteen. A bed-time, a curfew, a limit on desserts, a list of chores to complete—parents make rules. Children flout them.

"I decided that I was going to do it," Travis said, "and I did."

Most of Moses's earliest accomplices fit the Travis mold—Black girls with a sense of purpose who were eager to bring change to Mississippi and needed little more than guidance and support in how to do it. Jessie Divens later remembered her eagerness to join the cause: "To me, it was a revolution that had started."

"Revolution" was the apt term. As in 1776, a band of true believers was prepared to rebel for representation. At least the colonists had had guns. Girls in the Jim Crow South were both unarmed and under-age. The centuries-old terror campaign that had led to the murders of thousands of Black people was not in some distant past. Emmett Till had been mutilated and murdered in Mississippi less than a decade before—an attack that Travis later cited as foundational to her own sense of American injustice. And while the brutalization of Black men was better documented and more common, Black women were not spared.

In a state like Mississippi, where such violence was no secret, it didn't take a man like Moses to awaken Black girls to the realities of their circumstances. Divens knew she deserved opportunities equal to white people. She just had never had the tools to demand them. She knew she was entitled to more than what she'd been told to expect, but she needed other people to believe it too. In Moses, she and her peers met a man who was prepared, as Divens said, "to prove that to us."

In August 1960, just weeks after the riders were released from prison, the volunteers that Moses had corralled to take on the ballot notched their first win and helped half a dozen new Black residents register to vote. Moses was focused on voter registration as protest, and he'd proven that that kind of organizing was possible—even in Mississippi. It was admirable and essential and prescient work. But it was not as explosive as coordinated direct action. Moses preached the polls. In the meantime, other SNCC organizers had their own ideas about how to grow the cause. The girls who had rallied to support Moses weren't old enough to vote. Travis was a capable volunteer, but she couldn't do the thing that Moses was fighting for. She couldn't go to the ballot box and be heard. Door knocking was nice. But it's not hard to understand what it was about civil disobedience that appealed to a fired-up teenager. She wanted in on the action.

To keep up the momentum in McComb, activists proposed a sit-in at a raucous mass meeting of over two hundred people. Just three out of the hundreds volunteered—Travis and two others. She was the lone minor and girl. In her memoir, she describes making the decision on instinct. She was sure the action was just. She knew on an emotional and intellectual level that someone would have "to step forward at great risk and that someone was me."

The sit-in would be the next morning. Like a kid headed for a sleepover, Travis packed a spare pair of underwear. Essentials were essentials—slumber parties and jail had that much in common. Her mother had no idea what was planned, but Travis did kiss her before bed. She knew it could be a long time before she saw her again. When Travis woke up, she met up with her fellow volunteers and the three went down to the local bus station. The group lasted about a minute in the white waiting room before getting arrested.

Travis later said she felt more exhilarated than scared that first night in jail. McComb had been the kind of place where, as Travis put it, "there wasn't much going on." The influx of SNCC activists changed that. Their arrival was "the highlight of our being, the highlight of our existence," Travis said. In her quiet neighborhood, her arrest was a bona fide event. For the children of McComb then, activism was more than a call for justice. It was something to belong to. Protest had its own rites and practices. Its own leaders and stars. It was a lot like high school, and Travis became an instant cool kid. Soon she was hauled before a judge, who demanded to know how much a teenager had to be paid to be willing to get sent to jail. "He could not believe," Travis recalls, "that a . . . girl had conceived of doing this on her own." She told him no one had paid her. Who could put a price on freedom?

In an outcome that shocked McComb's Black residents, Travis was sentenced to four months in jail for her sit-in. And though she was released after just one (with Martin Luther King, Jr. signing her bail check), even her truncated sentence meant missing the first few weeks of the semester at Burglund High School. Her friends had been impressed. The school principal, C. D. Higgins, was less so. When she tried to return after her incarceration, he blocked her at the door and told her she wouldn't be readmitted. Perhaps if she'd been expelled for some other reason, no one would have made much of a fuss. But Travis was suffering for representing all of them. Her classmates wouldn't tolerate her ouster. With signs prepared the night before and in a scene that would have delighted Barbara Johns, two dozen teenagers marched out to protest her punishment. Some convinced their friends to join. "The kids ran out after us," said Annie Pickett, one of the girls in the first wave. Not because Moses or someone else from SNCC had told them to, but because one of their own had been insulted.

Parents throw out admonishments about groupthink. But there's something to be said for the power of a little peer pressure. Is a clique so different from an organizing committee? Another Bob Moses recruit was in her classroom when she saw people start to stream out of the building. It felt like the beginning of something.

Over a hundred students marched down the streets of McComb that morning, with SNCC volunteers doing their best to keep them from getting arrested or beaten or worse. Some from the organization had opposed the protest. When it became clear that deterrence would not work, Moses and others diverted the students from their initial and riskier plan to march on the jail where Travis had been held. The group settled on a new route and set off.

That didn't appease the police. The students were arrested and released to their parents later that evening. The SNCC workers were kept in cells. When *The New York Times* printed a short report on the walkout in the paper, it identified Bob Zellner, a white SNCC field organizer, as the instigator. But Zellner had just arrived in McComb. The demonstration hadn't been his idea. Later, he remembered sitting in the SNCC office downtown when he heard the sound of the students marching past him. "For those of us sitting inside it was a moment that brought back that great quote from Gandhi—'There go my people, I have to go and run and catch up because I am their leader.'" It must not have occurred to the reporter who credited Zellner that no one needed to coax 114 high school students into action.

The walkout should have communicated to the school's administration that its students were serious, not just about advancing the civil rights movement in America but about defending and expanding their own freedoms as well. But staff did not cheer on their declaration of independence. Their defiance was met with a show of force. Travis was not welcomed back to Burglund High School after the walkout in her honor. Principal Higgins forced students who'd taken part in the demonstration to either swear off further activism or be expelled. It wasn't an idle threat; sixty-four children refused to submit to the demand and were forced out. SNCC set up alternative classes and scrambled to find schools to accept them. Most ended up at Campbell College, the African Methodist Episcopal school located eighty miles north of McComb, in Jackson.

The costs of the walkout rippled outward.

Divens wasn't old enough for Campbell, so she had to travel to a local Catholic school instead. On the bus one morning, she refused to give up her seat for a white rider and was arrested. She had a criminal record at the age of twelve.

Travis was an unequivocal hero. And for her service, she was sent to the glorified prison that was a reform school for "delinquent" children. The walkout had constituted a violation of her probation.

The week before the walkout, a local white state representative murdered Herbert Lee, a Black farmer with nine children, for collaborating with Moses. A witness was coerced into claiming that the assassination had in fact been an act of self-defense, a claim he later recanted. Lee's killer was nonetheless acquitted. The witness was later shot and killed too. SNCC volunteers were devastated. Lee's heartbroken wife confronted Moses at her husband's funeral and accused him of killing her spouse.

The organization lost support in McComb. Activists, aware that local sentiment had turned, moved elsewhere in Mississippi. Volunteers didn't return until 1964. From the perspective of the movement workers, it was at least a disappointment if not an outright failure. But for the girls—who had gotten their first taste of activism and who had banded together to face off against their parents and the police—it wasn't a defeat. The voter registration effort, the bus station protest, the walkout—it was as Divens had predicted. It was a start.

In public and with no apologies, the children of McComb "stood up and went against the grain," Divens said. The walkout in particular, undertaken on behalf of a Black girl just like them, made a statement about their own value. It said that what happened to them mattered.

McComb had not just shown what Bob Moses could do. It demonstrated that the kind of intense relationships and alliances that form in high school could be marshaled in service of the movement. However incomplete, their actions made it clear: "Here we are," Divens said. "Deal with it."

A KEEN SENSE OF JUSTICE motivated the likes of Nash and Smith and Castle and Travis. But to understand their drive, it helps to understand the social and cultural environment in which their ideas were shaped. For independent girls, it was the dawn of a new age.

For her book *Linked Lives: Adult Daughters and Their Mothers*, the author Lucy Rose Fischer interviewed girls born between 1948 and 1958 and found that most either saw themselves as different from their mothers or were determined to *be* different from them. Fischer admits that she found her own mother's preoccupations and habits to be "a waste of time." She was not interested in her bridge games or monotonous routines. Her mother had been content to live her life between the parlor room and the kitchen. Fischer wanted more than matching dinner plates. So did her peers. Letters poured into magazines attesting to girls' horror at the smallness of women's lives. In one, a daughter decries the "emptiness" of her mother's existence. The writer couldn't stand to witness her "helplessness and dependence" on her father. She was determined to carve a different path.

We associate the 1960s with student protests and generational upheaval, but the notion of an adolescent culture is older. Even in the repressive 1950s, an awareness was blooming: Teenagers had the potential to be a blazing, hormonal phenomenon. For the first time, magazines, movies, music, and television were being made for and marketed to them. That customization of the wider culture to please them, the rise of entire sectors of entertainment that depended on them, demonstrated that their interests and attention had real, material value. The women's movement was still off in the distance, but even when girls like Travis and Divens were growing up, there was an understanding that their generation, as Steven Mintz writes in *Huck's Raft*, was destined for "more open and exciting" opportunities than their mothers' had been.

The concept of adolescence—like all teens worth their salt—took some time to come into its own. With the publication of the two-volume *Adolescence* in 1904, researcher G. Stanley Hall had introduced it into the mainstream. But it did not quite grip the public. At the time, social reformers were focused on the simpler and more innocent issue of grade schoolers. An increasing number of researchers and parents had concluded that children needed to spend time in school and were entitled to a basic education. With the launch of progressive programs during the Great Depression, it became conventional wisdom that children, as sociologist Viviana Zelizer writes in *Pricing the Priceless Child*, "occupied a special and separate world" and deserved individual attention and investment. Activists and politicians had focused on white children, but the "sacralization" of childhood drove some to take up the cause of Black, poor, and immigrant children too. Perhaps the advocates who championed the less fortunate believed that those who benefited from their efforts should have been grateful—that is, quiet and "well behaved." Not quite.

No sooner was childhood rendered precious than teenagers were tugging at its constraints. In her book *Teenagers*, Grace Palladino recounts an iconic anecdote of adolescent impetuousness: In 1936, a man slapped a teenage girl sitting in the row behind him at their local movie theater. She had been talking and laughing during the showing, which he found disruptive. The girl wanted him to apologize, but he wouldn't. He felt justified. The press sided with him. When the *Los Angeles Times* covered the incident, it headlined the report: "Talking Girl in Film Show Gets Slapped." Implied: She had it coming.

The girl was incensed. It wasn't that she took issue with an adult telling off, or even accosting, a child he didn't know. It was that she didn't see herself as a child at all. To be infantilized in public! How embarrasing. She contended that an adolescent was in fact something closer to an adult. The girl called the police and had the man arrested. Her complaint was dismissed, but she made an argument that was just beginning to find its footing in the public discourse. It might sound like a small distinction, although the encounter went about as viral as a run-in between two people could in 1936. Still, it exemplified an evolving attitude: The teen moviegoer was a person with rights. She had a voice and could use it.

For movie chatterboxes and independent-minded adolescents, high school was transformative. It had once been reserved for the studious and privileged. But in the midst of the Great Depression in 1936, a full 65 percent of teenagers were also high school students. That figure reached 73 percent in 1940. The formal invention of the term soon followed when in 1941, *Popular Science* introduced what it called the "teen-ager" to audiences nationwide. Members of this new cohort weren't peeling off to go to work. Most were spending their time in classrooms and halls doing something much more fearsome to adults than hard labor—interacting with *one another*.

There were of course teachers and administrators, whose job it was to enforce the rules, grade papers, and discipline troublemakers. There could also be crushing social pressure and heartbreak. But high school had become one of the few places where students could meet and socialize out from under the thumb of their parents. Most American children were now expected to spend their developmental peak in its cramped desk chairs. The shift, writes Palladino, "helped to create the idea of a separate, teenage generation"—one made up of adolescents who wanted the freedom to make their own choices. An awareness was seeping into the mainstream like Miss Clairol at the salon. What had once been a period of developmental maturation was now a cultural phenomenon.

Grown-ups were left scrutinizing the roommates who'd sprouted up where their beloved and familiar children had just been. The press was just as fascinated—and freaked-out. Its assessments of the teenage girl tended to be limited to white subjects in loafers and skirts. Yet even such innocuous creatures were met with mild horror. In December 1944, *Life* published a photo series that promised to take readers inside the lives of white teenage girls in Missouri. It found them inhabiting a blissful, upbeat "world of slumber parties and the Hit Parade" in which other concerns paled compared with the most important one: "to be one of a crowd of other girls." The text reads a little like *National Geographic*, inaugurating a tradition of treating teens with equal parts exoticism, condescension, and total befuddlement. But the piece does what American businessmen with daughters had come to realize: Their girls might be aliens to them, but these aliens liked to shop. The magazine concluded that adolescents could soon constitute a "big and special market."

Their parents had cash to spend. In the decade between 1939 and 1950, wages for managers grew 45 percent. Production workers saw their incomes rise 106 percent. Economic indicators were up. Manufacturing boomed. Deliberate obstacles prevented Black families and other minorities from taking part in the windfall. Still, consumption on a national scale rose. There were more cars on the road and a glut of new houses. The number of households in the United States with a television set—that organ of advertising—exploded, with double the number of shipments to dealers in 1950 as in 1949. Ads pushed consumer spending. The children who watched them wanted their wares. The critic Dwight Macdonald—bearish on the advent of the teenager—wrote in *The New Yorker* in 1958 that not just the teen market, but perhaps the notion of the teenager itself, was a creation of "the businessmen who exploit it."

The consecration of the teen—as demographic and as consumer—came down in part to numbers. There were just more of them than there used to be as the United States recovered from its Depression-era low birth rate. More of them wanted to earn their own dollars. More of them were born to parents who didn't have to depend on their children's wages to supplement their income and thus more of them who could spend without much restriction. In 1956, 35 percent of teenage boys who were eligible for after-school jobs had them, double the figure from 1944. Girls earned less money and held fewer jobs but still made on average—between work and their allowance—just over $6.50 per week. In 1959, *Life* pegged the amount that teenagers had to spend at $10 billion. That cash propped up local restaurants and lunch counters. It sustained shopping malls. The movies raked it in, with teens making up three quarters of the entire American theater-going audience. Girls were spending $20 million on lipstick alone. Cosmetics rang up over $1 billion in sales in 1952. Teenage dollars were valuable, coveted, and battled for—and that was true for Black girls as much as white.

Girls like Brenda Travis didn't wake up one morning and just decide to wreak havoc because of a commercial. The rise of girl groups like the Shirelles and the presence of Lucille Ball on TV were not responsible for earthshaking social movements. But consumer culture did have a relationship to the upheaval—first to the civil rights movement and then to the antiwar movement and second-wave feminism. The Shirelles—four Black girls who'd founded their group at a school talent show in 1957—sang about crushes and romance. Their outfits matched. Nothing about their presentation spelled iconoclasm. But their 1960 hit "Will You Love Me Tomorrow" marked the first time a Black girl group had ever topped the charts. The song was about sex. Would having it deepen a relationship or cheapen it? Would the girl doing it regret it? It sounds retrograde, but pitching sex as a choice at all made it bold.

In her retrospective on girls and mass media, the writer Susan Douglas parses acts like the Shirelles, which were radical in their existence and at the same time forged in a capitalist machine. Douglas concludes that pop music, despite its trafficking in saccharine tropes and its reliance on convention, was one of the few cultural phenomena to center adolescent female voices—to put them behind the literal microphone. The girls "sang about the pull between the need to conform and the often overwhelming desire to rebel, about the tension between restraint and freedom, and about the rewards—and costs—of prevailing gender roles."

What girls listened to. The movies and TV shows girls watched. Where their friends shopped. *Trendiness.* That disdainful thing! It helped shape them.

The factors that drew Black girls into the civil rights movement were varied and personal, but it's no accident that several of their accounts note a similar moment of reckoning. The inciting incident tended to happen when their wallets were open.

For Claudette Colvin, it had been hat shopping.

For Diane Nash, it was an outing to the Tennessee State Fair, where it occurred to her that while she was welcome to shell out for activities and snacks just as white attendees were, she could not purchase access to their restrooms.

Annette Jones White, a pageant queen who together with her friend Bernice Johnson became a prominent student organizer for the movement in southwest Georgia, tied her determination to fight racial oppression to the humiliations of shopping downtown as a kid. One of her earliest memories was of a clerk at the local department store refusing to let her use the bathroom while she and her mother were running errands. She wet her pants, and a crowd of white shoppers—adults and children—pointed at her and laughed. She was four.

It was the incongruousness that aggravated Jones White. Her cash was welcome. The small matter of her human existence was the problem.

The magazines that had launched to cater and sell to girls replicated the same exclusion. The monthlies treated both the consequential matter of shopping decisions as well as adolescent anxieties and ambitions with a level of seriousness that girls craved. But not all teenagers were given equal consideration. The women that mainstream magazines featured were white. Their targeted demographic was white and middle class. *Seventeen* didn't cast a Black model for its cover until 1972.

Still, despite their utter failures at representation—never mind their often hopeless gender politics—magazines like *Seventeen* and Black girl groups like the Shirelles reached an astounding portion of American girls. The market was saturated, with high schoolers in postwar New York and Milwaukee and Birmingham developing the same musical tastes and experimenting with the same fashion and watching the same shows on television. And while cultural products favored and catered to white sensibilities, "Black and white teenagers of all classes participated" in the new and dominant cultural conventions, as Wini Breines writes in her assessment of the period. Adults complained about the fads and trends that gripped their children, but even that horror just emphasized and reinforced what one historian calls adolescents' "generational status, their social position *as teenagers*." How electric: to be seen.

Mass media had arrived, and it set off the kind of panic that gives rise to movies like *Footloose*. Racist parents were up in arms over what was deemed the "'jive' talk and 'hep-cat' antics of the modern juvenile." White supremacists fretted that the "minds, morals, social values, and customs" of their children—not to mention "their language and dress"—were being corrupted. If high schoolers discovered shared taste in entertainment or clothes, it would be harder to maintain the line that races were *just not meant* to mix. The would-be harrowing possibilities of interracial friendship and romance were so evident that "teen canteens" were built in segregated neighborhoods, lest not just Black and white teens meet, but Jewish and Christian teens, or even the children of Protestants and Catholics.

Alas, isolated rec centers could not keep them all apart.

Sisters Susan and Liz Wilbur met their Black peers in Nashville, introducing themselves to students at Fisk and Tennessee Agricultural & Industrial. Both Wilburs had a baseline interest in the civil rights movement, but their friendships drew them in deeper. Long nights of strategizing and organizing often ended downtown. Susan remembered dancing and singing, delighting in the presence of her friends. "Although the goal was serious, there was a lot of laughter," she said.

Joyce and Dorie Ladner, another set of sisters, experienced those same thrills when the pair enrolled at Jackson State College in 1960.

The two arrived with a particular advantage: Both had been active in statewide student organizations as high schoolers, which meant that both knew student leaders from all over the state before so much as stepping on campus. Several of those acquaintances were now classmates. "We all recognized one another," Joyce later explained.

That well-developed network made the sisters instant fixtures of campus activism. The two liked to work in concert and reveled in the subterfuge that their organizing required. The administration did not welcome movement activities, which forced their efforts underground. Dorie once asked her sister to bless a group meeting just as its members were preparing for their first sit-in. She knew better than to make an explicit reference to the imminent demonstration. Instead, she said: "Oh, dear Lord, there are perilous times ahead. Please protect us as we go into this danger."

The next morning, the dean of students—who was also an ordained minister—called the sisters into his office and demanded to know what "perilous times ahead" meant. The Ladners brooked no accusation. Joyce demanded to know what *he* meant, asking her about what she had said to *her* God. Dorie doubled down: "As a man of the cloth, how could you?"

When the dean let them go without punishment, the girls hustled out laughing.

The rush of inside jokes and doublespeak, the pleasure of a clever retort, the particular performance of showing off and talking back and knowing too how to evaluate whether a threat is real—these are the eviscerating talents that girls have developed to survive in a world that denies them more obvious forms of power.

It's not just that their friendships helped girls feel supported and united in their movement work. It's that their friendships sharpened them—made them better and keener and more strategic.

The same skills that girls are socialized to hone in adolescence helped fashion them into superlative activists. Girls are raised to be resourceful and collaborative; to develop a knack for consensus building and a flair for drama. Even the aspects of female friendship that continue to be denigrated worked to their advantage in the movement. Cliquishness could mean protection. Emotion reinforced the bonds of activism. How else to establish trust? And what is adolescence if not finding purpose in shared anguish? Girlhood turned out to be training.

Girls are forced to be attuned to their vulnerabilities. Who could understand better that there is power in numbers?

BERNICE JOHNSON HAD HEARD about the sit-ins and Freedom Rides. The school walkout in McComb had reached her like a morsel of tantalizing gossip. In southwest Georgia, she felt impatient and—that woeful teenage condition—out of the loop. Johnson complained to friends, including the like-minded Annette Jones White: "[W]e would say, 'When is it going to happen here?'"

"Here" was Albany State College, where Johnson was a student. She had gotten a head start on organizing while she waited for SNCC. On campus, she and her peers dealt with constant harassment. White men drove past them and hurled raw eggs or bags of urine. Some snuck into dorm rooms and propositioned them. The local police were not just useless but hostile. Jones White once reported an incident involving a man who had tried to attack her, attempting to force her from a bridge onto the embankment below. "When he *does* something . . . let me know," the officer replied. The situation was so grim that women learned to call the football team instead of the cops when an intruder broke into their rooms. It was obvious which group would sooner come to their aid. It bothered Johnson that the police didn't seem to care about the students' predicament. But she reserved much of her ire for the Black administration. Reluctant to take up the issue with the white Board of Regents, school staff, it seemed to Johnson, refused to intervene.

In 1961, Johnson organized an event to protest the lack of support for Black female students. The president fired the dean of women—a lone source of support for the school's female population—in response. He suspended student government for good measure. He must have hoped that would quell the insurrection. He miscalculated.

SNCC arrived at last that fall, and two practiced activists—Cordell Reagon and Charles Sherrod—led the effort. Best friends and NAACP Youth Council members Johnson and Jones White were their first points of contact.

In November, just before Thanksgiving break, two college students were arrested for breaking into the white waiting room at the local bus station. To protest their incarceration, Johnson planned a march and—in an echo of Barbara Johns in Farmville and Brenda Travis in McComb—went from room to room with fellow activists to convince her classmates to take to the streets. Five hundred people decided to join the demonstration.

SNCC wanted to keep up the pressure. Another march was organized and girls rushed to take part. Sisters Joann and Lavetta Christian were still in middle school when Reagon and Sherrod came to town. When the protest was announced, Joann, fourteen, went home and worked up the nerve to ask her father: Could she join it? "Yeah, sugar," he told her. "Lead the line."

Around seven hundred people, including the Christian sisters, were taken to jail. Joann and sixty other girls were squeezed into a single cell. "That night in jail was something!" she said in an interview. She felt a deep sense that she was where she needed to be. "It was strange, frightening, funny, and enlightening—all at the same time."

King negotiated with local officials to secure the release of the jailed activists. His presence galvanized support and press. It also made it seem as though the movement revolved around his travel schedule. Not so, as Bernice Johnson had demonstrated. It was students—most of them girls—who had turned the embers of discontent and protest into organized and blazing resistance. It was students who remained after King moved on at the end of 1961.

King had extracted a promise from officials that public transport would indeed be desegregated and the jailed protesters released. But after he left town, local leaders reneged. The compromise fractured. Arrests continued. The dustup was called "one of the most stunning defeats" in King's career. It was in some sense the making of the girls of southwest Georgia.

Expelled from college for their arrests and civil rights involvement, Annette Jones White and several of her friends enrolled at Spelman. The elite college had made scholarships available to qualified students who had been penalized for their participation in movement activities.

Jones White spent those first months of 1962 volunteering at the SNCC office in Atlanta with Johnson and another close friend named Janie Culbreth. The three were inseparable. When it came time to book a ride home for spring break, the girls opted to travel as a group. "Bernice, Janie, and I decided to make a statement," Jones White recalled. Not with posters or even conventional protest but with coordinated outfits. Each of them embroidered a word on the left side of their white blouses. The finished tops blared their dearest values in sewn script: "Freedom," "Justice," "Equality."

In an interview in 1978, Jones White said her involvement in the movement gave her power. It allowed her to confront what terrified her. She had found her people. She seized her place in the world. At least once, she did that in matching blouses.

A DECADE AFTER *Brown v. Board of Education* mandated an end to the doctrine of "separate but equal," and not long after Police Commissioner Bull Connor turned his hoses and dogs on the children of Birmingham in what became known as the Children's Crusade, Joann Christian integrated her local all-white high school. She was one of six volunteer students. The next ten months were torture.

Administrators must have understood what Christian—who would be arrested over a dozen times—had learned on that first night in jail. Friendship meant survival. So the school's first move was separating the six Black children into six different classrooms. Isolation as a tactic.

The white students that Christian and the others encountered were not like the Wilbur sisters or Joan Trumpauer. (Most white teens in the South were in fact not like the Wilbur sisters or Trumpauer.) Just one white girl befriended Christian. She had been a star student, but her grades dropped after word got out that she had been spending time with Black girls. Her friends ostracized her. She lost her scholarship to college.

"She would call me and we would talk," Christian remembered. "I told her she had to take care of herself. Do what she had to do to heal herself."

At the end of those awful months, the girl wrote in Christian's yearbook. She could have recorded her ideals. She could have scratched out a diatribe about the evils of racism. But she kept it simple. Her inscription bore one line of adolescent declaration: "No one picks my friends for me."

THE INTENSE AND INTIMATE BONDS of friendship among girls helped to fuel the civil rights movement. In oral histories and interviews and memoirs, activists recall their dependence on one another; how their relationships kept them going in even the most dire circumstances; how their relationships inspired them to get involved in the movement at all. Friendship was the bedrock.

But girlhood is not an answer to racism, and friendship is not necessarily a progressive force for good. In cities like Chicago and New York, students themselves planned strikes when their schools tried to push for truer integration. In photos of the mobs that harassed the Freedom Riders, there is no dearth of sneering white teens. Decades after the abolition of Jim Crow, cliques of white girls continue to learn how to make the most of the social bonds that connect them to one another—excluding Black and brown girls. These are not the problems of 1964 or 1974 or even 1994, but of 2016 and 2023. Can even the wisest legislator write a law that matters as much to a teenage girl as the judgment of her peers?

Even within the movement, friendships were not a panacea for the deep divides between participants. There were romantic entanglements and dramas. There were hurt feelings and genuine slights. Some Black activists cooled on their white counterparts, finding them to be insensitive and sometimes oblivious to the stakes of the movement. While plans for Freedom Summer—which would unite hundreds of out-of-state white students and Black volunteers from the South—took shape in 1964, relationships between some white and Black activists strained to the point of fracture. In an earlier phase of the movement, women like Susan Wilbur and Trumpauer had grown so close to Black activists. Now even those Black organizers who had been friends with white students, like Dorie Ladner, kept their distance.

The movement trucked on. Demonstrators marched across the Edmund Pettus Bridge. With the Civil Rights Act of 1964 and the Voting Rights Act of 1965, activists notched two critical legislative wins. The organizations that powered such victories underwent their own transitions. SNCC reframed its mission. King was murdered. Millions of people mourned not just a leader but all he would have gone on to do had he lived.

In 1964, the same year that Christian integrated her high school, the activist and eventual doctor Jean Smith Young headed down to Mississippi to participate in Freedom Summer. She was an undergraduate at Howard but remained with SNCC until 1967. She later went to medical school and became an adolescent psychiatrist. Her clinical training gave her a new appreciation for what had allowed the movement to thrive. She later studied the concept of relatedness—a phenomenon she qualified as a deep human need. In her writing, she cites the principle, theorizing "that a woman is functional, effective, and happy in the world to the extent that she is able to call on her strength as one in relation to others."

"This posture of being in relation to others," she continues, "was the central fact in my organizing work in SNCC." Young came to believe that the fact that SNCC survived as long as it did and led to as much progress as it had was a testament "to the strength of human bonds and relationships."

Friendship—and female friendship in particular—is an overlooked cultural force. We put much more stock in romance. We prize ambition, without thinking of the relationships that achievement can compromise. We admire the people who stand behind podiums.

Some of the girls who devoted themselves to the movement occupied such exalted places. Others are harder to see from our place in the future: The girls whose corporeal forms seem to dissolve in the presence of their friends. That almost indistinguishable mass of singing, laughing, sobbing, screaming, arms-locked-in-protest teenagers. Two sisters, scheming in the face of a hapless administrator.

Look: You found the leader.

7

TALKING BODIES

SEX AND SINGLE GIRLS
IN SECOND-WAVE FEMINISM

n 1966—a little less than a decade before *Roe v. Wade* was decided (and more than five decades before it was overturned)—at least two hundred thousand illegal abortions were performed in America. Some estimates put the number much higher, at just around one million.

Who were the women receiving them? In a *Washington Post* feature published that winter, the reporter Elisabeth Stevens tries to paint a picture—mothers who couldn't afford to raise another child, unmarried women who didn't want one, and an inevitable number of sex-uneducated teenagers. In her reporting, Stevens describes the state of abortion in the kind of dispassionate tone that would thrill journalistic standard-bearers. She didn't need to editorialize. The horrors spoke for themselves.

Stevens cites abortions gone bad that ended in expensive surgeries and permanent injuries. She notes the case of a woman who had gone deaf after spending almost three months recovering from a botched procedure, and the experience of another, who testified about an illegal operation performed without anesthetic: It felt like her "whole stomach was coming out." The chief medical officer in D.C. General's Department of Obstetrics told Stevens about a recent patient. She had been sixteen when she died. The chemicals she'd ingested in an attempt at an abortion killed her.

In her conclusion, Stevens quotes Dr. Alan Guttmacher, the then president of Planned Parenthood, who called laws banning abortion "puritanical punishment." Then she lets slip a hint at her own convictions: Such "punitive laws" would be hard to repeal. And in the meantime, it would be women—more than so-called abortionists—who would suffer for them. Desperate women and girls would continue to end unwanted pregnancies, Stevens explains. And some would die in the process.

Margery Tabankin had seen up close the kind of despair that drove women to pursue underground abortions. In 1966, she was in the middle of her freshman spring at the University of Wisconsin–Madison when a high school student approached her. The girl told Tabankin she was pregnant and scared. She didn't want to be. Tabankin was a well-connected activist on campus. Could she help?

"I asked around and someone in the movement told me to call a woman in Chicago named Jane," Tabankin recalled. When she dialed, the phone rang in another dorm. Heather Tobis picked up and said, "This is Jane."

In June 1964, Tobis had been one of hundreds of volunteers to convene for a quasi–boot camp on the border between Ohio and Indiana. The cohort would be headed down South to galvanize Black voters for what activists were calling Freedom Summer. Bob Moses and the remarkable organizer Fannie Lou Hamer were on hand to prepare them. Tobis had enrolled in what was to be the second session of the summer. She was still waiting to be dispatched to Mississippi when the news broke that Andrew Goodman, who had been part of the first session a week earlier, had disappeared. Two CORE organizers, Michael Schwerner and James Chaney, were missing too. Goodman and Schwerner were white, as was Tobis. Chaney was Black.

Tobis's parents had been supportive when she said she wanted to volunteer. Now both of them pleaded with her to come home. "You're killing your mother!" her father told her. But Tobis didn't leave.

It was a relentless, hot, hard summer. When Tobis returned to campus, she could see that she had undergone some of the same transformations that Bernice Johnson and Annette Jones White articulated. The experience had given her confidence. It made her reconsider her insecurities. She had spent so much of her adolescence wondering whether she had the mettle to make a difference. Then she watched her Black peers mobilize entire communities without equivocation. In Chicago, Tobis looked around and saw familiar inequalities and injustices anew. Did she need to wait for someone to organize her, or could she respond to sexism as she had racism? Did she need a leader, or could she be one?

Tobis had witnessed what direct action could do. She had learned to be decisive and to take risks. She could find a use for such skills. She spent a lot of time on the phone.

Tobis founded what would become Jane (so named to conceal the identities of its members) when she was nineteen—not so long after Freedom Summer. The sister of a friend had discovered she was pregnant and needed an abortion. The movement had given Tobis chutzpah. It had also given her a Rolodex. She reached out to her contacts, hoping that someone could introduce her to a doctor who would do the procedure. She found T. R. M. Howard, a Chicago-based Black practitioner who had been a civil rights activist before his name appeared on a Klan death list and drove him out of Mississippi. Howard charged five hundred dollars for the appointment—over four thousand dollars now. It was expensive, but Tobis wasn't about to shop around for a lower price. She knew Howard could be trusted. When the girl went home, she was no longer pregnant. She felt free.

Tobis—who later took her husband's name when the two married and became Heather Booth—had not intended to become an abortion activist. She had been able to help someone who needed it, and she was satisfied. "But she must have told someone, because someone else called," she recalled. "And then someone else called."

Abortion providers like Howard didn't need to advertise their services. Friends told friends. Desperate acquaintances knew with whom to inquire. The calls flooded in. Tobis realized demand would soon outpace what she could handle on her own, so she enlisted the help of a few friends.

When Tabankin dialed the Chicago-area area code and found Tobis, Jane had been operational for months, and what it lacked in legal soundness, it made up for in efficient service. "We negotiated on price. We negotiated on the service—how did it go," she remembered. Jane's volunteer staff learned not just how the procedure worked, but what kind of support women and girls who came in for it needed.

It took a few weeks, but the girl who had confided in Tabankin made it to see Howard. She was out five hundred dollars and a round-trip bus fare to Chicago—not quite a steal, but a decent price compared with the emotional and literal costs of having a child.

Just as in the *Washington Post* article, all kinds of women turned to Jane for help. Married women and single mothers, girls and women who were in their teens and twenties and forties. Some were introduced to Tobis and her coconspirators. Others knew them from school. Several had snatched up their not-so-discreet flyers, seen pasted up all over Chicago: "Pregnant? Don't Want to Be? Call Jane."

· · ·

WHEN TOBIS FOUNDED JANE, abortion was both stigmatized and common. Rich and well-connected women could place a quiet phone call to a doctor who would do the procedure, or take a well-timed trip abroad for the operation. Poorer women could find services on the black market. Results varied.

For unwed girls, it was more taboo. Before *Roe*, the misfortune of being pregnant meant almost certain ruin. For those who lacked fortuitous connections, it could mean disaster. Even in better circumstances, the ordeal was expected to be borne in silence. Couples who got married in high school and gave birth a handful of months later did not talk about what had forced them down the aisle. People who had an abortion often didn't tell friends, let alone discuss the procedure in public. A thick stench of scandal hung around the middle-class white teenagers whose parents shipped them off to homes for unmarried girls to finish out their pregnancies in near-total isolation. One such high schooler was sixteen when she found out she was pregnant. She was given no information about what birth would entail—so total was the sense of embarrassment and shame about her condition. There was no internet and she had no access to books. When she went into labor months later, she endured contractions in silence. In the sheen of an overhead lamp, she could see her child coming into the world. The attendant noticed and pointed it another direction to obstruct her view.

It's sadistic to bar someone from bearing witness to the birth of her own child. It's also a fact that the conventions of the era dictated such callousness. Since the infant would have to be given up, there was no point in letting a mother get attached. People theorized about how women and girls should relate to their bodies; the conclusion was that women and girls should not.

Advertisers marketed makeup and skincare to women and made clear that their looks were their most valuable investment. But the mechanics of the female form—sex, birth, aging—were considered far outside the bounds of polite conversation. Bodies and their violation were not up for discussion. In the rare cases when sexual assault was reported, the crime tended to be cast as the fault of the victim. Tobis had a friend who was raped at knifepoint in her own bed. When she went to student health, she was informed that the school did not cover vaginal exams and was denied further treatment. There were no resource centers for mental health care. No one mentioned counseling or used words like "trauma." The staffer who saw her did, however, see fit to give her a lecture about her "promiscuous behavior." Tobis was so furious she held a sit-in in the office in protest.

Cracks in such repressive attitudes were starting to show just as girls like Tabankin and Tobis were enrolling in universities and entering the workforce. The first FDA-approved birth control pill was introduced in 1960. It was banned in several states, as were advertisements about all flavors of contraception. Still, its mere existence spurred nervous conversation over what would become of the "good girls" who were supposed to wait for wedded bliss to have sex.

The agita turned out to be justified. Single women were indeed developing new attitudes toward sex. The cost-benefit formula—risks and pleasures—had changed. Campuses became fertile ground for experimentation. A still-green journalist ventured into this new landscape for a 1962 *Esquire* piece titled "The Moral Disarmament of Betty Coed." Her name was Gloria Steinem. It was her first major magazine assignment.

The piece delves into the latest in campus sexual politics, introducing readers to girls who were feigning imminent weddings to trick doctors into fitting them for diaphragms or referring friends to "nice doctors" who refrained from inquiring about the marital status of their patients before offering them contraceptive advice. It was scandalizing. It was the future.

"The names of such doctors and clinics are handed from one girl to the next," Steinem reports. Not unlike a favorite brand or a book recommendation, the advice circulated.

It had once been the case that angst about sex was the obsession of a girl who was having it: What if she got pregnant? What if no man wanted her? Now Steinem wrote that the girls who were not having it were the ones who worried. Did being a virgin mean something was wrong with them? Sex had become so routine that some had started to take it for granted. Steinem quoted a "bewildered" women's college dean who told her that it had ceased to be even a real point of focus for her students. "It isn't that they're preoccupied with sex, it's that they accept it so easily and then turn to you and say, 'And now what?'"

It was the question of the hour.

Steinem concluded her article with the prescient warning that "the contraceptive revolution" would forever change gender roles in America and that it required a shift in the thinking of both women and men. If women were to be able to make the most of their new opportunities in sex and in work, men would have to evolve in their attitudes toward them. The danger was that men might not want to.

A few months later, a new book hit shelves nationwide.

The Feminine Mystique was published in 1963. The landmark book identifies what its author Betty Friedan calls "the problem that has no name." Friedan was describing the unhappiness that dogged capable women who remained in their kitchens and dens while their husbands went to work. It was a book for and about housewives.

Still, the book had radical underpinnings. It had not grown out of Friedan's sewing circles with privileged mom friends. It was grounded in conversations that Friedan had been having with her former classmates. Friedan graduated summa cum laude from Smith College. She became a writer and contributed to newspapers as a journalist. She met her husband and had babies just as her friends did. But she kept up her writing even as she raised her children. Her friends for the most part did not. In 1957, she attended a class reunion and started interviewing her peers about what had happened to them since the proverbial mortarboard toss in 1942. Friedan observed the women whom she had last known as adventurous girls. It seemed each had transformed into a mother who "made the beds, shopped for groceries, matched slipcover material," cared for her children, and tossed and turned next to her husband as she contemplated her private horror: "Is this all?" Her friends had been audacious. Now her friends were catatonic.

The Feminine Mystique was criticized even when it was published for its narrow focus on a particular slice of American womanhood. It drew on the memories Friedan had of girlhood, but it was not for girls. It was not even for most women. It emphasized women who were white, middle class, heterosexual, and married.

In 1966, Friedan seemed to take a somewhat more inclusive tack when she cofounded the National Organization for Women. NOW launched around the same time as Tobis was dreaming up Jane in the Midwest. It was the brainchild of over two dozen women—including several prominent labor and feminist leaders and the multitalented activist and eventual minister Pauli Murray—who met in Friedan's hotel room on the sidelines of the Third National Conference of Commissions on the Status of Women in Washington, D.C. NOW would focus on getting the government to enforce anti-discrimination law, which meant it would focus on working women. Less attention was paid to another population brimming with activists determined to secure equal rights for their sex.

Where were the girls?

Young women had good reason to organize. Laws denied them access to abortion. Social convention empowered a medical professional to hold forth on the supposed moral lapses of a rape victim. Girls were barred from certain schools, certain classes, certain clubs. Girls did not become activists in anticipation of future problems. Their work responded to the conditions of their lives now. In the present.

It is true that we have fewer records of student feminists than we do of high school civil rights organizers or antiwar demonstrators. In her influential work on student protest, the historian Gael Graham tries to explain the differential. She theorizes that racism and the war were deemed lethal evils while sex-based discrimination was seen as more of an inconvenience than a threat. Gender roles were still often considered "natural"—even in liberal circles. Was revolt against the social order genuine activism? Or a distraction?

But sexism did kill and continues to. The havoc it wreaks is minimized but no less real. Botched abortions, sexual violence, disparities in health care—women have died at its hands for centuries. Girls like Tabankin and Tobis and the students who Steinem interviewed knew it.

In classrooms and bedrooms and out in the streets, girls started to claim their bodies as their own. That led not just to underground organizations like Jane, but to audacious lawsuits that pregnant teenagers initiated and zines that provided sex education, including one that would spawn one of the best-known and most reprinted manuals in the United States. Resistance was multifanged and ferocious. It bit back.

The women behind such efforts were in their teens and twenties in the 1960s—born into an era that never saw them coming. How had the restrictive 1950s birthed this?

EDITOR HELEN VALENTINE offered up a sweet narrative when she talked about founding *Seventeen*. In an interview with *Newsweek*, Valentine explained how she had told the media impresario Walter Annenberg that she had just seen a photo taken as the doors were opening at the still-new United Nations. A line had formed outside, and she estimated 90 percent of those who had queued up were teenagers. The girls filled her with hope. "They are really thinking about very important things," she said. She wanted to start a magazine for them. Annenberg was in. He offered her the job on the spot.

One quibble: *Seventeen* launched in 1944. The United Nations wasn't unveiled until 1945. So perhaps not the most accurate account. But do we not love our lore? Valentine knew how to spin a pitch, and this one suited the magazine that would become *Seventeen* well. It would later specialize in "traumarama" and push-up bras. But it did indeed launch on an intrepid note.

The debut was frank. An editorial in its first issue told its audience: "You're going to have to run this show—so the sooner you start thinking about it, the better." It later warned readers not to depend on their future husbands for financial security and recommended that girls find their own source of income. When someone wrote in to complain that her parents made her do household chores but absolved her brother, the magazine admonished her: "[Y]ou have a job of education to do."

Cooking and cleaning were responsibilities that "all the citizens" of a home should share in.

Was it advocating a separatist commune? No. But *The Feminine Mystique* would not be on bookshelves for another two decades. War raged in Europe. The United States was still recovering from the Great Depression. Here was a magazine was talking to teenagers about household divisions of labor. Not bad for 1944.

The magazine sold 400,000 copies of that first issue in less than a week. In the second half of the 1940s, it claimed to be reaching over half of the total six million teenage girls in the whole of the United States. Its success was a tremendous shock to those who had never before considered the appetites and interests of American girls. The magazine christened its ideal reader "Teena" for the purposes of promotional material and circulated information about her to prospective marketing executives. The text in one flyer read: "Meet Teena. No one thought she could read!"

Being underestimated and then overperforming—Teena was more like her reader than a Madison Avenue hotshot could have known.

It was the beginning of a paradoxical era for girls. World War II was about to end with America victorious. The economic upturn would be undeniable. Good fortune was becoming an inheritance, earned and deserved.

"You are the bosses of the business," *Seventeen* told its readers—readers who were getting quite different messages from the world outside its pages. Men had the breadwinning jobs and the social capital. Women in families who could afford it remained at home and took care of the children. Men were in fact the bosses of business. Girls were the shop clerks who endeavored to work—as a 1962 Gallup poll reported—"until children come; afterward, a resounding no!"

So much bullishness on the American present. So little sense of what Teena should do with it. It was Steinem's question presaged: And now what?

Girls were starting to look for new answers.

Between 1955 and 1956, a decade after *Seventeen* launched, the researchers Elizabeth Douvan and Joseph Adelson studied over two thousand girls between the ages of eleven and eighteen. The two were interested in how girls pictured their futures. Douvan and Adelson found that most girls did not. It was so evident to them that an eventual husband would dictate the course of their lives that it was impossible to chart an autonomous path forward. Some would graduate. After that, a blank.

In a letter, a teacher at a women's college validate the researchers' basic premise. She had witnessed hundreds of students complete their papers and take their exams. She describes their modus vivendi: aimless, begrudging, dutiful. Girls study and receive their diplomas: "Few of them ever really see any particular future in it."

What filled the gap where ambition should have been? Douvan and Adelson reframed the popular accusation that girls were romance crazed or love obsessed. Fantasies were how girls modeled what the world told them to expect. Denied opportunities to plan for their own careers and futures, teenagers resorted to make-believe. Douvan and Adelson's research was an exoneration: Who could blame them for dreaming?

It turned out to be decent practice for what was coming next. In a contribution to the book *The Adoring Audience*, the scholars Barbara Ehrenreich, Elizabeth Hess, and Gloria Jacobs recount a scene: News footage shows police lines "straining" as hundreds of girls race forward. Dust rises from the ground, swirling in response to a thousand running feet. Cops shout orders to disperse. Their commands are met with chants and shrieks. The girls rush to the front. The police line breaks like a tidal wave.

The description paints a vivid picture of the era. It calls to mind marches and protests—sit-ins or perhaps the blazing demonstration outside the 1968 Miss America pageant. Careful now: "This is not 1968 but 1964," Ehrenreich and her cowriters explain. The girls do not shout an activist chant but instead call out in frenzied voices: "I love Ringo!" How's that for a reverie? Beatlemania had come to America.

Later, the band would be associated with the antiwar movement and with free love and the dream of a peace-seeking utopia. But at the time it had no particular activist valence. What made the Beatles radical—Ehrenreich, Hess, and Jacobs maintain—was how the band emboldened its fans.

The girls who fell all over themselves for it had been given almost no outlet for their emotions, let alone for their desires. When the music arrived, it landed "with the force, if not the conviction, of a social movement."

America had seen such mania from its repressed girls before. In 1944, Frank Sinatra had inspired tens of thousands of them to cram into Times Square to hear him perform, a month before *Seventeen* debuted. *New Republic* editor Bruce Bliven compared the scene to "the dance madness that overtook some German villages in the middle ages." A decade later, Elvis mesmerized girls nationwide on *The Ed Sullivan Show*. A smaller population grew infatuated with Beat poets. Their restlessness perhaps foretold a broader revolution, with some of those same women becoming pioneering civil rights and campus activists and committed members of women's liberation groups.

But nothing compared to the Beatles, whom thousands of girls greeted at the airport when the band landed stateside and whom seventy-three million Americans watched on television that winter. The effect was not just galvanizing, but all-consuming. Beatlemania gave girls permission to "abandon control—to scream, faint, dash about in mobs." Whether it meant to or not, that kind of fandom protested "the sexual repressiveness, the rigid double standard of female teen culture," Ehrenreich and her coauthors write. "It was the first and most dramatic uprising of women's sexual revolution."

Fandom offered them a taste of what it would be like to be heard. Having a favorite Beatle, shaking and dancing in public, fantasizing—it was an act of defiance. It planted a seed. The shifting sentiment that Steinem documented on college campuses gave a girl space to ask herself what that professors' former students hadn't been able to a decade prior: What do I want?

WHERE THE TENDRILS of revolution were taking root, Heather Tobis was there to water them. That had been true long before she'd gotten involved in the civil rights movement. In high school, she quit the cheerleading squad when she decided its members were not committed to a true progressive agenda. With more free time on her hands, she protested capital punishment in Times Square and joined CORE to oppose the racist policies at her local department store. She was fifteen. Decades later, when the *Chicago Tribune* profiled her, the newspaper titled the article "A Woman Born to Be Riled."

For all her varied efforts—political, social, cultural—gender had not been an initial focus. When she arrived in Chicago for college, she made her first protest appearance at a demonstration to publicize the subpar facilities in which Black public school students were educated. It was after Freedom Summer that her perspective started to shift. She had inequalities to face closer to home.

Others in the movement had reached similar conclusions.

In 1964, the activist Mary King, who joined SNCC as a staffer after graduating from college, wrote a controversial paper for a national conference that tried to envision how women could have a more central impact on the structure and organization of SNCC. She gathered several cowriters, including the esteemable Casey Hayden. Still, the document landed with a thud.

In 1965, undaunted, the women hazarded a second attempt and called for further examination of the role of women in not just social movements but the wider world. It was headlined "A Kind of Memo"— as tentative a title as a manifesto has ever had. The text, which King and Hayden cowrote, spoke to not only the profound inequities between men and women but also the extent to which both sexes seemed to have made their peace with female subordination. It was not optimistic about the potential for a women's movement. It placed the odds of one at a rousing "nil."

Even so, the document made the rounds. The memo reached Tobis, who read it and was electrified. The authors had learned as student organizers that matters of justice were not to be dismissed as "private troubles." These were social concerns in need of structural solutions—personal woes in need of a political response.

Tobis grew up. She founded Jane. She later launched a women's discussion group on campus. She was one of an astonishing 70 percent of women and girls who went on to immerse themselves in the battle for women's liberation after participating in Freedom Summer. She married Paul Booth in 1967. But she did not fade from view as Diane Nash, Mabel Ping-Hua Lee, and Anna Elizabeth Dickinson had. The work that she did contributed to the expanded set of possibilities available to her.

Feminism abhorred the idea that a woman had to disappear once she had a spouse or children. Booth continued in her work to advance that precise conviction. Her activism fortified her powers. Booth had two children and named one after Eugene Debs. She marched in support of universal childcare with her son on her hip. She founded a center to train the next generation of progressive activists and has continued to house student organizers in her basement apartment. Is it possible to teach the kind of activism that she practiced as a girl? She hopes so.

Booth has seen women and girls fall out of organizing even as she sticks with it. What can she tell them about how to continue? Teenagers look out at the world and see promise and potential. That is the feeling that Booth would like activists to hold on to: the conviction that it is all possible.

SECOND-WAVE FEMINISM and the push for reproductive freedom moved in tandem. The most consequential dates follow one after another and overlap. The pill was invented in 1960. *Sex and the Single Girl*—the now retrograde treatise on financial independence and sexual freedom—was published in 1962. Friedan published her opus in 1963. Contraception was legalized for married couples in 1965. Then came revised guidelines on sex discrimination in the workplace in 1968, and Title IX in 1972. *Roe v. Wade* was decided just over six months later.

In the span of a decade, women gained rights and access to choices that would have been unthinkable a generation before. We would lose at least one of them two generations later. But back then the revolution marched ahead: Women could have sex without risking the prospect of childbirth. New kinds of careers and educational paths unfurled.

It was not all progress and enlightenment. Some of the earliest proponents of birth control demonstrated a hideous interest in eugenics, with an emphasis on providing contraception to minorities and single women of color. Margaret Sanger, the activist and sex educator who helped found Planned Parenthood, was one of them. In 1927, she backed the Supreme Court decision that allowed the state to sterilize those it deemed "unfit" to procreate, without their consent. Over two dozen states sterilized their citizens, a practice that continued for decades. Programs limited the number of children that Puerto Rican and Native American women and girls had. Others targeted people with disabilities. The women who ran the programs might have called themselves feminists. In 1967, Elaine Riddick was sterilized after giving birth to her son. She was fourteen and he was the product of rape, but doctors took one look at Riddick's grades and her supposed "promiscuous" behavior and ruled that she was not suitable for motherhood. She did not find out what had been done to her until she wanted to have more children. In North Carolina, where Riddick lived, forced sterilizations continued until 1974, and the law that permitted them was not repealed until 2003. Riddick had been ensnared in a project that had been designed to "improve" the state's population. It left over 7,600 victims in its wake. And like Riddick, most were Black and poor.

Even in less extreme circumstances, pregnant girls struggled to find their place in women's liberation. The movement advocated independence. Teen mothers could not be so unencumbered. In a letter to *Ms.* magazine, one mother explained her desperation to be as "free and liberated" as other burgeoning feminists. "I want to fight battles and make changes, but some nights I lie in bed too frightened to move, too crushed by my own insecurity," she wrote. "[I]t seems the bonds I chained myself with are inescapable." She was seventeen.

Who could blame her for feeling constrained? Never mind the pressure and responsibilities that having a child entails—a set of duties that had for a time overwhelmed even the crusading Claudette Colvin. There were also the punitive measures that unmarried teen mothers were forced to endure. Girls who were not sent to homes to wait out their pregnancies were often kicked out of school or at least separated from their classmates. Girls who had jobs often lost them. It was hard to find a reasonable and affordable place to live, and brutal to attempt to earn enough to support a child as a single woman.

All over the United States, tens of thousands of girls experienced isolation, humiliation, shame, punishment. In 1957, the teenage birth rate swelled to 96.3 per 1,000 women—almost 10 percent. In 1965, that number had declined somewhat but still stood firm at 7 percent.

Adult women seldom came to their rescue. The predicament in which girls found themselves proved the need for access to contraception and stigma-free abortion and sex education. But what to do with the teenagers who were pregnant just then? What did feminism have to teach them?

Just as the courts were careening toward their decision in *Roe*, another kind of case was under judicial review. It too was rooted in that familiar and contentious question: What are women and girls allowed to do with their bodies? Its plaintiffs looked a little different than the others. When Estelle Griswold became the defendant in *Griswold v. Connecticut*, the case that legalized birth control for married couples nationwide, she was in her sixties. When the woman who would become known as Jane Roe was hoping to get an abortion, she was in her twenties. In contrast, this new set of cases had literal if unconventional poster children: pregnant high school–aged girls.

In 1966, the prospect of pregnant teenagers was not the top concern of school officials in Grenada, Mississippi. Administrators were instead

154

preoccupied with the more immediate concern of integration, which had started to seem like a losing battle. White leaders were vehement in their opposition. Black parents were determined to see the district follow the law. That fall, the SCLC and local Black leaders registered over four hundred Black students to attend the two all-white schools in town as the district geared up for a new semester. Black students who arrived on that first morning of classes were attacked while police looked on. Several had to be hospitalized. Just over one hundred Black students lasted through the spring and decided to stick it out the following fall. Two of them were Clydie Marie Perry, seventeen, and Emma Jean Wilson, fourteen. Within a matter of months, both were pregnant. Perry and Wilson had been capable students and well liked, but the school wasted no time expelling them. It cited "moral unfitness" as the cause.

The NAACP Legal Defense and Education Fund seized on the case and sued. It argued that the law protected the girls and claimed that their pregnancies were being used as a pretense to rid the school of Black students. When Judge Orma Smith issued his decision, he hastened to make clear that "lack of moral character" was a legitimate reason to exclude someone from a public education. He just didn't think that all pregnant teenagers were such hopeless causes.

"[T]he fact that a girl has one child out of wedlock does not forever brand her as a scarlet woman," he wrote.

The decorated Black journalist Carl T. Rowan celebrated the decision. In the *Toledo Blade*, he heralded it as perhaps as important as the "school desegregation policies of the Nixon administration or the new voting rights proposal of the Justice Department." The case had "reopened the door of hope for tens of thousands" of girls who had once been conscribed to lives as "the scorned, the accursed, the bitter." A few progressive newspapers also noted the case. Otherwise it passed without much fanfare. Elizabeth Eckford and dozens of other

Black girls had worn their best virginal white dresses to desegregate white schools for a reason. Claudette Colvin had been sidelined on purpose. With expanding bellies, two pregnant Black teenagers gave the press less to root for.

The media did go on to find a somewhat more palatable face for teen motherhood. Fay Ordway was eighteen when she learned she was pregnant in 1971. She also happened to be white. Petite and attractive, Ordway had been a model student at her suburban high school in Townsend, Massachusetts. She was planning to attend Fitchburg State College the following fall. But when it became undeniable that she was pregnant, she was expelled.

She was in a disadvantaged class: single female. Married girls were permitted to finish their studies. Expectant fathers were allowed to graduate—no matter their marital status. Unwed mothers were not welcome.

That did not sit well with Ordway. She appealed her expulsion. And when the school board came back with a proposal that she continue with her coursework and meet with her teachers after normal classes had been dismissed lest she be seen on campus, she was even more incensed. If she had consented to a quickie wedding, she would have been free to pursue her education. But because she had not wanted to get married, she was seen as a threat. Too radioactive to be allowed on campus with her friends. Too shameful to sit in class.

What relevance was her marital status to the matter of her education? she wondered in an interview with the *Chicago Tribune*: "[E]veryone needs an education. So I decided to fight for mine."

Ordway took the school board to court and won. The judge in *Ordway v. Hargraves* affirmed as Smith had that "a public school education is a basic personal right." The soon-to-be mother was readmitted and graduated on time with the rest of her class. She gave birth two weeks later.

The cases established a firm legal precedent. Soon Title IX—the federal law that prohibits gender discrimination in educational programs receiving government dollars—would inscribe the rights of pregnant students into law. The legal argument rested on an understanding that children had a right to education—a finding that doesn't seem to have much to do with the precepts of feminist thinking. But the discrimination that pregnant girls experience opens the door to a host of moral and legal judgments. It returns us to old questions: Who is entitled to be seen as innocent? Who gets to be independent? Who is allowed to make choices, and who has her choices made for her? The girls who refused to slink off into oblivion forced courts and their own communities to recognize them as capable. In the present, the battle to have all girls seen as trusted guardians of their own bodies continues.

Social victories are seldom complete. Each requires tending, nurturing, furthering. The promises of Title IX remain unfulfilled. In 1999, the ACLU settled a case on behalf of two teen mothers who claimed that their grades qualified them for membership in a national honors program, but their status as pregnant and parenting teenagers had been used against them. In 2002, the New York Civil Liberties Union submitted a letter to the schools chancellor to call attention to the harassment and discrimination that were driving pregnant girls and teen mothers out of state public schools. Executive Director Donna Lieberman put it in terms schools could understand—she gave New York an F.

We still don't trust girls to make their own choices. In dozens of states, minors must obtain parental permission to have an abortion. In

August 2022, a Florida court denied a request from a high school student to seek an abortion because it ruled she was too immature to make such a consequential decision. It made the call for her that she was not too immature to become a mother.

When teenage mothers decided to assert their right to an education, their cases formed an underappreciated legal backbone. Their outspokenness—even when it was just an errant *Toledo Blade* reporter who cared to acknowledge it—was an act of self-declaration. Colvin had been cast aside as a pregnant teenager. Two decades later, girls demanded that their schools continue to recognize their potential—as students and thinkers and as people who wanted to define themselves as something other than "mother." That conviction put them at least in conversation with if not on the same side as the activists we tend to think of when we talk about feminism. The dream is the same: women's and girls' lives, on their own terms.

In a strange sense, the cases and their plaintiffs testified to a new value of the age: frankness. Bodies would be mapped and explored, in all their unruliness. Women and girls would demand it. In a piece first published in an underground journal and later reprinted in one of the first issues of the magazine *Off Our Backs* in 1970, Diane Devlin—self-described as a "rather militant" lesbian—seemed to speak for her generation in seeking answers. She had just graduated high school, where in a new sex education course she had been taught that "homosexuals are poor . . . pitiable creatures" and that "the average good, clean, 'normal' teenager would do well to avoid [them]." "Must we sit in classrooms and hear ourselves characterized as sick, immature, and incapable of loving and being loved?" she asked. Devlin didn't want to be passive or quiet or even tolerant of those who might be moved to silence her. She wanted a voice.

. . .

IN HER MEMOIR *Where the Girls Are,* Susan Douglas writes about her adolescence before and after *Roe.* The book is a chronicle of a person looking for a mirror in the culture—some piece of the world in which she might get a glimpse of the universe as she experienced it. Douglas recalls the girl groups she listened to in high school with particular warmth. The songs were not at all political anthems—more bubblegum pop. But the women who performed them seemed to give literal voice to her inner world. Groups like the Shirelles—emphasizing love and experimentation—primed Douglas and her generation to see sexual freedom as a legitimate pursuit, just as Ehrenreich had insisted. That revelation became a step on the path toward "other freedoms as well." The girls weren't some band of activists, but their music helped female fans practice a defining element of second-wave feminism: talking.

"What we have here is a pop culture harbinger in which girl groups, however innocent and commercial, anticipate women's groups, and girl talk anticipates a future kind of women's talk," Douglas writes.

That "talk" drew on intimate high school chatter—preoccupied with the same topics that earned them little respect from adults: bodies, romance, ambitions, indignities, gossip.

In 1970, *The New York Times* dispatched Susan Brownmiller—who would become famous for her treatise on rape, *Against Our Will*—to sit in on the meetings of a women's circle not unlike the kind Douglas describes. Founded in the fall of 1967, the New York Radical Women counted Shulamith Firestone and later the feminist giant Ellen Willis as members. When Brownmiller arrived to bear witness, she encountered several alumni of the civil rights movement. The environment was confessional and compassionate, and whatever awkwardness persisted at the start petered out and was replaced with passionate testimonies. There was so much that needed to be said, a member of the group told Brownmiller. "[A]nd most of us had never said it to another woman before."

Brownmiller headlined her dispatch "Sisterhood Is Powerful." The feminist Robin Morgan later gave the collection of articles, poems, photographs, and manifestos she edited—all contributions from activists for women's liberation—the same name. The eventual book features a trio of entries from high school students, with one titled "Excerpts from the Diaries of All Oppressed Women." The piece documents just how hard it was for even this new generation of enlightened girls to write about the movement—to name its aims, to devise a plan to realize them. It expresses no clear idea about how to move forward. It does not enumerate policies to pass or bills to debate. Still, its writers were sure on one point: There was an inordinate amount of pleasure and relief to be had just in sharing—in talking and recognizing points of overlap. That can be its own kind of protest.

"Getting together and rapping about hang-ups that have arisen as a result of our being females helps us realize that we aren't shits," the girls write, "that we aren't docile and reticent because of something fucked up inside us, but it's like that because we have been programmed into that."

The things that women dismiss or hide as personal failings turn out to be common, the girls continue: "We've all been fucked over and show it."

The women who joined groups like New York Radical Women tended to be fresh out of college or in their midtwenties, but their example inspired high school and college students—like the *Sisterhood*

Is Powerful contributors—to establish their own conversation circles, several of which transformed into activist groups committed to sex education and reproductive freedom. In New York, the High School Women's Liberation Coalition passed out leaflets that prompted women to think about their responses to cultural norms. Pedestrians were asked to consider street catcalls and the cost of makeup. One of the group's most straightforward questions asked whether respondents liked their bodies. The coalition later embarked on a campaign to sell almost one hundred municipal high schools on a feminist sex-education curriculum. The girls organized a five-week training course for students in their peer leadership program, not just covering STDs and contraception but inviting participants and their parents to discuss them together. In Michigan, the high school faction of Youth Liberation of Ann Arbor published an eighty-page pamphlet as a feminist outreach tool.

Some girls went further, flouting the Comstock laws that, until 1972, banned sending "obscene" materials—a class that included information about birth control—via the USPS to circulate information about women's reproductive health. It was a radical gambit, but it squared with the priorities that teen girls listed in a 1974 Planned Parenthood poll. Receiving information about sex education ranked second, just after career training.

Grown women tried to be supportive. NOW published a report on gender bias in schools. The organizations that backed girls' legal bids in court were full of like-minded adults. But girls led the charge. Their experiences informed their strategies. Their issues dictated their actions.

Their work demonstrated that gender bias found unique expression in their lives. No one wanted to wait for liberation.

. . .

EIGHT MONTHS AFTER the 1968 Miss America pageant, during which protesters held signs that featured women's bodies labeled like cuts of meat, a group of twelve women met for a workshop about women's bodies. The session was part of a female liberation conference held at Emmanuel College—a Catholic women's college in Boston. The school's undergraduate vice president, Barbara Deck, had convinced the administration to approve the unconventional event. But then, she had never been a conventional student candidate. When she ran for government, she did it on a "Student Power" ticket.

Over five hundred women attended the conference—a mix of undergraduates and activists and varied ardent believers in women's liberation. The program opened with a karate demonstration. The next morning, a volunteer held a session titled "Women and Their Bodies." Participants traded horror stories about how medical professionals had treated them. Women recalled doctors who refused to tell them how birth control worked. Doctors who manipulated them into unwanted courses of treatment or disregarded their pain. Doctors who delivered their diagnoses to their husbands, leaving them in the exam room alone. The workshop ended, but the women weren't finished. A resource group was started to continue the conversation. The group would go on to publish the results of months of discussion and research in a compendium titled *Women and Their Bodies*.

It was the first of its kind. Printed on cheap newsprint and rendered in accessible prose, it offered reliable information about bodies and sex—topics that could make even committed feminists blush. Heather Booth remembered attending one of the first National Women's Liberation conferences and running into Anne Koedt, the audacious activist. Koedt was handing out a questionnaire that would go on to inform her cult classic essay, "The Myth of the Vaginal Orgasm." Even Booth, who had spent her time in college recruiting doctors to give women underground abortions, felt a little frisson of scandal.

"I was shocked!" she recalled. "I didn't know about that! We all would be talking about it, and we learned about our own bodies in part from one another. We realized we could turn to each other not in shame or embarrassment but in support."

When Jane was founded, it existed to connect women and girls in need to doctors who would perform abortions for a reasonable rate. But around the same time as the Boston collective formalized to build on the momentum from the conference, the women who were now in leadership positions with Jane had started to do the procedure themselves. Their cutting out of the middleman also cut the cost to a hundred dollars, and less if a patient couldn't afford it.

More than ten thousand women ended unwanted pregnancies with Jane's help. Its work became as communal an effort as a medical procedure can be. The volunteers who oversaw the abortions developed a practice. Two women would conduct each procedure, switching off between holding the dilation and curettage tools and holding the hands of the patient. A sisterhood, gathered around the plastic-covered bed.

Laura Kaplan, who joined Jane in 1971 and wrote a book about the group, remembered sending patients home with copies of *Women and Their Bodies*—later reworked as the iconic *Our Bodies, Ourselves*. The group purchased hundreds of the pamphlets at a time and stacked them in the makeshift waiting room.

In an interview, Kaplan noted how radical it was for her patients to read about their bodies in plain language. The text was often "the first piece of detailed information for women on how your body worked," Kaplan said. "It was the beginning of a revolution."

In 1972, eight months before the *Roe* decision, police raided the apartment out of which Jane was operating. Seven women were arrested, including one college student. In the police van, the women ripped up the index cards inscribed with patient names and swallowed them. Each was booked on half a dozen charges. But after the Supreme Court ruled in *Roe*, the state dropped the case. The procedure had been made legal.

We have been forced back into a moment in which prosecutions over abortion are all but inevitable. Women and girls are subjected to laws that render their bodies organs of the state. Carve outs for cases of rape or incest or even the health of the mother are so limited as to be almost irrelevant.

Abortion clinics have had to pick up and move out of states where abortion is now illegal. New ones have been built near borders and airports to make the procedure as accessible as possible to those who will need to travel to obtain one. Networks that help ship abortion pills through the USPS are fundraising and beefing up their legal counsel.

Not all girls are pro-choice—as a recent parade of Gen Z anti-abortion activists marching through Washington, D.C., attests. Not all girls who get pregnant want abortions. But an astonishing number do back abortion access. A 2022 poll found support among emerging adults at close to 75 percent—a twelve-point jump compared with adults a decade older.

When Senate Bill 8 passed in Texas, one Gen Z activist based in the state railed against the law in an op-ed for *Ms.* magazine. In an interview, she was bitter: "We should be teenagers; instead, we're having to worry about what could happen to our bodies."

Larada Lee, who had an abortion as an adolescent, told a reporter in 2022 that she would continue to organize no matter what became of *Roe*. The women of Jane had done it. The high schoolers who launched their own talking circles had too. "We need to be thinking more expansively about what abortion access and rights look like without this ruling," Lee said, "because when *Roe v. Wade* falls, we still have each other."

8

GOOD GIRLS

CRUSADERS IN MINISKIRTS
AND THE RIGHT TO AN EDUCATION

n the fall of 1968, two girls plotted a stealth attack in the lunch-room. Both were enrolled at their local public school in New York. Both were dissatisfied. Alice de Rivera was thirteen and a fresh-man, having skipped third grade. Mia Rublowsky was a sophomore. The pair met in the student union, where the girls bonded over their shared aptitude for math and science and disdain for their lackluster classes.

Rublowsky had been the first to suggest an act of insurrection. She told de Rivera that she was thinking about submitting an application to Stuyvesant High School—reputed to be one of the nation's best. The institution was well-known for its investment in math and science—the same subjects in which the girls felt their current education was so deficient. It had never accepted a female student.

Rublowsky wanted to challenge the gender rule. She was the daughter of out-and-proud radicals who had introduced her to activists and antiwar demonstrators as a child. She knew she would have their support. But as in late-night escapades, so too in acts of revolution: It's never a bad idea to bring a friend. She invited de Rivera to join her and de Rivera agreed.

Trust good girls to do their research: Within a matter of weeks, the two set up a meeting with Ramona Ripston, an activist with the National Emergency Civil Liberties Committee (NECLC). The NECLC had backed conscientious objectors to the draft and Black Panthers. Now it would take up the cause of a rarer species of rebel: the overachiever.

The girls presented their plan, of which Ripston approved. But she had some news to break: Rublowsky had no shot. In addition to not accepting girls, Stuyvesant would not consider junior or senior transfers. Rublowsky would be too old to enroll the following September. Ripston pointed out that de Rivera, on the other hand, had an actual chance. But if she wanted to tackle the problem, she would have to pursue the case alone.

De Rivera had come this far. She was game. So Ripston approached the lawyer Eleanor Jackson Piel, who agreed to represent de Rivera in court pro bono. The trio began meeting to strategize the case. De Rivera took her notes in a three-ring binder.

GIVEN HOW OFTEN GIRLS have had to advocate for themselves (who else is going to do it?), it is perhaps surprising that girls were not the drivers of the earliest efforts to secure their own education. The most famous enthusiasts were grown women, and the likes of Catharine Beecher and Emma Willard did not start schools with the aim of gender advancement.

While her contemporaries were pushing for abolition and universal suffrage, Beecher was determined to make the case that women did not in fact need the same opportunities as men. What women needed was to be shown their place. Men went to school to prepare for professional life. Women needed to be trained for *their* futures. Beecher envisioned school not as some great equalizer but as a reinforcement of what seemed to her to be the natural order. Men went out into the world. Women tended the home front.

Still, she believed that girls were capable learners and had real ambitions for her approach to their education. She was prepared to work to realize her vision, even as she ratified the gendered inequalities of her moment. (She never did come around on suffrage.)

Beecher founded her first institution dedicated to higher education for women in 1823—an instant hit. It had to expand to keep up with demand from new pupils, and Beecher got to work establishing and canonizing her curriculum. In 1841, she laid out her central contention: The "proper education of a man decides the welfare of an individual," but the education of women ensured that the interests of entire families could be secured.

You can thank Beecher for home economics. She is credited with creating the course.

Schools became more bureaucratic and formalized over the subsequent decades. The institutions started to offer job preparation and civics instruction, taking over for the tutelage that families and churches had once provided. Both sexes attended. Both were rewarded—or penalized—with graded papers and tests. Girls were supposed to perform in school, whether their multiplication tables would serve them as wives and mothers. Students have long whined: "When am I going to use this?" For girls, the answer was often a firm "never."

But in the Cold War, school became a patriotic enterprise. Teenagers streamed into classrooms with no less "than the survival of the free world" resting on their "puff-sleeved shoulders," Susan Douglas remembers in her memoir of the era. Girls might not be expected to serve in battle. That did not let them off the hook at home. In the struggle for world domination, "we had to get As well," she writes. The fate of the republic depended on it.

The reward for girls' achievement could not be acceptance letters to the most elite universities, which still barred women, or a leg up in a competitive job market, where bosses were still allowed to discriminate on the basis of sex. An entire education—for what?

WHEN DE RIVERA decided to take on a formidable school board and a storied institution, she did so at a time when weighing whether to meet the intellectual and social needs of women and girls was still a question evaluated in terms of the impact it would have on men.

In 1966, when Yale considered a partnership with Vassar to import women to New Haven, it did so not out of some forward-thinking desire to offer women the same caliber of education that it gave men, but rather because some in the administration feared that Yale was missing out on top male students who preferred—as one former dean of admissions put it—the "more natural, more realistic, more progressive" model of learning and living with women.

For the sake of Yale's reputation and its standing with men, at least some partial effort had to be made to include women. Kingman Brewster, then Yale's president, was explicit about that, telling a roomful of alumni that his concern was "not so much what Yale can do for women but what women can do for Yale."

Those who opposed coeducation—whether men were clamoring for it or not—had their list of accusations at hand. Women were distracting. Women would ruin male camaraderie. Women passed their idle hours, as one Yale alum wrote in 1966, with "gossip about the idiotic trivia." And while it could not be denied that there were certain pleasures to be had in what he called "the girl filled weekend," women were overall better in small doses. Too much exposure and those girls "get to be a drag."

In 1968, just as de Rivera was starting her first semester of high school, a Princeton graduate submitted a letter to the editor of his alumni magazine to express his outrage at the prospect that his alma mater might go coed: "What is all this nonsense about admitting women to Princeton? A good old-fashioned whore-house would be . . . more efficient, and much, much cheaper."

The results of a poll of Harvard and Radcliffe students released a few months later seemed to reveal a generational divide, with 90 percent of current students at both schools voting for coed accommodations in at least some dorms on campus. Their response pointed to an openness to the acceptance of women at Harvard, although Harvard did not take over the academic and residential functions of its sister school, Radcliffe, until 1977, and the two did not merge until 1999.

In 1970, a Dartmouth alum made his point short and sweet: "Keep the damned women out."

These were the kinds of schools to which students at the best high schools were expected to gain entrance. And "the best high school"— or one of them—was the one that de Rivera wanted to attend. She would have to sue to get her chance.

To accuse the school of violating the law, de Rivera first had to be denied admission. Piel had settled on a simple approach. If de Rivera was not permitted to sit for the entrance exam, Piel would claim that the school violated the equal protection clause guaranteed under the Fourteenth Amendment. De Rivera requested an application, as she was instructed. She received a response on the letterhead of the school principal. Dr. Leonard Fliedner had knocked down the request. A reporter later summed up his rejection in two simple words: "No girls." It was the slammed door that Piel had been waiting for. She and de Rivera filed a lawsuit against the New York State Board of Education.

News of the case was in *The New York Times* the following morning, paired with a photo of de Rivera in profile that made her look much older than thirteen. "I wasn't prepared for the press to twist things," she said. De Rivera didn't recognize herself in the photos. Some seemed to her doctored with fake lipstick that she never would have worn. She winced at the recollection of others that emphasized her legs. She went to court alone, taking the train. She was a kid.

The paper notes that the Manhattan Supreme Court had ordered the school board to either allow de Rivera to take the entrance exam or explain what valid legal rationale it had for preventing her from sitting for it. De Rivera did not speak at the hearing, but she could still remember how she felt. "I just was like, 'This is ridiculous. Last century, women got to start to be doctors. We're everywhere. I didn't realize this was still happening,'" she recalled. "In general, I've taken on things with a lot of chutzpah because I feel justice is needed for other people. It seemed to me something would work out."

In a retrospective on her stand, *The New Yorker* chronicles how the media received the girl whose presence seemed to pose such an existential threat to a few hundred math nerds: The *Daily News* dubbed her a "crusader in miniskirts." The *Washington Post* commented on her "inevitable jeans." A student reporter wanted to know whether she believed she would have a "disruptive effect" on the school, to which she replied, "I intend to be disruptive not with my presence, but with my ideas."

The case made national news, attracting the notice of not just wonks and administrators but none other than Jimi Hendrix, who sent de Rivera an autographed record, inscribed with a heart. "Good luck on the school thing," he wrote.

De Rivera kept most of the clippings, which—annotated in her adolescent hand—tell their own stories. Over one photo in *El Diario*, she wrote: "Oh Jesus these pics have got to go."

While the alums of Ivies panicked about the women who might share in their resources, credentials, and job opportunities, the male students with whom de Rivera was hoping to share classrooms were more amenable. A bunch of them started coming to court to show their support. One told a reporter that de Rivera would be a welcome addition to the student population. She started dating another. He was one of the few Black students at the school and her first kiss. The two, a pair of outsiders, have remained friends. In anticipation of her arrival, students hung a banner that read "Alice's Corner" in the lunchroom. It charmed her. "In retrospect," she said, "getting the support of kids my age mattered the most."

She looked back with less fondness on the adults who masterminded the case. "I didn't understand the consequences at that point," she said. "I had all this attention for something that for me wasn't that hard, and I experienced that whole thing about being smart and feeling like I didn't deserve it." She didn't feel like she had earned the attention. Was she *the* smartest girl ever to want to go to Stuyvesant? Or was she just the one who had somehow ended up in court?

She didn't know how to make sense of the hoopla. The case had gotten so much press that she started receiving disturbing phone calls at home, with men heaving and grunting on the other end. Her looks were scrutinized. She felt embarrassed and ashamed. She thought of the Black students she admired who had integrated their high schools. She tried to channel their courage. "I feel like it was a positive thing to do and to accomplish, but there was some pain associated with it," she said.

In the end, she could see her function. She was the clean case that Ripston had been looking for. What she needed to do was exist. She did not speak once in court.

Piel did the talking instead. She cited the final report of the President's Commission on the Status of Women, which had been released in 1963. The report stopped short of backing the Equal Rights Amendment, which would have enshrined equal rights for men and women in the Constitution, but it endorsed the view that the protections guaranteed by the Fourteenth Amendment applied to women. Piel also quoted "Jane Crow and the Law"—an influential law journal article on the relationship between gender, race, and civil rights that the scholars Pauli Murray and Mary Eastwood had cowritten and published in *The George Washington Law Review*.

It was an apt citation. Murray had embarked on a version of de Rivera's quest decades earlier. In 1938, she had applied to law school in her native North Carolina. Like de Rivera, she was rejected. women In her case, women were welcome. Black people were not.

Piel laid out persuasive claims. She also happened to have a receptive listener on the other side of the bench. Judge Jawn A. Sandifer had taken over the case in April 1969. He, too, had been excluded from the law school of his choice. He was Black. Duke had refused to admit him. He went to Howard instead and moved to New York after graduation, working with the NAACP and Thurgood Marshall. Later he would win a seat on the New York State Supreme Court. In the meantime, his work on civil rights was no secret.

The school board must have sensed its losing hand, so it reversed course before a judgment could be rendered. It would consider girls for admission, preempting a damaging ruling from the bench. With its repeal of the ban, the case was over. De Rivera told *The New Yorker* that the outcome had disappointed her. She had hoped to set a legal precedent. Later, she came to see the conclusion as its own kind of achievement. "It was a cultural precedent," she said.

The era had demonstrated that those mattered too. When de Rivera was growing up, student protest had a male face—even when women and girls participated. Columbia students barricaded themselves in Hamilton Hall. Youth-led civil unrest exploded in France. Men stood on the figurative and literal front lines as the antiwar movement spread around the world. De Rivera shrugged off the attention she got. But it is undeniable: She gave her cause a new look.

In April 1969, the same month that Sandifer took over de Rivera's case and prompted the school board to reverse its gender ban, a reporter for *The New York Times Magazine* was permitted to preview an exclusive selection process. A few months earlier, Yale had announced it would at last admit women. The reporter would witness the formation of Yale's inaugural coed class.

The writer compared the candidates to Nietzsche's *Übermensch*. So qualified! Such credentials. The nickname stuck: Yale's superwomen. But the 230 female high school seniors who earned a coveted place were not so sure. College was supposed to be a social experience. Would it be hard to make friends from their perch at the top of a pedestal?

In a recollection published decades later, a woman who started at Yale that fall remembers how her three soon-to-be roommates sent letters to introduce themselves. Each of them sounded the same note of caution: "No, I am *not* a superwoman." But like it or not, the women did stand out.

Professors started to call on the one or two women in each class to solicit "the feminine viewpoint"—a habit that *New York Times* reporter Harriet H. Coffin notes, often followed discussion of matters that had "no academic relevance." Their male classmates liked to pick their brains too, steamrolling conversations with observations and opinions and intimate confessions. Women—whom Coffin observes, had been "brought up to listen"—did not dare interrupt. Coffin pronounces that these new "Yale mothers" were fast replacing "old Mother Yale." When the first female transfers graduated in 1971, the campus was split between 4,000 men and 780 women. The gender imbalance meant, as Coffin puts it, a "ratio of five talkers to one listener."

The din could be overwhelming. Sexism was a constant and unavoidable fact of the coeducational experience that women had worked so hard for. Coping meant making as little fuss as possible, although several of the first female Yalies did voice their objection to a paragraph that appeared in the freshman handbook given to each new student: "Treat Yale as you would a good woman; take advantage of her many gifts, nourish yourself with the fruit of her wisdom, curse her if you will, but congratulate yourself in your possession of her."

A few months after women arrived at Yale, *Time* ran a major article on the movement for women's liberation. (Despite the hemming and hawing from its alumni, women had been admitted to Princeton that fall as well.) The *Time* feature noted the growing number of women who had now enrolled in higher education and declared that the girls who graduated high school and went off to universities instead of settling down with a husband were "having fewer babies, looking ahead to living longer, and thinking more about careers." The horror.

It was the kind of planning that had been unavailable to previous generations of women, and it came as a gross surprise to the writer of the piece, Ruth Brine. "Women's rising expectations" were not just

unprecedented but almost absurd. Brine notes that girls in particular—
who were "fertile ground for the seeds of discontent"—were flock-
ing to the movement. Worse still: So-called militant feminism had
"attracted a number of women who otherwise had no radical leanings
at all."

Its latest recruits included not just laborers and disaffected housewives but high schoolers. Hundreds of them were "learning karate,
tossing oft furious statements about 'male chauvinists,'" distributing
audacious pamphlets, and even quoting the likes of Frantz Fanon, Brine
continues. Toward the conclusion of the piece, Brine cites a sociologist who summed up what remains an aim of the feminist movement:
If children are not socialized based on the characteristics associated
with the gender assigned to them at birth, the perceived differences
between them will disappear. The inequities, the biases—those could
be overcome.

"To change such patterns and the resultant personalities is a formidable goal, but the feminists believe that it can be achieved," Brine
wrote. And while she could not quite get on board with their most
extreme biological theories, she did concede this much: "Girls are
seldom encouraged to think of themselves as anything but creatures
who will one day substitute babies for their dolls."

Brine was no great feminist theorist, but she understood the risks
of her transitional moment. Roles for men and women were growing
more alike. Soon women would have less tolerance for male machismo.
And if men could not learn to retire it or did not want to, an inevitable
backlash would follow.

"The radical women have opened a Pandora's box," Brine wrote.
But then: Pandora had been a radical woman too.

After de Rivera, dozens of Pandoras, not content to wait until college or graduate school or the professional workplace to unleash their

furies, protested the kinds of injustices that cropped up in their own lives. Their activism was a call for inclusion.

In 1970, Chris Robinson joined with four female classmates to sue her school district over its mandate of home economics as a requirement for girls. Soon after, Bonnie Sanchez convinced a federal court to force her school district to explain its decision to bar her from a metalwork class. She testified with seven other girls before the Board of Education in New York, arguing that their schools had shut them out of classes, sports, and activities that were considered more masculine pursuits. The historian Kera Lovell has written that their testimonies drove the school district's decision to list vocational and technical course options as coeducational.

The dam did not break all at once. Lowell High School in San Francisco admitted girls in 1970, but it still required them to have a higher GPA lest female students flood the campus. In 1971, *New York Times* reporter Eleanor Blau chronicled the successes of an initiative to keep underperforming students in high school until graduation. The program, which operated out of Thomas Jefferson High School in New York, offered participants a reduced course load and a job that both counted toward their credit requirement and paid them $2.31 an hour (over $16 now). Two cohorts of students had graduated from it, with impressive retention rates. In a single line, Blau explains that girls couldn't participate in the program. The cafeteria work was deemed unsuitable for them.

Lovell has argued that cases like de Rivera's helped form the basis of Title IX. The legislation was the result of the careful work of a corps of dedicated lawmakers, including Congresswomen Patsy Mink and Edith Green and Senator Birch Bayh, who said when he introduced the bill in 1971 that it would give women "a fair chance to secure the jobs of their choice." (He couldn't have intended to recall the precise language of Harriet Hanson and Charlotte Woodward Peirce, but isn't it nice that he did?)

Bayh refuted the notion that women were no more than "pretty things who go to college to find a husband, go on to graduate school because they want a more interesting husband, and finally marry, have children, and never work again." That kind of thinking led to discrimination against them, not to mention the fact that such biases were "corrosive and unjustified."

Title IX did not end inequalities in education or outside it. But its effects were far reaching. After *Time* published a piece on the new legislation, a girl marched into her principal's office with the magazine in hand. "I know my rights," she declared. "I really want to play soccer."

IN 1973, BERNICE SANDLER, director of the Project on the Status and Education of Women at the Association of American Colleges and the so-called Godmother of Title IX, spoke before the congressional committee on labor and public welfare. She noted the progress that had been made since 1970, when the first-ever hearings on sex discrimination in education had been held in Washington: Women and girls had since won federal protection through both Title IX and the expanded Title VII amendment to the Civil Rights Act. But while legislative stipulations outlawed what Sandler called "overt forms of discrimination," laws alone could not fix a broken culture.

The discrimination that girls and women experienced in the wake of Title IX was subtler than it had been before. Sandler described the kinds of books girls encountered in school—stories and textbooks about men in which women and girls seldom feature as central characters and spend most of their time waiting for men to rescue them, solve their problems, or otherwise respond to circumstances outside their control. She cited the observations of a high school freshman named Ann MacArthur, who had pointed out that not even her math textbook was free of gendered presentations of men and women. In algebra class, MacArthur found that problems concerning men involved dealing with large sums, making substantial purchases, and investing their earnings. Problems that focused on women and girls saw them handling just enough cash to purchase butter or eggs.

Title IX meant a school could no longer reject a girl because of her gender. But the message that girls internalized about themselves had not much improved. Sandler told her audience about professors who discouraged their female students from pursuing competitive jobs, who advised them against exploring graduate work, "who ignore women students in their class, or make 'jokes' about how the 'girls' wouldn't understand 'what we men are talking about.'"

She noted that women who graduated from college and worked full time earned about the same median income as the men who dropped out of high school. Imagine how horrified Sandler would have been to know the truth—that the wage gap remains an inexorable fact of American life even now.

Sandler and generations of activists since have fought for girls to have equal opportunities. But something is still lost in translation. No doubt the textbook that Ann MacArthur protested has long since been replaced. Girls now do as well in high school STEM classes as their male counterparts. But the real world remains unequal and stubborn. Men make more. Women are outnumbered in politics and tech and business—in all the places where power accrues.

Studies have disproved the old zombie theories—that girls just do not have the aptitude for math or science or that girls lack confidence or have different priorities in school and at work. The factor that does seem to be contributing to the dearth of women in these professions is what the researcher and social scientist Kim Weeden has called "occupational plans." When children and adolescents picture themselves as adults, girls still do not let themselves envision certain kinds of futures. Yes, even now.

Support groups for women in STEM and organizations that encourage girls to pursue computer science and engineering in college are nice. But Weeden's research has demonstrated that efforts to make real progress need to start sooner. Feminism can't wait for girls to grow up.

Do teenage girls have a home in feminism? The aims of girls and adult women are compatible and often overlapping, but their lives are not the same. For a 2007 issue of the journal *Off Our Backs*, Natalia Thompson wrote an article entitled "Confessions of a Teenage Feminist," in which she observes that while the relationship between feminism and happiness in the lives of grown women has been explored, "much less has been done to correlate feminism, happiness and the lives of teen girls."

She had a list of suggested reforms, from more opportunities for girls to share their views in public forums to better representation for women in elected office and the media. Thompson, then fifteen, cited as optimistic developments the movie *Real Women Have Curves* and the "girl-cott" effort that drove retailer Abercrombie & Fitch to pull shirts emblazoned with slogans like "I Had a Nightmare I Was a Brunette." "Sometimes, though, it's less about feminism and more about common sense," Thompson writes in her conclusion. "The question we need to start asking is simply, *What's best for girls?*"

. . .

IN THE DECADE after de Rivera's lawsuit was settled, most holdouts relented. Harvard subsumed much of Radcliffe. Columbia sanctioned the admission of women to its undergraduate college in 1983. The Virginia Military Institute spent months fighting a Supreme Court decision, but even it at last moved to accept women in 1996—the final state-supported single-sex school to do so.

Most of the movement's successes have not been quite so definitive. Even Title IX—parsed and expanded and reaffirmed—has faltered without clear or consistent enforcement. How well it works for the population it is meant to serve too often depends on zip code and race. In 2007, a Department of Education report measured what kind of access high school sophomores had to sports. It found that white girls had a 51 percent participation rate, while Black girls clocked in at 40 percent. Asian and Latina students ranked even lower. Dionne Koller—the director of the Center for Sport and the Law in Baltimore—blamed those uneven numbers on a failure of Title IX to make good on its promises. "There is unfinished business," she told *The New York Times* in 2012, "but we're not talking about it."

Gender holds girls back. But gender alone fails to account for the other kinds of inequalities that some girls experience—because of their race or class or their access to clean air and drinking water. Certain sports require certain equipment. Certain fields require certain preparation. Doing the drills or taking the tests is just one part of the equation. De Rivera knew that. You need to be able to see a future in it to succeed.

FEMINISM MADE WRITING this book possible. Yet the movement seemed distant to me when I was in high school. I had more immediate concerns. I devoted precious extracurricular time to climate activism. Even then, the warming planet was an obvious threat. I fundraised for food pantries. I was a good student and respected in class. I had grown up around adults who told me that whatever I wanted was possible—out there for me to achieve. What did I need from feminism?

Then I graduated. I worked for men who relegated me to the most menial tasks and called me charming. I learned how to placate and soothe people who might otherwise chafe at the confidence I had worked hard to feel deserving of. What did I need from feminism? I soon found out.

On the eve of a new decade, *Time* reported on women at the dawn of the 1990s. The issue is famous for the dour-faced woman who graces its cover. A headline demands: "Is there a future for feminism?" For the piece, the magazine interviewed a college student to find out how she felt about feminists: the kinds of women who had borne the debris to tunnel under the gender barriers of the '50s and '60s. The student said that when she pictured a feminist, she imagined "someone who is masculine and who doesn't shave her legs."

ALL THE TURMOIL and all the heartache and de Rivera never even attended Stuyvesant. She was permitted to sit for the entrance exam, but her parents decided to leave New York before she finished her application. She was never admitted or rejected. She moved on.

But when the fall semester did start in 1969, a dozen girls enrolled thanks to her efforts. There was still no bathroom for women that September, so one of the men's rooms was converted in a rush for their use.

For schools that went coed, a lack of architectural accommodations seemed to be a theme. Yale failed to prepare bathrooms for female students in time for the first coed class. When the women moved in, the mirrors were mounted too high for them to see themselves.

It took time, but circumstances improved. Men budged. Yale fixed its mirrors. In 1970, two hundred girls started at Stuyvesant. In 2020, girls made up almost 43 percent of its classes. Don't pat it on the back too fast. Black students total about 1 percent of the population.

De Rivera—who married and is now Alice Haines—has recovered from the whole ordeal. She thinks it turned out how it was supposed to. Because she never enrolled, she never had to come into a school with a reputation for rabble-rousing. She escaped the pressure that she has seen dog other former girl activists, who are never quite sure how to make the transition from child wonder to adult advocate.

In high school, no one expected her to be a firebrand. She pursued politics and savored time spent outdoors. She became a doctor. She helps people. She sticks to "things out of the limelight," as she put it. She never graduated from the school that had refused her. But she did get her diploma. In 2013, it awarded her one in recognition of her stand.

9

LOOK AT ME NOW

TINKER, TAILOR, AND THE
AESTHETICS OF A MOVEMENT

We all have to get dressed in the morning—CEOs, the president, Starbucks baristas, activists. We have identified service workers in uniforms; upheld the social contract by not wearing white to other people's weddings; acquired pink knit hats and pulled them over our ears on one cold winter morning; dissected a politician's decision to wear a purple tie to a consequential debate; decided to whom to introduce ourselves at parties; and otherwise assessed and examined the people around us on the basis of their outfits. And because of that we know that clothes can be a form of speech.

The fashion critic Vanessa Friedman once wrote a full-throated defense of her line of work, which has so often been derided as superficial. She insisted that to interpret the wardrobes of the rich and powerful—as well as the downtrodden or dissident—was an act of political and cultural excavation. Their clothes were biographies laden with sometimes inadvertent clues.

"Why does fashion matter?" Friedman asked, to assume for a moment the position of her critics. She answered herself: "The world is not run by naked people."

Women and activists—and those who are both—have debated the degree to which fashion can or should be weaponized. Is it a tool or a distraction? Must it be renounced? Can it be renounced? Or is its renunciation its own kind of aesthetic and political choice? Is opting out of fashion-as-personal-expression possible? Desirable? Essential?

Suffragists wore white, endowing generations of women with a visual language that still calls back to their struggle for equal rights. Antiwar protesters wore their hair long and questioned the value of a middle-class aesthetic in the face of bloodshed abroad and alienation at home. Afros and denim became the visual expression of Black power. The link between an article of clothing and the movement that adopts it can weaken or fade, but some signifiers retain their ideological edge. Red baseball hats were once an innocuous form of headwear.

There is no one wardrobe fit for revolution. There isn't one fabric or cut or silhouette. If people take it up, it becomes a shorthand. Fatigues. A uniform.

What an advertisement or logo can do for a product, an outfit does for a protest. It's a cue. In a meditation on what she calls "protest costumes," the writer Carli Velocci explains that an effective outfit "acts like a picket sign" at a demonstration and communicates in visual modalities that are simple and straightforward; telegenic.

Activists dressed alike can force attention from the individual onto the collective and erase distinctions between leaders and organizers, the famous and the unknown, the seasoned and the green. A uniform can be a comfort to those who would rather not stick out. If threatened, matching costumes—to borrow Velocci's term—can offer refuge and blankness. You know this as an activist or just as a graduate of a hierarchical high school. In the beloved teen movie *Mean Girls*, the Plastics wear pink once a week. In Zuccotti Park in downtown New York at the height of the Occupy Wall Street protests, demonstrators strapped on their Guy Fawkes masks.

Teenage girls—fluent in the semiotics of cheerleaders' uniforms, costume parties, dress codes, trends, and status—understand better than most what a potent tool appearance can be. Presentation is more than a first impression. In a culture fixated on women's bodies, dress is the one mode of expression to which girls know the market will respond. Their words are accorded middling value, but an outfit can do the talking.

Sometimes it makes so much noise it lands on the steps of the Supreme Court. Sometimes what people hear is not quite the message its wearer hoped to deliver.

In December 1965, several students mined their closets for megaphones. The Vietnam War had started, and their opposition to it was strident. In a quiet demonstration, a small coalition—including the sister-brother pair Mary Beth and John Tinker—decided to wear black armbands to class.

Nine months earlier, the United States had sent combat forces into battle on the ground. Tens of thousands of troops were soon dispatched. In November, a Quaker activist lit himself on fire and died in front of the Pentagon. The number of American soldiers in Vietnam ticked upward.

At the Tinkers' school in Des Moines, Iowa, the administration received a tip-off about the imminent protest and made a quick amendment to the school dress code. Students who wore armbands would now be suspended.

The Tinkers responded with the equivalent of a shrug. So did Christopher Eckhardt, sixteen, one of their literal comrades-in-arms. The students walked into school with their armbands on the preselected winter morning. Eckhardt marched straight to the office to turn himself in. The Tinkers—who were thirteen and fifteen—waited to be sent there. Within a few hours, all three were suspended and remained out of school for weeks. An offer was extended to them: Give up the armbands and feel free to return. The trio declined.

The group filed a lawsuit instead. The dress code swerve was a violation of their right to freedom of expression, protected under the First Amendment. Clothing was speech too—no different from a protest chant.

In the 7–2 decision in *Tinker v. Des Moines*, the court sided with the students. The opinion drew on the precedent set in a previous case, which had as it happened also involved siblings and free speech in school. In *West Virginia State Board of Education v. Barnette*, it wasn't some declarative statement of political resistance that had gotten students into trouble. It was its absence. Jehovah's Witness sisters Marie and Gathie Barnett were expelled from school after the two refused to recite the Pledge of Allegiance. The girls—with their parents—sued.

Justice Robert Jackson wrote the opinion in *Barnette*, decided in 1943, affirming that the girls were entitled to remain silent. He chose not to frame the decision as a vindication of religious freedom. He situated it in the context of speech.

Jackson declared that the Constitution protected not just adults but children too. He further argued that the republic depended on recognizing the rights of its littlest citizens. If children were not allowed to invoke their own freedoms, schools would be teaching them "to discount important principles of our government as mere platitudes."

America—then at war with the Germans—couldn't afford to be so cavalier with its dearest values.

Democratic ideals needed to be inculcated and reaffirmed from the earliest possible moment—at least for white children. (At the same time that *Barnette* was decided, Black children were barred from entering white classrooms in the South—never mind claiming their right to decline to recite the Pledge of Allegiance in them.) Still, the decision, albeit limited, validated the Barnett sisters as individuals with an interest in the civic sphere. It called upon schools to honor children and their choices.

The Barnetts wanted to opt out of speech. The Tinkers wanted to express their opinions. There is a difference—as the legal scholar Justin Driver has written—between sitting something out and speaking up. So when *Tinker* was decided, the court had to elaborate. In an iconic declaration, the prevailing opinion affirmed that students do not "shed their constitutional rights to freedom of speech or expression at the schoolhouse gate."

The court would later undermine *Tinker*, finding in the decision weak points that could be exploited to limit student freedoms. But the premise of the case stands. It doesn't have to be words read in front of a packed auditorium. It doesn't even have to be a picket line around the football field. Fabric—fashion—can count as speech too.

Books that mention *Tinker*—even books *about* the Tinkers themselves—tend to peter off here. The case was a landmark. Several subsequent cases limited its scope and application. It remains the go-to evidence in progressive classrooms that children can and should formulate their own opinions.

Tinker herself marvels at its impact. But her memories of that time diverge from the textbook version.

Despite the media attention that seized on her and, to a lesser extent, her older brother, Mary Beth Tinker was not a rebel or even an extrovert. She was far from the most outspoken of her five brothers and sisters. (That title belonged to Bonnie, who was older and had secured a stipend to attend the March on Washington in 1963 after winning a writing competition about the meaning of the Emancipation Proclamation.) But Tinker's parents had become involved with Quakers when their children were small and believed in deep engagement with the world around them. Her father, a Methodist preacher, was fired from his job for petitioning their town to allow Black children to swim in the local swimming pool. Her mother, raised in the South, did not consider herself political but was involved enough with CORE that when the Sixteenth Street Baptist Church in Birmingham, Alabama, was bombed in 1963 and four girls were killed, she rounded up her children to attend a local memorial service for the victims.

In the aftermath, civil rights leaders and activists like James Baldwin called on people to speak up on behalf of the girls who'd been killed. "That was the first time we wore armbands," Tinker remembered. Tinker, whose voice is still as bright and shimmering as an incandescent bulb, wanted to honor girls her age whose lives had been extinguished for the crime of being Black. Otherwise, she kept her head down and worked hard. No one seemed to notice or care about her demonstration on behalf of Black girls.

"Growing up, I was kind of the teacher's pet," she said. The profile fit—good grades, daughter of an educator. Still, she had absorbed the lessons of the people who raised her. Love and conviction and hope had to be turned into action for the sake of a better world. What she meant was: "It didn't just happen in a vacuum." She knew the war in Vietnam was wrong. She knew it as a child like she knew arithmetic and her own name. Quakers opposed all bloodshed. This one was a particular kind of senseless.

When she and the others drew up their plans for the protest that led them to the Supreme Court, Tinker knew what it would feel like to walk around with a length of black fabric that marked her and her opposition. She knew what could happen too to people who stepped out of line as her father had. She was nervous, but she found her resolve in her fellow protesters. "It was about being part of something," she said. She wanted the war to end. She believed she could help bring that about. She would wear her determination where people could see it.

After the case was filed, the press zeroed in on Tinker. Eckhardt received the least attention. But even John seemed to register less in the zeitgeist than the girl rebel—the sole female student to be suspended.

Perhaps it was because she would never be forced to enlist that her protest was deemed somehow purer. Perhaps it was that old impulse: to see a white girl taking on complex issues with aplomb as charming and charismatic. Tinker became a star plaintiff.

The narrative has made its mark on the historical record. Most people still do not know that she and John were not the lone Tinkers to wear armbands to school that morning. Their siblings Hope, who was in middle school, and Paul, who was in second grade, did too. Neither was suspended.

"It put us in such different roles in the future going forward, because I was this person out front," Tinker said. "The media loved to focus on me."

At first she couldn't understand the attention. Then the picture cleared: The press liked the idea of her. She exemplified the age-old conflict between innocence and darkness. She was a girl on the edge of womanhood with an independent streak. She became a sensation and, without her consent, a distraction from the cause that had driven her to protest in the first place.

Hope and Paul and even John—none of them fit quite so well.

"It became about me, without dealing with the whole context of this whole movement of people that I was part of to challenge the growing involvement in the Vietnam War," Tinker said. She had worn the armband to draw attention to the soldiers shipped overseas for no good reason. But the battle she had started was now being waged over free speech. The armband was the flash point.

There would be larger-scale intersections between fashion and protest, between appearance and politics. In each case, activists would do their best to point back to the cause. But *Tinker* speaks to the essential risk: a strip of cloth becomes the bigger of the two stories. The war went on.

Tinker can talk about it now and does. She grew up and became a nurse and then retired. She has made it a point to get in front of groups of students and tell them about the rights she helped win for them, to demonstrate that even if a position is the unpopular one, kids can speak out with armbands or on social media or in the streets.

But the stakes of what Tinker had accomplished were less obvious back then. She was not sure the media had made a good bet in choosing to turn its lens on her. She was racked with nerves before interviews. She sometimes canceled at the last minute—overcome with fear that she would get a fact wrong and embarrass herself. Her adolescence had been such a monumental part of her appeal. But turning girls into spokespeople is not so simple. Sometimes girls are thirteen. Sometimes girls act like it.

When the Supreme Court decision came down, Tinker was in fact seventeen and a junior at a new school in St. Louis. She had landed there in November and was just starting to make friends when a magazine reporter tracked her down, showing up in her science class to see how the girl hero felt about the verdict. "I was just mortified," Tinker recalled. "I wanted to hide under the desk."

It was less that she was embarrassed than that despite the decision, she felt defeated. The war that she had been so desperate to help end was still going on. The same week that the decision was announced, North Vietnamese forces and insurgents launched a series of attacks that came to be known as Tet 1969, in which over a thousand people were killed. While the American and the Vietnamese sides sustained brutal losses, Tinker had succeeded in consuming an institution as august as the Supreme Court with the implications of a rectangle of fabric.

"It made no sense to me at all," Tinker said. It was hard for her to feel pleased when she found out she had won. She remembered thinking, "Oh, now we can wear a little piece of black cloth on our arm. Whoop-de-do."

OUTRAGE OVER HOW TEENAGERS choose to dress is a generational rite of passage. Each new group of adolescents redefines cool to mean *something that will scare our parents.*

There have been short dresses and short haircuts and long pants and long haircuts. There have been shirts that were too tight and cropped, shirts that were too loose, and the societal scourge that is low-rise jeans.

In the *Tinker* case, the court sided with students—who happened to have the support of their parents—and ruled that public schools could not interfere in their protected activities. It was a conclusion that the press hailed with dramatic flair. The *Des Moines Register*—which John Tinker himself used to deliver before school—calls the outcome "an admonition to school officials that panic is no substitute for calm judgment and common sense when free speech is at stake." The *Boston Globe* writes that the decision had "struck a ringing blow" for American values. *The New York Times* declares that "[f]reedom of expression—in an open manner by those holding minority or unpopular views—is part of the vigor and strength of our schools and society."

But the *Times* also stresses another aspect of the conclusion to which the court had come. The headline on its report says it all: "Armbands Yes, Miniskirts No." The reporter outlines "the jurisdictional bounds" that the Supreme Court had set in its decision—one to which few outlets had paid much attention.

The justices who signed the opinion write that while public schools could not police student protest, the court would not object to schools that wanted to discipline "hair length, clean ears, blue jeans or miniskirts," as the *Times* puts it. The court distinguished between a standard dress code devised to mandate proper decorum and good taste and the "legitimate protest" in which the Tinkers had engaged.

Armbands, buttons, or placards, the *Times* writes, were real exercises in activist dissent. A miniskirt was a nuisance.

The court, however, either failed to recognize or did not want to contend with an emergent element of countercultural dress. If there had once been clear boundaries between dress designed as a form of protest and dress that was content to just violate social norms, those lines had begun to blur. Did once clean-cut college men grow their hair out to signal their alignment with hippies and antiwar activists, or was the appeal in how much their lustrous hair aggravated their fathers? Did girls wear miniskirts—or worse: pants!—to reject a constrained, outdated definition of feminine dress or to show off their legs? Which came first: the trend or the protest? And did it matter?

Did the court know the answer and choose to disregard it, or was it blind to what we all recognize about dress and the chase of that ineffable cool—that changing how we present ourselves to the world can change how we view it? The historian Deirdre Clemente has written about this process of material self-invention—a practice at which teenage girls are maestros. Some adolescents who first picked up a pair of bell-bottoms later wore them to protests and became ardent believers in the social causes associated with them—from civil rights to the antiwar movement. Some adopted the aesthetics of the beatniks without meaning to nod to the activists of an earlier era. Others discovered in their clashes with parents and school administrators over hemlines and denim that their disputes went deeper than sartorial preferences. The clothes themselves became a first step toward embracing political activism. Fashion choices that began as exercises in personal expression became imbued with collective consciousness.

"The clothes were what made them radicals," Clemente said of the activists of the era. "That's the trick," the piece of the puzzle that people for whom clothes mean little never seem to understand. "People wear clothes to live out identities that are still forming," Clemente added.

Was that not true for Tinker too? She had been to marches. She had participated in demonstrations. The armband was a spotlight. It illuminated her just as pink hats made millions of suburban women visible post 2016 and festooned crowns helped show the discipline and force of the suffragists on their march up Fifth Avenue in 1912.

Fashion can respond to and be reflective of change. Ideals shift and so do the uniforms of the people who believe in them. But clothes can also be transformative as a shared experience. The clothes make the girl. You want to be an activist? Dress like one.

What is evident—from the Tinkers, from generations of marchers and demonstrators, from the suffragists to the civil rights organizers—is that it's impossible to pretend clothes are irrelevant to the success or failure of a movement. At best, uniforms, or at least a unified aesthetic, give literal shape and texture to a gathering of individuals. At worst, clothes hijack attention, distracting the press and potential audiences from the aims of the people who wear them.

THE TINKERS WERE NOT the first or last to realize that humble accessories—when well coordinated—could make a more impactful statement than even the cleverest assortment of posters. And girls—who are seldom afforded a chance to make a second first impression—have made particular use of the power that clothing has to communicate a set of ideals and to inspire a sense of shared purpose.

If the point of fashion in protest is to raise awareness or to bolster the odds that a charismatic PR offensive will work, then the pink-hatted marchers of the post-2016 era demonstrated its use. If it is meant to cheer on the activist equivalent of team spirit, then department store hats sold to suffragists came as close to merch as 1912 could offer. Civil rights activists however needed their clothes to do more. Fashion was not just a tool to shape stories in newspapers or bond demonstrators to one another. It had a political aim.

The clothes that Black women and girls wear have long had to *make an argument.* Their appearance has had to counter racist tropes about Black women—the jezebel, the temptress, the "welfare queen." The historian Stephanie Shaw has written that Black parents in the Jim Crow era "reared their daughters not to present themselves in sexual or sensual" fashion. When Angelina Weld Grimké—named after her white aunt, the famed abolitionist—wrote to her father in 1897 to ask for an evening dress for Christmas, he refused. She was seventeen and a Black schoolgirl, not some debutante. Miriam Matthews, later a trailblazing librarian, was permitted to wear "pale pink pomade lipstick" during the Roaring Twenties, but she and her friends were never allowed to use blush or other makeup. That kind of adornment was not for nice Black girls.

After *Brown* was decided in 1954, white families who opposed integration relied on familiar strategies to delegitimize the rights of Black people, taking aim at the moral character of Black women. That meant targeting the dress and conduct of Black girls too—and making them seem older and dangerous.

Later, the civil rights movement would deemphasize the importance of full skirts and suits and ties in protest, embracing natural hair and denim to connote a new kind of pride. But at the first sit-ins, middle-class dress was considered essential—for the media narrative around the protests, but also for the demonstrators themselves.

For Black women, presentation in protest as in life was complicated. The standards of dress were drawn from white and bourgeois values— church clothes, modest hem- and necklines, "neat" hair pressed into submission. At the same time, a girl who showed up in her best clothes to a sit-in was making a statement about how she valued herself. A white mob could throw food and cigarette butts and glass bottles. She would not be demeaned. Her clothes were her tactical gear.

In 1963, Tougaloo College students were pelted with "ketchup, mustard, sugar, pies" at a lunch counter during a sit-in in Jackson, Mississippi. Two of them were the white Freedom Rider Joan Trumpauer and the Black activist Anne Moody, who would go on to write an acclaimed memoir documenting her experiences in the movement, *Coming of Age in Mississippi*. The group withstood three hours of abuse. The women were dragged off their seats. One man had his face kicked in. Moody lost her shoes in the melee. She watched a white man trawl the store with an open knife.

The sit-in ended with her hair "stiff with dried mustard, ketchup, and sugar." Her stockings were stuck to her calves. She staggered out in a daze. But she had a stop she needed to make before returning to campus. She went to the salon. Three women had been waiting but let her go ahead. She wanted to get her hair washed.

Not narcissism, but survival. The historian Tanisha C. Ford has written about how salons functioned as "places of refuge and sister-hood" for Black women. The civil rights movement endowed them with even greater purpose, transforming them into protected spaces for planning, organizing, and catharsis.

It was about more than hair. Ford writes that Black girls who had been raised to stamp out all evidence of so-called unruliness would have been desperate to restore themselves after a sit-in. Their bodies, so scrutinized, were the vessels of their action. Girls learned to tend to them. Salons helped them reclaim pieces of themselves that had been warped in protest—internal and external. Whatever beatings the activists had taken, at least the condiments could be washed down the drain.

How essential was such self-fashioning to the girls who populated the civil rights movement? When the incandescent Ruby Doris Smith Robinson was serving her first stint in jail in South Carolina, she wrote a letter to her sister. She had been sentenced to a month behind bars. She missed her classes. She missed her friends. But in the letter, one humiliation stood out above the rest: "My hair is awful!"

When SNCC and the civil rights movement started to engage in direct action in the Deep South, conventions of dress adapted to suit their new mission. Debbie Amis Bell remembered how she and her fellow volunteers had taken to calling themselves soldiers. With the new identities came new uniforms.

Girls who had spent their childhoods tracking the rise and fall of trends adapted. A-line skirts, cropped sweaters, and wide belts were out. Denim and simple cotton dresses, borrowed from the sharecropper families who housed Black and white student volunteers, were in. The clothes were easier to wear in the hot weather and more practical. Girls who started wearing overalls found that their wide pockets could hold voting materials and pamphlets, which meant not having to tote around a bag for their supplies. Compared with knits, denim showed less dirt. The volunteers learned to stretch their wardrobes between washes.

A girl might leave her best clothes at home and transition to workwear down South, knowing she could return to her dresses in a few weeks or months. Other aesthetic choices made bigger statements. Hundreds of volunteers transitioned from salon-attended to natural hair. Their curls were easier to maintain and it was cheaper than making trips to a salon. But it wasn't just about time or cash. SNCC volunteers had come to feel, as one organizer put it, that an "activist with straightened hair was a contradiction. A lie. A joke, really."

In her memoir, *Pushed Back to Strength*, Gloria Wade-Gayles describes natural hair as a "badge"—a marker of certain values. When she saw other women and girls with natural hair, she felt connected to them. There was no easier and more evident sign of shared ideals than one a woman could never take off.

Those who joined the movement learned fast that to fit in, a certain look was expected. Judy Richardson—one of eight Black students accepted to Swarthmore in 1962—could pinpoint the moment she realized that she needed a makeover. Another Swarthmore student warned her that if she wanted to feel at home with other organizers, she would have to start forgoing chemical relaxers.

When she looked back on it later, she described the clothes and hair as a kind of flare—a visual cue that activists threw up to find their people. It was an "outward manifestation that we had broken from the traditional norms," she said.

Activists rebelled against segregation and demanded justice. Their hair and dress were how women and girls could express the same opinions without even having to open their mouths.

Students who returned to campus after a stint volunteering discovered that the aesthetic that had helped them blend in in Alabama or Mississippi now identified them as troublemakers at school. Such is the difference between the risks that white girls who opposed bans on miniskirts accepted and the ones that civil rights activists and later antiwar and feminist organizers withstood. The threat was heightened.

There are people who would draw a thick line between doing battle for "real" rights and demanding the right to wear silk. But Ella Baker, godmother of SNCC and mentor to Richardson, was not one of them. She got one of her first tastes of the power of activism not at a formal demonstration, but in composing a letter of protest to her own administration at Shaw University in Raleigh, North Carolina. In 1923, a group of older girls had asked Baker, then nineteen, to challenge a rule that prohibited students from wearing silk or colored stockings on campus. Baker had no interest in the garments themselves, but the cause spoke to her. Shouldn't she and her friends be entitled to choose their own accessories? It took her entire undergraduate career, but the ban was lifted.

If what Deirdre Clemente said is true, and clothing makes the activist, then insisting on the right to wear it should be at least as affirming. Baker understood that. She supported the girls who went back to schools like Spelman and Tougaloo in their casual clothes and natural hair, despite the fallout. She knew, as Ford writes, "that such forms of embodied activism could spark a more radical consciousness among college women." These were her advertisers. She embraced them.

In the act of asserting themselves in fashion, girls awakened to other desires. It became clear to them—just as it was clear to those who wanted to stamp out countercultural modes of dress—that how women and girls present themselves can be bold expressions of personal and communal pride. That was true in the civil rights movement. It was true in other protest movements as well.

In the time it took *Tinker* to shuffle through the courts between 1965 and 1969, students waged their own wars on dress codes and elevated a spate of cases and demonstrations to national attention. In several incidents, girls were dismissed for wearing pants, culottes, or even sandals without socks. Some were sent home for a glimpse of bare thigh. In at least one case, girls were penalized for wearing dresses that were too modest—students had set out to mock their restrictive dress code and their teachers did not like it.

In an era of political and social upheaval, dress codes were implemented as visual manifestations of good citizenship. Girls' bodies became a place where order and containment could be enforced in an out-of-control world. Not for the first time. Not for the last.

That girls refused to submit to these rules en masse has been seen as an expression of the teen rebellion for which the period is known. But for female students, it is possible to locate in these acts of dissent a more concrete ideological stance: a substantial kind of resistance to the same forces that push women out of workplaces and deny them basic health-care procedures. Our bodies, our choices.

Tinker serving as the named inspiration for some of these protests was the last outcome that Tinker herself could have predicted. She had not worn her armband to inspire feminist teens to protest rules about culottes. But the students who partook in the demonstrations did feel empowered. In the feminist manifesto *Sisterhood Is Powerful*, an eighth grader named Connie Dvorkin put language to the idea that clothes could be a source of confidence and that girls could reclaim a rare-for-them kind of control over themselves in the act of choosing their own. "I read all the literature on women's liberation and still wore skirts," Dvorkin writes. But when she heard about the decision in *Tinker*, she realized what it could mean for her too. She went to her principal and informed him that she intended to wear pants. He couldn't stop her. He did tell her he felt slacks, as he called them, "were in bad taste."

Whoop-de-do indeed.

In her piece for the compilation, Dvorkin reflects on what she had learned since she started wearing pants. The first was that she felt "more equal" with men. The second was practical: She didn't have to concern herself with how her legs were placed. She didn't find herself competing as much with other girls for male attention. She was less worried, she wrote, about "all that bullshit." In general, she concludes she was "much more at ease with the world."

With one success under her belt, Dvorkin went on to upend the school rule that sent girls to home economics instead of shop. (Take that, Catharine Beecher.) Her request to join the class had to be filed with the superintendent, but in the middle of the semester she was granted permission. The clothes came first.

Dvorkin was on her own. She was in fact so notable for her presence in shop that she knew as soon as she walked in the door that she would never be able to skip class. The teacher would spot the missing girl in two seconds. But other girls organized coordinated civil disobedience, staging sit-ins in their administrators' offices and sometimes even tag-teaming their efforts with their female teachers, who were often also forced to wear skirts to work.

Restrictions and expectations around dress were one of the most obvious manifestations of sexism in the lives of girls. Rejecting their objectification became a powerful form of dissent. In 1974, less than a decade after feminists picketed the Miss America pageant, the female students at Terra Nova High School were invited to assemble in the cafeteria. The mayor had come to speak to them to encourage the girls to enter a local pageant. Zoe Joyner, sixteen, was seated with a few dozen of her friends when she decided to interrupt. She didn't want to be squeezed into sequins or paraded around in a gown.

"I said, 'Excuse me. Since the important thing about a woman is her measurements, as this gathering demonstrates, would you tell us the measurements of your penis before you speak, so we can tell if you're important enough to listen to?'" she recalled. "He didn't say anything, so I continued, 'If you don't know them, I've got a tape measure.'"

An account of the face-off between Joyner and Mayor Aubrey Lumley is included in a compendium of documents and manifestos related to the women's liberation movement, published in 2000. Its editors cite an untitled news clipping that noted the punishment for Joyner's outburst. When it was clear that she would be disciplined for her comment, she sprawled out on the floor to prevent her own removal, but that just staved off the inevitable. She was kicked out of school for a week.

"Zoe didn't seem to mind though," the editors write, "and neither do we."

. . .

IN 1969, WOMEN'S LIBERATIONIST Ellen Willis writes with evident displeasure in *Mademoiselle* that "a girl is trained . . . to be what the culture defines as feminine" from the time of her birth. Such primping and priming used up her time and resources—the exact treasures that Dvorkin got back when she started to wear pants. "That means," Willis adds, "being preoccupied with clothes and makeup—with how she looks instead of what she does."

When girls reject exploitative clothing or otherwise use fashion to undermine patriarchal expectations, that is activism, whether men behind podiums believe it or not. Dvorkin insisted on her pants. Girls have made headlines for attending prom in suits—with their girlfriends. Girls have forced amendments to restrictive, racist dress codes that ban braids. That is activism.

The so-called girl-cott that teen girls launched to protest Abercrombie & Fitch shirts emblazoned with slogans like "With These, Who Needs Brains?" and "Gentlemen Prefer Tig Old Bitties" in 2005? Activism. And effective activism too. Abercrombie & Fitch caved and pulled both tops from its stores within a few months.

When Tinker went to school to express her opposition to the war and used fabric as the form for her demonstration, that was, of course, activism.

When Annette Jones White and her friends embroidered their blouses with words like "Freedom" and "Justice" and then wore them to ride a bus in the heart of Georgia, despite knowing that the simple combination of that thread woven into those letters paired with their bodies made them a threat, that was activism.

And it was in fact the precise kind of activism that another group of girls echoed in 2017 when fifteen of them took to the steps of the

Texas State Capitol in Austin dressed in their finest. "The colorful scene melded two time-honored Texas traditions: political protest and the quinceañera," NPR reported at the time. The girls were expressing their opposition to Senate Bill 4, an immigration enforcement measure that would permit local police to request proof of legal status in even such routine "detentions" as traffic stops. The group could have made speeches or held signs. But the outfits spoke louder.

"In Latino culture, quinceañeras are an important tradition to bring families together, to unite communities, to unite culture," Magdalena Juarez, then seventeen, told NPR. She would not, she added, "meet this law on its hateful level." Instead, she promised to resist it with a celebration of her culture. Dozens of media outlets picked up the demonstration—not just NPR but *The Dallas Morning News*, *Refinery29*, *Teen Vogue*, and the *Chicago Tribune*. Some of the girls had worn sashes over their gowns, with phrases like "No SB4" and "No Fear" written in Spanish. In photos, the sequins on their dresses glint in the sun.

Would fifteen girls in jeans have gotten the same attention? Would fifteen grown women in evening wear? A dozen women in formal dresses might have looked ridiculous, but the girls pulled it off. Their demonstration alchemized the components of protest and culture with which we have decided we are most comfortable: the invocation of a coming-of-age ritual, the hint of selflessness that we expect from women and dutiful daughters most of all, the pomp and circumstance that makes a protest feel American—patriotic in its coupling of dissent and personal anguish.

Young and vibrant women have long helped frame conversations about immigration reform in the United States—from Clara Lemlich to Mabel Ping-Hua Lee. The latest generation is no exception. In 2010, activists in favor of immigration reform—including high school senior Greisa Martínez Rosas—sat in the United States Senate and watched leaders vote on the DREAM Act, a bill that would have cleared a path to citizenship for some immigrants brought to the United States as children. It fell five votes short. In 2012, the Deferred Action for Childhood Arrivals program (DACA) was announced. President Barack Obama devised it as a creative stopgap measure meant to shield that same vulnerable population from deportation. One of its cheerleaders and masterminds was Cristina Jiménez Moreta, a formerly undocumented high school student who later cofounded United We Dream, the largest organization of immigrant youth in the States. DACA has been the target of legal challenges since it was announced, even as it has protected well over half a million recipients from being sent to countries most of them do not remember.

The quinceañera demonstration was a valiant and beautiful and zealous effort of the kind that girls have been staging forever. It draws to mind the work of the activist Mari Copeny, who has been agitating and organizing since she was eight to raise awareness about the water crisis in Flint, Michigan. She is often identified in media reports as "Little Miss Flint," a nickname that stuck after she won a pageant in her hometown in 2015. She met two presidents wearing her trademark sash. She is a teenager now, but continues to push for clean water and environmental justice. She is often pictured wearing her tiara. Would we know her without it? Juarez and her friends earned as much press as a single protest in which fifteen people participated perhaps ever could. But a few months later, the law took effect. And despite several legal challenges to it, a federal appeals court went on to uphold portions of it in March 2018. That's not a failure on the part of the girls. Most protests don't raise even a tenth as much awareness. But it emphasizes the kind of paradox that hovered over the group. The one that sounded almost like ambivalence.

Back in 2017, Juarez told a reporter from *BuzzFeed* that the dresses made a statement, but she found them hard to move in: "[Y]ou step on them and you fall and you're not used to being in this giant thing that gets in your way." The dresses were what people looked at. But that didn't make them effective. It also didn't make them comfortable.

Conscious of it or not, Juarez seemed to nod toward Willis's old contention—that consumer goods as creations of a sexist media and marketplace can never be as effective a form of protest as renouncing them would be. Far from *Seventeen*'s hopeful founding, magazines aimed at "empowering" girls have entrenched an obsession with their looks and peddled for-sale solutions that have turned girls into the policers of their own bodies. No patriarchal superstructure required.

With the notable exceptions of editor Jane Pratt's *Sassy* and its spiritual descendants, *Rookie* and *Teen Vogue*, teen magazines have centered and featured white girls and prioritized pleasing advertisers over the activation of their readerships. In August 1986, a memorable *Seventeen* headline promised to advise readers on what to do "When Your Best Friend Is Better-Looking Than You." In 2012, a group of girls protested the magazine for its continued use of superthin models with photoshopped skin and bodies. Julia Bluhm, fourteen, started an online petition to call for . . . not quite an end to the practice. In an indication of the hold that teen magazines have had over their audience, Bluhm didn't dare demand that *Seventeen* eliminate its use of photoshop. She asked instead that the magazine include just one photo spread per issue that was not retouched. In that environment, or even the improved one in which we now live, what can fashion do? How free are we to use it?

We encode our clothes and appearances with our own intentions. But it's impossible to divorce them from a culture of norms. That's less than ideal for teenage girls, whose most exercisable forms of power are their dollars and their attention. The consumer marketplace, not the ballot box, is where their voices can be loudest.

The feminist scholar Rosalind Gill has made the point that individualized aesthetic choices are no substitute for concerted activism. In fact, she writes that movements that emphasize external presentation often do so at the expense of collective action. A slogan tee has not forced Congress to protect abortion access. It hasn't stopped sexual harassment or protected LGBTQ+ kids.

But fashion does allow girls to claim what is so often held against them: their looks. For Juarez, the dresses were cumbersome. But wearing one still subverted expectations. The dresses recalled pageant queens and the practice of performance. Protest is a performance too.

Before the internet, fashion and makeup helped girls find one another, their flags high. With social media, those old tools—at the cross section of personal expression and commerce—have gotten their own kind of makeover. On TikTok, the activist Feroza Aziz used makeup tutorials to issue a call to action about the treatment of Uyghurs in China. Twitter users have turned male disinterest in the tastes and bodies of women and femmes into a meme. Tweets start with lists of the kinds of items "all women should own," tips about how to best use a concealer brush, or musings about what to wear while shopping for tampons and conclude with some variation of "OK, now that the men have stopped reading: We strike at dawn."

The format—familiar to people who have spent time on Twitter since 2016—is a Trojan horse and a joke. Most men do tune out in the glare of Sephora. Women organize rebellion under their noses. While conservative politicians belittled girls who led marches in the name of climate action, *Allure* published an explainer about which kinds of skincare product formulations should be avoided at rallies and protests because certain ingredients can exacerbate the effects of tear gas. In a primer on how to prepare for a protest, *Teen Vogue* devoted several bullet points to matters of dress. It advised dark, label-less clothes and closed-toe shoes. It recommended sunglasses—not to complete the look but to counter law enforcement's surveillance measures.

OVER TIME, TINKER came to feel a new appreciation for the case that bears her name. "The heart of this case to me—besides being against war—also became about the idea that teenagers should have a voice in the policies that affect their lives," Tinker said. She believed not just that girls would grow up to be adults and thus deserved to command a stake in their future, as the Supreme Court had implied in *Barnette*, but that teenagers had their own interests. Their perspective was important, even if it is a condition of adolescence that its members age out.

It's strange to be a child. The world claims to operate on their behalf—designed and structured to ensure their welfare. Yet children are seldom consulted when it comes to the conditions of their own lives.

The paradox reminded Tinker of the predicament in which women have found themselves for centuries—placed on a pedestal and worshipped without being accorded real respect. Girls suffered a double disadvantage—marginalized as children and as women.

We so often hear men vow to do better "for their daughters" or promise to build the kinds of worlds or companies or political apparatuses that might benefit girls. Sometimes these proclamations are well intentioned. Other times girls are a cover. Helpless and innocent. In need of rescue. How confounding it can be when a girl asserts her own will. How fast forces can mobilize to push her back into place. To cast her as small and pure and grateful.

It's no wonder that the media response to the *Tinker* decision focused on the girl and not on her cause. It was so much easier to treat her—white, middle class, Midwestern—as a kind of universal American daughter than to emphasize what she believed. The war was unjust and those who expanded it were complicit in its crimes. *Tinker* set a vital precedent for students, but Tinker herself has worried about the paradigm she provided. When an issue is complicated, isolate the girl. Make it about her.

Parts of the case were difficult or invasive for Tinker. But she knew she had been treated with literal kid gloves compared with what a Black girl would have experienced. Tinker's father was threatened, but the Ku Klux Klan was not about to hunt him down in Des Moines. She would sometimes feel weighed down by the expectations people had for her—what de Rivera was so glad she had escaped. But she also knew much of the public backed her. It was true that in some sense that little cloth made her. The act of wearing it turned her into a public figure. It sharpened her activism. It also mattered that it was she who was wearing the armband.

10

IN HER FEELINGS

GIRLHOOD AT THE END
OF THE WORLD

A girl sat down to write to her president. She was twelve—a kid. She should have been doing her homework or out for a bike ride, but she couldn't relax. Her worries consumed her. She was scared that the world was on the brink of total destruction. Children were starving. Families were desperate. Her government seemed more interested in producing weapons of mass annihilation than protecting the future of the planet. Her planet.

"I do not think it is my business to have to think about such things," she wrote. But if she didn't speak up on behalf of her generation, who would?

The letter continued in the same tone of grave alarm. She was reconsidering whether she wanted to have children of her own. The world seemed too unstable—too dangerous. She wondered what kind of future she might face. She was declarative. She was emotional. She couldn't even quite articulate what it meant to be alive in an era of such extreme fear. She loved her friends. She loved her planet. It felt precarious. "[W]hen I think about the world situation," she wrote, "I get a horrible feeling."

It was not 2023 or 2020 or 2016 but 1981, and a Vermont native named Nessa Rabin was beseeching President Ronald Reagan to act—not to curb the effects of a warmer climate or to ban AR-15s but to prevent the outbreak of nuclear war.

The letter reached the White House, and Rabin received a response. It thanked her for writing. It did not outline a concrete plan to ensure the future of the literal planet. Without a pledge, Rabin decided she needed to escalate the issue.

Rabin later told a reporter that she and her friends were terrified. She might not have had a newspaper subscription in her own name, but conversation about nuclear war was inescapable. She picked up on it—the concern that the situation had become a full-blown crisis, the sense that the threat level was rising. She was attuned to a growing national alarm: When Rabin wrote to Reagan, fears over nuclear war had hit a peak for the period. Almost half of respondents in national polls estimated that odds were good the United States would become involved in nuclear conflict within the next decade. Some research pointed to an even more dismal outlook among students in particular, who rated their own chance at survival as lower than their parents had. No wonder Rabin and her older sister, Hannah, were crazed with nerves.

"We just had to do something," Hannah said in the same interview.

That spring, Rabin called a meeting. Nation-states would not choose to demilitarize because children were panicked in their bedrooms. She needed to organize. She assessed her aims and considered her resources. She composed a to-do list. Her first order of business would be roping in influential supporters—the kinds of people who moved public sentiment and knew how to throw a bit of a tantrum. In an interview, she outlined her plan: "Get in touch with kids."

She and her friends named their new coalition the Children's Campaign for Nuclear Disarmament (CCND). With Rabin's initial—albeit not quite requited—letter to Reagan as a model, CCND invited children nationwide to write letters protesting the funding and development of nuclear weapons. The girls would hold a public reading across the street from the White House, reciting each letter aloud. To raise awareness about their campaign, CCND circulated a notice for pro-peace organizations to print in their newsletters. It struck an ominous note: "We are children who fear for the future of our world."

IN 1945, the United States dropped atomic bombs on Hiroshima and Nagasaki, ending the war. But the decision to do so had grievous consequences. It decimated communities and killed civilians. It also ushered in an era of genuine nuclear terror. For people around the world, the fear was real and frightening. For children and adolescents, it hit with a particular force. This was their inheritance.

At a conference on child studies held in 1964, the renowned pediatrician Dr. Benjamin Spock used his coveted speaking slot to tell the sixteen hundred assembled parents and professionals that he had come to believe it was "no longer sufficient to protect children from the usual physical diseases and the typical emotional stresses of the past" when "the greatest threat to their . . . survival is from nuclear disaster." He had come prepared with a list of recommendations for people in positions of actual power. But he spoke to children and adolescents themselves when he urged them to join activist groups devoted to peace, participate in marches, write to their elected officials (as Rabin would), and "learn to be a little bolder than their parents seem to be."

For those who had committed themselves to the movement, boldness did not seem to be a problem. In 1962, two girls were convicted and sentenced to three months of probation each for sitting down in Times Square to protest nuclear testing. Deborah Nagin was sixteen and Gale Packer was eighteen; the two were born just as the world ushered in the nuclear age. Nagin testified that when the police came to remove her, she was beaten with clubs and fists. Packer, who had until then been training to be a nurse at Bellevue Hospital, said in a hearing that she had quit the course. She wore a button to court that advocated banning the bomb. In 1966, another "girl pacifist"—as *The New York Times* called her—spent over two months in jail for trespassing and resisting arrest at the launching of a nuclear submarine in Groton, Connecticut. She was seventeen.

When Rabin wrote to Reagan in 1981, she expressed a sentiment that dozens of scientists had started to track. Researchers in the United States and around the world were attempting to calculate what the threat of nuclear devastation was doing to children. In the mid-1980s, the reports came in. The determination was: nothing good. In 1982, a paper tracked high awareness of nuclear catastrophe among adolescents in particular. In 1986, a Canadian paper found that those who reported the most suffering from a condition termed "threat of annihilation" were the most vulnerable citizens—the poor, caretakers, children. Most research did not break down the data across the gender divide, but in Finland, when close to seven thousand children between the ages of twelve and eighteen were polled, 81 percent listed war as one of their three main fears. The paper's lead author noted that the prospect of war provoked a stronger and more negative reaction in girls, speculating that girls had not been socialized to associate combat with positive values.

The Cold War ended without nuclear incident, but the fears it stoked in children and adolescents didn't resolve because a wall fell. In one woman's recollection of her childhood, she remembered how during the peak of the crisis she and her friends were made to stand in the hall for air-raid drills. Girls were instructed to line up shoulder to shoulder and face the wall, crouching down and covering their heads, while their male classmates were instructed to stand above and "protect" them. Never mind that some girls were bigger and taller than their would-be saviors. The decision to cast victims and heroes left its mark. It was a miserable period: "We learned a sense of helplessness."

Resisting the ideologies of the era meant rejecting the idea of their powerlessness. Girls who were activists had to believe that—despite the era's backlash to feminism, the unquantifiable fears of global oblivion, and the general disenfranchisement that is just the nature of being a child beholden to adults—it was still possible to act with purpose and conviction.

The Rabin sisters both gave frequent interviews about how fear inspired their activism. For ten hours in front of the White House in October 1981, CCND read the thousands of letters that its headquarters had received. In the afternoon, the lawn sprinklers came on and soaked them—a development that raised Nessa Rabin's hackles. "We have good reason to believe that sprinklers are not turned on every October afternoon," she commented to a reporter. The event went on despite the downpour. After the last letter was read at dusk, the mail was loaded up and handed over to an officer of the administration.

Reagan's "machine"—as Rabin put it, derision leaping off the page even now—later sent the children a letter in response to the protest, doing the familiar parental dance between praise and condescension. It congratulated their efforts and reaffirmed the importance of the national arsenal. It did not meet their standards.

In March 1982, the group gathered once more in Washington to raise awareness about nuclear war. The girls chose Easter weekend and the optics were stark. On the White House grounds, children rolled Easter eggs down the lawn. Outside, others pleaded for their future. The *Christian Science Monitor* observed the scene, noting that CCND had collected over a thousand additional letters since its last demonstration and had drawn up plans for another trip to Washington in June. "While some may consider those who favor disarmament to be naive," a reporter with the outlet wrote, "CCND founders [said] it is the letters' guilelessness that makes them powerful."

Politicians could triangulate or focus on rhetoric at the expense of action. But "for children it's life or death—nothing to do with politics," Hannah Rabin told the newspaper. She didn't care about partisanship or about the relative positions of the United States and the U.S.S.R. in Cold War standings. She cared about whether she and her friends would survive.

The movement kept growing and girls rallied for it. Around the same time, *The Christian Science Monitor* profiled the president and founder of another group—the Children's Peace Committee. Monique Grodzki, fourteen, led 250 members across several dozen chapters in both the United States and abroad from her headquarters in New York. In San Francisco, Children as Teachers of Peace compiled thousands of notes and drawings about what peace meant to them to give to world leaders and published some of them in a book. In 1982, when *The New York Times* published a guide for parents to help them handle their children's fears of nuclear war, it included the voices of several members of Future Generations—a still-new pro-disarmament organization in New York. Five out of the six students it interviewed were girls. Nessa Rabin made an appearance, as did a girl named Tijuana Jackson, who told the reporter that war seemed unfair to her. "[W]e're little children," she said. She hadn't even had "any fun yet." Two of the other activists echoed Rabin's initial letter to Reagan, focusing on how the threat of disaster was complicating their desire to have families of their own. Read at once, the anxieties seem to describe a generation suspended in amber: Young enough to feel entitled to the delights of childhood. Wracked with the worries of grown men.

Over time, the menace of the end times has weighed with particular heaviness on girls. While America fizzed with cash and pleasure in the 1920s, thousands of girls preached evangelism, predicting imminent and divine catastrophe to desperate crowds who were urged to repent. The prophetesses sold out arenas. In the 1980s, Rabin and her ilk agonized over the threat of nuclear war. Now, in the battle to address our climate catastrophe and roll back the gun violence epidemic, it's the same marchers and protesters and disenchanted letter writers: girls, girls, girls.

Of course, adults have organized to oppose disaster too. Tens of thousands of demonstrators protested the Vietnam War and later advocated for disarmament. Women have launched organizations like Women Strike for Peace and Another Mother for Peace, not to mention Mothers Against Drunk Driving and Moms Demand Action. In 1986, six hundred people marched from one end of the United States to the other to raise awareness about and voice their opposition to the nuclear arms race. It took the participants nine full months. Some were greeted with public interest. Some were interviewed. Several made compelling cases. In 2019, the international environmental movement Extinction Rebellion disrupted traffic and public transport in London to call attention to the climate crisis. The organization's logo is an hourglass inside a circle to represent that time is running out to save the planet.

The media marks these efforts. And sometimes casts aspersions. But the mainstream response to our grown Cassandras tends not to be compassion. At best their actions are deemed commendable. And viewed from a distance.

But children captivate. Children move us—from our entrenched positions and from our stasis. And these children—who have emphasized not a set of policies but the destruction around us; who have held protests on the White House lawn and collected doodles for peace; who have protested the massacres that threaten grade-school classrooms—draw an outsize measure of attention.

When adult activists parade down streets, screaming about worldwide doom, people avert their gaze. Girls who foresee disaster inspire in us the opposite—a desire to stare. We tolerate more from them. We expect in our adolescents the occasional outburst. So goes the narrative: Adult women who weep in public have lost control of themselves. But a girl who cries for her future tugs at us. Women must strategize and comport themselves—put their developed brains to work and make alliances and concessions in the name of political gain. Adolescents and girls in particular—emotional, passionate, determined— can be more unbound.

The genocide scholar Eric Markusen wrote a paper in 1982 in which he outlines how schools could become sites of more rigorous antiwar and disarmament education. He says that it was imperative that children be recruited, both because children were aware of the threat and deserved real information about how best to combat it and because it was their lives that nuclear war imperiled. "The familiar cliché—that each generation of children inherits the accomplishments and mistakes of its parents and forebears—has a special relevance in the nuclear age," he writes. What he meant then is what we mean now: The time we have to correct the errors of our elders is running out.

In 1983, Hannah Rabin traveled to the International Conference on Children and War in Finland. In her speech, she sounded at once resolute and nervous. She described the efforts that CCND had undertaken to make their case. It seemed exhausting. Peace walks, rallies, letter-writing drives, events, in-school education, speeches, fundraising—the list went on. "The work is sometimes frustrating," Rabin conceded, "but working to help prevent the destruction of our future gives us hope."

WHEN WE LOOK around and tell ourselves *the kids are all right*, are we applauding their efforts or are we outsourcing our own? Armies of girls take to the streets while adults applaud. The emotional burden bears down on children, and instead of easing it, politicians praise their resilience. We force them to grow up and confront the most catastrophic problems. We admire how mature their generation is. We stoke the problems. We tell them to learn to problem-solve.

The baggage is a load. And girls—activists or not—are not well. In 2011, 12 percent of girls reported major depression. Less than a decade later, the number clocked in at 20 percent. Between 2007 and 2015, suicide rates doubled among girls, hitting their highest point in four decades. In 2019, a full 70 percent of teenagers identified mental health as a big issue. That was before a pandemic closed schools and cut adolescents off from their lifeblood—one another. Social media has not helped. In an internal presentation delivered in 2020, researchers for Facebook (now known as Meta) said that 32 percent of teen girls reported that Instagram made them feel worse about their bodies. It's the competitiveness and the comparison and the internet and the insecurities and the photoshopped pictures and the pressure to do well in school and to look good and to be good. And it's also the not-so-small and ever-present prospect of an unlivable earth.

For one recent paper, researchers spoke to ten thousand people in ten countries—all of whom were under the age of twenty-five—to ask them about the state of the climate. The scientists reported a correlation between the incidence of negative emotions, like fear, and the sense that governments were not doing enough to save the planet. More than half of respondents—spiritual descendants of Rabin— said the climate crisis itself made them feel "afraid, sad, anxious, angry, powerless, helpless." Some said it made them feel guilt ridden. The essential developmental narcissism of adolescence had made it seem as though the burning planet was their fault. In the poll, over three quarters said the future was frightening. That was their word choice: "frightening."

The paper concluded that not just Earth but the wellness of those who stand to populate it was at stake if world leaders continued to sidestep the issue. One of the participants wrote that the threat of climate change was different for her generation: "For us, the destruction of the planet is personal."

Perhaps that explains a feature of the stories that teenage climate activists tell about how they came to the movement—the admission that mental health and their work are intertwined. That the relationship between them is impossible to tease apart.

Greta Thunberg, who turned student strikes for climate into a worldwide phenomenon at fifteen, has given dozens of interviews in which she has tied her acute childhood depression to her awareness of environmental destruction. "I kept thinking about it and I just wondered if I am going to have a future," she told *The Guardian.*

Later, she stopped going to school. She obsessed over the fate of the planet. Her parents tried to reassure her, but she knew that in fact it would not be all right. She was almost hospitalized. She received a slew of diagnoses. She also started to compile data. She didn't want to be soothed. She wanted change. She showed her parents graphs and documentaries. She pointed them to articles about the effects of warming. It worked. Her mother gave up plane travel. Her father became a vegetarian. "That's when I kind of realized I could make a difference," Thunberg said. Her parents' willingness to be convinced didn't snap her out of her depression, but it gave her real motivation. It was a "waste of time" to feel so despairing, she said. She needed to be out there, fixing the problem.

In 2019, *Teen Vogue* ran an article headlined "5 Ways Climate Activism Could Make You Happier" and soon after published an op-ed in which a freshman in high school details how climate activism has helped her cope with "a hopeless sense of loneliness, lack of motivation, and a deepening sadness." Learning about the ravaging effects of climate change could have sunk her into more severe depression, but instead she found it galvanizing. "I didn't want to just sit back as it happened. For the first time, I felt as though I could do something radical," she writes. "Rather than hopelessness, I felt a sense of purpose."

Dig a little, and even subtler connections between mental health and climate activism reveal themselves. In 2017, *The New York Times* revisited the origins of the movement at Standing Rock, which saw a coalition of activists set up camp on the north end of a Sioux reservation to protest the Dakota Access Pipeline. At the center of the protest was a little-known coalition, most in their late teens and twenties. It was called the One Mind Youth Movement. A trio of friends founded it after a period of crisis on their reservation in South Dakota. In one summer, over two dozen kids had attempted suicide. Eight were dead. The group started out advocating for counseling services to address mental health issues and addiction, but its leaders became interested in a local campaign demonstrating against a pipeline that would have bifurcated the river on which their reservation sat.

When the Obama State Department nixed that pipeline, One Mind turned its attention to Standing Rock. Youth led the crusade: Bobbi Jean Three Legs, who was twenty-four, helped plan a five-hundred-mile action to deliver a letter asking the Army Corps of Engineers to block the Dakota Access Pipeline from crossing the Missouri River. Other activists planned another—two thousand miles this time. In a video announcing the race, women invited people to take part and come to Standing Rock. Eryn Wise was twenty-six when she arrived, having survived a suicide attempt at eleven. She was drawn to the scale of the movement—how it appealed to something bigger than her. When she walked into the camp, she saw familiar faces. Her siblings had beaten her to the site.

There's a certain exhilaration in finding a community. That's the work of adolescence. It's also essential to building a coalition. Movements aren't sets of one. Nuclear standoffs and warming planets aren't problems to be solved alone. It's fine to scream into the void to cope. It won't convert the masses.

People like Thunberg and the members of One Mind find respite in protest because it introduces them to like-minded people. It's no substitute for treatment and it's not a cure-all, but activism can validate a person's fears and show them at the same time how that swirl of emotions can be productive—converted and stored like renewable energy, and then channeled for power.

The bigness of these issues was no longer something to pretend to ignore. It was a potent force that activists could tap into and let themselves feel. It's what drove the work. A parent or a mentor might have been an able listener. She might have had advice on how to balance the demands of organizing and of living out in the world. But who could let herself dissolve like a teenage girl?

Jamie Margolin, cofounder of Zero Hour, an organization that advocates for climate action and whose staff is for the most part in high school, has dealt with depression and obsessive-compulsive disorder since she was little. The conditions returned with a vengeance when, in the span of a few weeks in 2017, three hurricanes battered the Southwest and wildfires turned the sun red in Seattle, where she had grown up. She'd had a sense of what climate change could do. But the rapid succession of disasters put a sharper point on it. She decided to get involved in the movement.

Margolin led her first international climate protest when she was sixteen. She soon published a book for which Thunberg wrote the introduction. When she was eighteen, Margolin was asked about the time she had invested in her activism—work that kept her up late, that gave her the inbox and calendar of a CEO, that made her answer questions from children about whether the human race would survive. She said that organizing helped her handle her emotions—those that came with adolescence and the unique set of feelings that stemmed from growing up in a dire era. It wasn't quite that her work made her feel better or helped her find equilibrium. It was that activism as she practiced it had become almost meditative. The intricacies of it, its bureaucracies and processes—it gave her a means to put one foot in front of the other. She told a reporter that she thrived on the constant alerts and texts that poured in. She immersed herself in the endless refinement of planning documents. The more she did that stuff, the less time she had to stress about what might come next. Other kids blocked out the world with TV marathons or video games. She had spreadsheets.

It is an approach she has since wanted to revisit. Margolin started her first semester of college in 2020, amid another crisis of monumental proportions. She had gotten into film school, a long-held dream of hers. The pandemic had emphasized how ill prepared the world is for real disaster (as she had been telling people), and it forced her to slow down. She was no longer traveling to speak to audiences that numbered in the tens of thousands. She was spending more time with her friends. She realized it was a fast-forwarded version of the process most girls had undergone while she had been consumed with marches and preoccupied with "being 110 percent focused on the movement."

"I've been in a place where I've been navigating finding balance," she said. She was on the precipice of her twenties. It felt like a good moment for some reevaluation. She had graduated from high school burned out and exhausted. She had almost lost sight of what she was fighting for. She was raised in the beautiful and transportive Pacific Northwest, but she spent most of her time indoors, sitting in front of a screen. The summer before she moved to New York, she resolved to hike more and walk around and just bask in the presence of trees. It reconnected her to the present. She had to relearn to take pleasure in the world as it existed. Who knew what flower or plant or animal would disappear next?

Later, when she took stock of her path in the movement so far, she could see three distinct phases.

In the first, she was "super anxious about the future but still like, 'We can stop this,'" she said. It energized her.

In the second, which she now calls "climate depression," she read more. She got acquainted with the latest science and the papers that foretold of millions displaced and entire countries rendered unlivable, creating a refugee crisis of unprecedented proportions. Seasoned researchers came to speak to her. Their audience did not make her feel important. It made her feel sick. "I hadn't quite grasped that there was some damage that is locked in," she said. "That was a bad place to be. That is a place of overwhelming existential dread." She mourned the world she might never experience. Adults cheered her gumption. "There's no guaranteed tomorrow," she said in an interview from around that time, "and I haven't lived."

In the third, she realized she had inner work to do. She could see she had mastered a skill our culture teaches girls to develop: Margolin poured herself into her commitment to others. She blew past her own limits in their service. The movement was her entire universe. The work she did became a measure of her value.

"And because this is such an important cause and I felt so much like, 'There's no more time left to act,' I thought that meant that I had to just sacrifice," she said. She viewed herself less as an actual person and more as "a vessel to get work done." She gave up her free time and the hours she could have spent with loved ones and friends. She didn't hesitate to cancel plans when protests or movement work came up. She believed the crisis called for a total denial of personal needs in the face of collective disaster. Sometimes that served her. It was easier to fixate on her to-do list than to face the truth. How could she sit with her desperation when the people with the power to save what remained of this beautiful planet sat on their hands?

She called the third phase "climate acceptance." "I'm not a child," she said later. She knew she wasn't quite old. ("God forbid!") But she was getting used to the idea that she would soon age out of her most defining characteristic: adolescence. She had founded Zero Hour over Instagram. Her public persona was based on her girlhood. She would soon grow out of that. "The cuteness factor has worn off," she said. "I'm not the person that I used to be when I was sixteen."

She was still involved in the movement, but she had more nuance to offer than she did at fourteen or eighteen. She talked more about self-care, more about balance—more about how important it is that activists give themselves permission to internalize the timeline of this crisis. "When people ask me about it, it's like, 'We are in the process of getting into a traffic accident. We could have avoided said accident if we would have hit the brakes a while ago.' Now it's not hopeless, but it's a matter of, 'Do we want a lot of people to survive this crash? Do we want it to be catastrophic? Or do we want it to be survivable?'"

That mindset has helped her focus her efforts. It has made her far less interested in the kinds of sound bites that get repeated across the social media landscape. The proclamations that adolescence helps people compose. She has started to view the present as something sacred and worth savoring. "I've been motivated to go out, have experiences, spend time in nature, cross things off bucket lists, see sunsets—all the cheesiest stuff," she said. She was growing up.

The Rabin sisters said that working with children to protect the world from nuclear weapons gave them hope. It was impossible to hide from the problem, and doing something about it felt better. At the same time, it exacted a toll. Nessa Rabin had never planned to be a public speaker. In the hours she might have spent experiencing and taking pleasure in the normal rites of adolescence, she was organizing. Was it a choice to become an activist? Or had the grown-ups failed her in such spectacular fashion that she had no choice but to become one? Was her childhood the sacrificial lamb, so that other children might have their own?

Margolin gave and gave. But then she decided she wanted to hold a sliver back. She was also a part of the planet—an entire world—and she was worth protecting.

THERE IS A REASON WHY photojournalists camp outside the United Nations when Greta Thunberg addresses world leaders but not outside the colloquiums on climate science where dozens or sometimes hundreds of researchers recount in painstaking detail how damned we are. Girls make better celebrities. Even on a burning planet, we need those.

Naomi Wadler was eleven when she—as one reporter put it—

"captivated the nation" during the 2018 March for Our Lives. The event was an anti–gun violence demonstration planned in the wake of the lethal school shooting in Parkland, Florida. The main march drew at least two hundred thousand people to the streets of Washington, D.C., although some estimated at least twice that number of attendees. Adding up the people who had turned out for hundreds of satellite events held nationwide, the total number of demonstrators was pegged between 1.2 and 2 million people.

In the month between the shooting and the protest, the names of several of its organizers had become well known: Jaclyn Corin, X González, Samantha Fuentes, Delaney Tarr, Cameron Kasky, David Hogg.

Wadler was a later addition to the lineup. Activists reached out to her after learning about a local walkout she had helped lead in Virginia. She was one of the few speakers not even in high school.

"I am here to acknowledge and represent the African American girls whose stories don't make the front page of every national newspaper, whose stories don't lead on the evening news," Wadler said. "I represent the African American women who are victims of gun violence, who are . . . statistics instead of vibrant, beautiful girls full of potential."

"For far too long, these names, these black girls and women, have been just numbers," Wadler added. She had come to declare it: "'Never again' for those girls too."

In the speech, Wadler positioned herself as a microphone and a conduit—the girl through whom the stories of other women and girls could be told. But in a sprawling profile, the *Washingtonian* wondered what it was like to be "the voice of [her] generation." The piece centers on her—her explosive fame and her growing social media presence. It noted that "balancing the demands of child stardom is something of a high-wire act." When had she become a child star? She thought she was an activist. She wanted to be able to do the interviews and the speeches and watch old episodes of *The Office*. She wanted to be her whole self and be all of that in public. It seemed to dawn on her mid-interview: "I'm not going to be *that* girl."

To become a visible girl is to be singled out. It has its benefits: If a girl can make activism feel personal and emotional and urgent, she might be able to reach people who might not otherwise be moved. It has drawbacks too. Anna Elizabeth Dickinson never could translate her appeal as a girl into a viable career as an adult. Claudette Colvin experienced the worst of the consequences: at once known and dismissed. Alice de Rivera never planned to make headlines. The instant attention came with fame but not much help or advice. Wadler's mother sat near the phone when I last interviewed Naomi. She knew the trap.

Movement elders are aware of the risks too. Gloria Steinem once offered up this assessment of how she spent her time: "I learn, I give." She does not believe in minting activists or in some passing of the torch from one to the next: "There shouldn't have been a 'first' Gloria Steinem, and there won't be a last one." The seasoned organizer Dolores Huerta focuses much of her work now on training the next generation of activists. Her foundation helps them develop not just sharper tactics but a more expansive perspective. She has said that her advice to them is simple: Be patient. You want change. You work for it. You wait for it. She was and remains in awe of students, but she has pushed back on the idea that the world rests on their shoulders. She has not let them do it alone.

The girl-power trope can be a burden. It can be a menace to movements too. Public precociousness makes the results of collective action look like individual excellence. It makes for a snappier headline. It does not tend to represent the whole truth. The media impulse to turn activists into stars has a downstream impact in even the best cases. Attention is good for raising awareness. But is the issue elevated, or is the girl?

Emphasizing the girl—so smart and furious—has made it easier for those who should have to respond to her to stop at admiration. Her activism becomes a referendum on her potential instead of a battle for a cause. What a shimmering future she has ahead of her! This girl—she is going places.

An organizer wants to inspire action. Instead, she gets praise. That can feel far too much like a pat on the head. It is the fate that befell girl preachers and abolitionists, who were marked as special and who were selected as the exception to the rule. Their political heirs do not want to be so famous and so sidelined. Margolin never craved attention. She knows she will need to figure out how to make her voice heard once she is freed from and too old for the girl narrative. The prospect thrills her.

In an ideal world, the press would learn. Reporters would stop emphasizing the new wunderkinder and focus instead on the substance of what activists call for. But Margolin has not been holding her breath. "The headlines tend to be less about the actual legislation or cause or thing that we're fighting for and more like, 'Isn't it cool that these kids are articulate and can speak,'" she said.

Girls are enthused over. No one seems to hear them. Margolin started to feel like a freak whom people paid to see. "It was like, 'The cat can talk!'" Soon the carnival sideshow would be over. Margolin laughed when she said it, but it is true that people think of her—a college student—as an elder of the movement. Part of the reason she decided to pursue film was because she liked the idea of making art that could speak for her. She was done being the girl behind the podium.

AFTER THE *Washingtonian* profile—and the covers of *New York* magazine and *Glamour* and the features in *Elle* and *Teen Vogue*—Wadler took a step back from the crush of the speaking circuit. She had made it to high school and had found new friends who didn't know her first and foremost as the girl from the Parkland speech. She was proud of what that work represented. She was less sure about what her impact had been or what it might be still.

"No matter what came out of my mouth at that time, the stories would end up being about how old I was and how crazy it was that I was aware of these things," Wadler said. "People listened because it was like, 'There are these big things coming out of this little girl!'"

She had dedicated her viral speech to Courtlin Arrington, a Black teenager who had been shot and killed a few weeks after the massacre in Parkland. Wadler noticed that her death had gotten little media attention. At the walkout, she marked an additional moment of silence to honor Arrington. Wadler had tried to elevate the experiences of Black girls and women who had been overlooked or erased. But the media wanted to herald Wadler. More people know her name than know Courtlin Arrington's.

The compliments were flattering. But the praise started to feel like a minefield. She worried she would make a false move and blow it all up. "It was so hard to navigate," Wadler said. "I feel that if all of that had happened now, I would be so much more equipped to handle it. But I also feel like the experiences I've had have shaped me as a person. It was good and bad."

In her close study of the March for Our Lives demonstration at which Wadler spoke, the scholar Emily Bent explores the popular fixation on girl activists. She breaks down the invocation of "girl-power rhetoric" in the media and examines how such vocabularies fed an old conviction: "the power of individual girls to change the world."

She does not believe that the girls aren't committed to feminism and justice and to doing critical, overdue work. She doesn't even believe that girls are unsuccessful when their talents are applied to such movements. What interests Bent are the limits of the narrative we have built around them.

Theorizing that girls will save us is a convenient position for people who have actual power to hold.

Girl-power feminism—the kind that propped up de Rivera and Tinker and Margolin and Wadler, and which all of them both used and resisted—sees girl activists as endowed with particular and unusual abilities. Their charisma and determination allow them to have an outsize influence. There's some truth to that. But that framework doesn't ask what comes next. It doesn't need to. Because girl-power feminism holds that the fame and relevance girls achieve are themselves movement accomplishments. It claims that the empowerment of one girl or ten girls will lead to improvements in the lives of millions more.

That posture "gives the impression that sociocultural and political change happens as soon as one exceptional girl puts her mind to it," Bent writes. Its scripts and conventions turn girl activists into what the academic and activist Lyn Mikel Brown has called "blank screens onto which we can project our hopes and dreams."

For the girls themselves, it can be a bewildering experience. Wadler mentioned her favorite TV shows. She credited her mother for helping her with her schedule and its attendant pressures. Margolin stressed her commitment to other forms of activism besides the one for which she became best known: her commitment to LGBTQ+ rights, her participation in Black Lives Matter marches. She was a person—a full person. Not just someone else's idea of a superhero.

Margolin and Wadler and girls like them have given countless speeches. People like the wrenching ones best.

In 2018, in the middle of her speaking time at the March for Our Lives demonstration, Samantha Fuentes—who'd been wounded in the Parkland attack—vomited while dozens of live TV cameras rolled. News outlets praised her for continuing with her speech.

In 2019, Greta Thunberg cried at the United Nations as she delivered a scathing address to world leaders. The moment was entrancing. But Thunberg bit back her sobs. She and fifteen other children around the world have sued five countries for failing to act to protect the environment. The suit has never gotten even a fraction of the attention her public appearances have. (Young people in America have tried a similar tack, filing *Juliana v. United States* in 2015. The suit claims that the government's failure to act on climate violates their constitutional rights. It is one of several suits that the public-interest law firm Our Children's Trust has represented in court.) When she stood before diplomats and politicians at the UN, Thunberg knew better than to use her time to reiterate the science that has been obvious for decades or to outline the legal case for hauling entire governments before judges. She did her best with the tools she had. The most visible "exceptional girl" used her time to subvert expectations. She did not want to be an inspiration.

"This is all wrong," she said. "I shouldn't be up here. I should be back in school on the other side of the ocean. Yet you all come to us young people for hope. How dare you! You have stolen my dreams and my childhood with your empty words."

It was an indictment. It was a sensation.

A few months after her UN speech in New York, Thunberg was invited to speak at COP25—another United Nations climate conference—in Madrid. She tried a new tack. "I've given many speeches and learned that when you talk in public, you should start with something personal or emotional to get everyone's attention, say things like, 'Our house is on fire,' 'I want you to panic,' and 'How dare you,'" she said. "But today, I will not do that because then those phrases are all that people focus on. They don't remember the facts, the very reason why I say those things in the first place." Instead, Thunberg spoke about carbon emissions. She invoked budgets and percentages. She cited reports and listed numbers. She tried to redirect the attention heaped upon her.

"Girl-power scripts assume that celebrity girl leaders have all of the answers to complex societal issues," Bent writes. The stories suggest "that girls can shoulder the burdens and responsibilities associated with changing the world." But girls are not static. Girls grow up. So far we have not done a good job of letting them.

Thunberg has been subjected to an avalanche of attacks. Margolin has been condescended to. Wadler—an exception as a Black girl in an activist landscape that tends to elevate white ones—has described wishing she could go back to being unknown. She has tens of thousands of Instagram followers but continues to feel conflicted about whether she should use social media at all. She knows that the account is hers to operate. But she has a hard time shaking the sense that selfies are not what people want from a girl who once was seated on a panel with Diane Nash. "I shouldn't have to be stuck in this mold," she said. "I'm still working on that."

The hazards of activism are enormous. The media whirlwind it inspires is reductive. And even so, when *Time* magazine named

Thunberg its Person of the Year in 2019 and featured with her girls like the climate activist Xiye Bastida, who helped lead at least sixty thousand people on a climate walkout in New York, and Howey Ou, who was sixteen when she was taken to a police station in her native China for a solo demonstration of climate protest, it was frank about the fact that researchers have spent decades struggling to get leaders to recognize the climate threat. At last someone had gotten the world's attention. The article revealed that Thunberg had been anxious about the fate of the environment for most of her childhood, but she could pinpoint what had moved her to start speaking out about it: She had been watching the Parkland students—all those visible and burdened teenagers. It made her think another world was possible.

We herald our girls as saviors. How is it then that we treat them with so much scorn? How is it that their feelings—those same sensitivities that drove them to act—are deemed embarrassing, over the top, too much? "What is a teenage girl?" Samantha Hunt asks in *The New York Times*. Hunt wanted to understand what it was about girls that inspired people who saw her daughters walking down the street to respond with, "Here comes trouble." She wasn't sure she had a good answer. But she knew what the world pretended: that most girls "fit into narrow categories with shallow concerns—selfies and shopping and TikTok dances." It galled her.

In the piece, Hunt invokes *Parable of the Sower*, the Octavia Butler novel in which a girl is endowed with the power to feel the emotions of others. It sometimes leaves her miserable and incapacitated with pain, which might not sound like science fiction to the teenagers who have devoted their adolescence to repairing the world.

"Our girls are explorers and experimenters," Hunt writes. She quotes bell hooks, who observed that love has been deemed "women's work, degraded and devalued labor," when in fact learning to love—

to feel—should be revered as a fierce undertaking. Isn't that what girls have shown us?

"I feel a shift," Margolin said. She had noticed it in the climate movement, but she has seen it happen with Black Lives Matter and March for Our Lives too. She was part of the first generation of activists for whom the mainstream press cheered—even if their outlets failed to cover environmental devastation, police violence, and the gun epidemic with the same enthusiasm. "We were in high school during the peak of when the media cared," Margolin said. And that meant—though there were no paparazzi waiting outside her door—that she and the others got a taste of what it could feel like to be a little famous. To have to be *on* and working, no matter what. "I think a lot of us burned ourselves out and became unhappier or became overwhelmed or overstimulated or spent so much of our development focusing on fighting these issues that we didn't focus on coming into our own like teenagers often do."

Wadler decided to take a break in the hopes that she might avoid the same fate. She was in high school. She still had time. It dawned on her that her focus on "saving the world"—on making sure that things were "equitable and inclusive"—had come at her own expense. She had never stopped to think about how the issues to which she was bringing attention affected her. "I started to feel like, 'I am so well versed on how women of color are treated in the media and in America that I feel like I forgot that that included me for a little bit.'" Her quest to see Black girls honored and respected would have to start with her respecting herself.

IN TERMS OF balls and strikes—America's preferred math for calculating wins and losses—Standing Rock failed. In December 2016, the

United States Army Corps of Engineers denied a request to continue construction of the pipeline under the Missouri River. But the next month, the still-new Trump administration reversed that decision. It was operational the following June.

But in March 2020, a district judge ruled that the government needed to conduct a new environmental impact review of the pipeline. Its overseers tried to appeal that decision to the Supreme Court, but it declined to take the case. The environmental review continues, as does the pipeline's operation.

The activists who stood firm on the ground know that Standing Rock changed something profound for them, whatever the eventual outcome of the latest legal battle. Aliya Eagle, then seventeen, had experienced the suicide of a close relative and the murder of her brother. The world had not seemed lovely to her back then, but the protest drew her out into it. Tokata Iron Eyes, then thirteen, had craved a more definitive victory. Still, she could see that a movement that had started as an effort to halt a pipeline had grown into something much bigger. It had given people a cause to believe in.

"Our communities have such a hard time," she said. "With this generation, with the youth, we're just trying to pick ourselves up and start over and live in a good way."

11

STREAM OF CONSCIOUSNESS

HOW GIRLS USE THEIR VOICES

Youth voting has been a perpetual source of handwringing for the pundit class. These kids! The kids are tuned out. And obsessed with their own reflections. The kids spend too much time with their video games or on social media and listen to too much music or care too much about what their friends think. Young people need to get serious. Or at least get back to class. Young people need to make *better choices*.

The next generation—each next generation—is supposed to improve on the one that came before it. But kids have also been a historic letdown to the people who think children can be controlled and made obedient. Young people are never so predictable.

Speculation about voter turnout was a fixation ahead of the 2020 presidential election—with a particular obsession over whether millennials and Gen Z Americans would show up at the polls. Young people would be essential to the success of the Democratic ticket. Joe Biden and Kamala Harris needed them to win. The trouble was numbers from previous elections were not promising. Youth turnout had clocked in at around 43 percent in 2016—lagging almost 15 points behind eligible citizens overall. Rates of participation in the presidential contest were similar in 2012.

Still, there was evidence that 2020 could be different. In the midterm elections in 2018, the rate of campus voting had doubled—from 19.3 percent in 2014 to 40.3 percent. Voter registration efforts had paid dividends—from around 65 percent of the demographic in 2014 to 73.3 percent in 2018. Activists knocked on doors and reported enthusiasm. Students reached out to their peers via text, via postcard, via Instagram. Volunteers organized and held their breath. Girls jumped in.

When then candidate Joe Biden decided to air a campaign ad during the MTV Video Music Awards, the sixty-second spot centered on Adrianna Williams—a senior at Duke and the cochair of the national organization Black Students for Biden.

After the pandemic put an end to in-person gatherings and canceled scores of planned voter registration events on campuses nationwide, a freshman at Columbia and four of her friends launched FroshVote, designing the organization to boost freshman and first-time voting in swing states.

Older women have long made up the bulk of poll workers. But when that corps of volunteers was sidelined amid the public health crisis, their granddaughters stepped forward to replace them. In 2016, over 50 percent of poll workers had been over the age of sixty-one. When voters went to the polls in 2020, 60 percent were under fifty and 40 percent were under thirty-five.

Princeton student Ella Gantman was one of the people who decided to staff the ballot box. But she did more than sign up to be a poll worker. She had helped develop a platform that recruited fellow students to the cause. What she christened the Poll Hero Project registered more than thirty thousand volunteers—almost two thirds of whom were sixteen or seventeen and ineligible to vote themselves.

Poll work is underpaid and requires both attention to detail and patience. It is an essential public service, but when it operates without incident, volunteers are more or less invisible. Its existence embodies the ideal of a democratic republic as a team sport: something we do and build and maintain in the collective without expecting much credit. "It's Gen Z reaching out to Gen Z in order to create a tangible change within our generation," Gantman said in an interview. No surprise: Women and girls filled an overwhelming number of the open roles.

The vote exploded expectations in 2020. Turnout for people between the ages of eighteen and twenty-nine surged 8 percent, and most broke for Joe Biden and Kamala Harris. Young people helped flip at least three swing states for Democrats. Polling data suggests that Gen Z and millennial voters delivered the Senate to Democrats too with Jon Ossoff and Raphael Warnock winning the Georgia runoff races and representing the state in the chamber.

When Tufts's Center for Information & Research on Civic Learning and Engagement (CIRCLE) and other organizations dug into the data, they drew clear links between the stances candidates expressed on issues that mattered to Gen Z and millennial voters and the likelihood of their participation. In 2018, CIRCLE found that the March for Our Lives demonstration led to a consequential bump in voter participation in the midterms. In its own postmortem in 2020, the Sunrise Movement—a Gen Z–led organization calling for action on the climate catastrophe—cited research that found that telling Gen Z voters about the plan Joe Biden had to address the issue was the single best intervention to increase enthusiasm for him.

Politicians needed their vote. Young people said: "Talk to me."

THE CONSTITUTIONAL AMENDMENT that lowered the voting age to eighteen was passed in just over twelve weeks in 1971. The historical context makes it seem inevitable. America had been plunged into the Vietnam War, and high school seniors were on the front lines—old enough to die for their flag, but not old enough to vote for their leader. Girls were not going to help make the case. This was about soldiers and the appeal was for their enfranchisement. The appeal was instead grounded in gut-wrenching patriotism with a whisper-shout of machismo thrown in—that beloved American combination.

The gambit had been tried before. In 1942, after an amendment to the Selective Service Act lowered the age of the draft to eighteen, several politicians made the case that the voting age should be adjusted to match. But critics rejected the pitch. Congressman Emanuel Celler did not accept the rationale that the same qualities that made a soldier qualified for war made a citizen qualified to vote. The New York representative claimed the opposite. New soldiers were trained to take orders and honor the chain of command. Voters should be able to think for themselves. Adolescent vigor could be an asset on the battlefield. It would help less at the polls.

When the effort failed, an odd mix of people were to blame. There were the politicians like Celler, the paternalistic activists who urged greater protection for children rather than more responsibilities, and, in some cases, students themselves. The rise of Hitler in Europe resulted in well-publicized photos of German Hitler Youth—arms raised in lockstep. Young Americans shared in the skepticism over the sound-

ness of their own judgment. Could adolescents be trusted to make political decisions? One student bemoaned his own generation: We "are
quick to grasp at panaceas for obvious wrongs." Shrug: Voting was
best left to adults.

But in the time between the two eras of war, fundamental attitudes
toward adolescence had shifted. When elected leaders and the public
first debated lowering the voting age, advocates for children were describing childhood as a period of innocence and naïveté. Their work
was grounded in the conviction that the state had to smooth the transition to adulthood as much as possible, with extended welfare, limited work hours, and expanded access to education for people who
could not quite be trusted to handle the shift on their own. When
Vote 18 rocketed back into the national consciousness a few decades
later, it made less sense to claim that those who happened to be under
the legal voting age were not equipped to shoulder adult burdens. Students had helped to end Jim Crow and kicked off the antiwar movement. Children had shut down traffic. Their demonstrations made the
news. Their protests were defiant and effective but their power was
indirect. When a politician was corrupt or ineffectual, their best recourse was urging other people to vote him out of office. In Connecticut, a committee that supported lowering the voting age decried
laws that barred young people from having "a real voice" where it
mattered most. Others framed the case in terms of the future of the
nation. Allow those who were at least eighteen to vote or risk alienat-
ing them from the political process—a *Tinker*-like pitch.

In 1968, a few months after a Gallup poll found that 56 percent
of Americans believed those over eighteen should be able to vote, a
movement called Let Us Vote (LUV) launched in Stockton, California. It had a national presence within six weeks, establishing chapters
at thousands of high schools and on more than three hundred college

campuses. Its members were photographed for *Time* in 1969. Writers who had composed hits for the Monkees released a single titled "LUV" in its honor.

Then a network called the Youth Franchise Coalition built out the on-the-ground infrastructure. It was made up of over two dozen organizations, including labor, education, and student groups. It united such disparate interests as the National Education Association, the American Jewish Committee, and the National Association of Autoworkers. In 1969, it planned to host a pivotal summit to make a final and slam-dunk case for the cause.

The NAACP decided to sponsor that event, sending the indomitable Carolyn Quilloin, then in her twenties, to draw untapped groups of supporters. Youth mobilization was her focus. One movement fed another—Quilloin had been arrested with two other Black high school students almost a decade earlier for refusing to leave a segregated lunch counter in Savannah, Georgia. To demonstrate the wide support for Vote 18, Quilloin invited two thousand people to attend what one historian called a "coming-out event" for the push in Washington, D.C. Most of them were students. Quilloin obsessed over the details, wanting to ensure that teenagers represented themselves well. But when the conference was covered in the media, it was the leaders of the Youth Franchise Coalition—all male—who dominated.

In 1970, movement leaders were invited to appear at a Senate committee hearing, but Quilloin was absent. Almost a month later, the members reconvened. This time, two female representatives from the NAACP were invited to join. Philomena Queen, chair of the Middle Atlantic Region of the NAACP's Youth Division, introduced herself to the committee as a future voter. She believed she and her peers deserved the ballot, not as soldiers or antiwar protesters but as citizens. She called the vote "sacred" and framed the issue of the "voteless" people her age as a matter of civil rights. Then she hit her stride. In front of some of the most powerful men in the nation, she testified on behalf of her generation.

"We see . . . wrongs which we want to make right; we see imperfections that we want to make perfect; we dream of things that should be done but are not; we dream of things that have never been done, and we wonder why not," she said, an echo of Dr. King. "And most of all, we view all of these as conditions that we want to change, but cannot. You have disarmed us of the most constructive and potent weapon of a democratic system—the vote."

Less than a week after Queen's appearance, the Senate moved to attach an amendment to the 1965 Voting Rights Act extension that would lower the voting age to eighteen. The bill passed in June—a few weeks after National Guard troops fired on a crowd at Kent State and killed four unarmed students. The amendment was seen as a "steam valve"—something to ease the pent-up pressure.

When newspapers covered the momentous occasion, the Youth Franchise Coalition was credited for its efforts. Queen and Quilloin were not.

With the 1972 presidential election on the horizon, candidates turned their attention to courting the newest voters. Democrats exhaled. Presidential nominee George McGovern expected at least 70 percent of the new demographic to back him. Strategists predicted a landslide.

Credit to the pollsters. The race was definitive—just not in favor of McGovern. Incumbent Richard Nixon won. When the ballots were tallied, just about half of the voters whom the amendment had enfranchised turned out. Their vote split down the middle between McGovern and Nixon. Young people had not behaved as the adults anticipated.

The kids had not saved them.

. . .

ACTIVISTS CONTINUE TO build on the work that gave the vote to millions of people, but activists think we can do better. In 2019, Colorado passed a law that allowed teens who would turn eighteen before an election to vote in primaries. Thousands of the people whom the new law enfranchised did so. New Era Colorado, which was launched in 2006, had helped write and pass the bill that created voter preregistration. Its founders were recent college graduates who hoped to engage their own generation in politics. Most of its staffers are women. One had just graduated high school and had come to see her value as a girl in politics. She could relate to the people she wanted to reach. She could invoke their "shared language"—as she put it in a 2020 interview—without it feeling contrived. Her pop culture references and her affect and her clothes made the case for her—that the issues she was describing were relevant concerns. In her presence, she got "the wheels turning," she said. Voting wasn't just "something for adults." In 2022, Senator Elizabeth Warren and Congresswoman Nikema Williams introduced the Youth Voting Rights Act, a bill that would expand on the work that New Era Colorado has done. It would require colleges and universities to have on-campus polling places. It would allow teenagers nationwide to preregister to vote after turning sixteen.

Of course, even these attempts to expand the franchise would empower just a fraction of the activists mentioned in these chapters. The Youth Voting Rights Act would not have let Harriet Hanson cast a ballot, let alone Brenda Travis. Alice de Rivera sued her school board but was not old enough to vote to replace its members. Girls have had to make themselves heard, with or without the vote.

At least now, girls have the internet. To establish meaningful relationships with voters in 2020, coalitions like NextGen Nevada and

Georgia's Black Voters Matter hustled to meet them online. NextGen integrated several of its organizing initiatives into the popular Nintendo game Animal Crossing. Voters could download slogan tees and other merch to wear in its virtual world. Phone banking is considered the gold standard in voter outreach, but volunteers tried their hands—and thumbs—at DM banking too. Yaniliz Rosario, an organizer in Wisconsin who had just graduated high school, stressed in an interview how important it was that organizations reach people, whether a presidential election was imminent. She coordinated student attendance at school board meetings and pointed peers to specific initiatives to support issues that mattered to them—from police reform to funding for education. She curated musical selections on Snapchat to galvanize attendees at local events.

"It's not just about elections," a writer reporting on Rosario's work explains. It was instead about establishing a relationship with an essential demographic of voters. It was about ensuring that political engagement had a good vibe.

Ahead of the election, activists in their teens and twenties drew on similar tactics. Some marshaled memes for the cause. Others coordinated TikTok explainers in support of candidates up and down the ballot. Adults own the social media platforms. Parents can make decisions about screen time. Young people, however, shape and define what constitutes "cool." Fluent in the varied dialects of the internet, girls have learned to use it to communicate with a flow that no consultant can teach.

When Greta Thunberg was named *Time* Person of the Year in 2019, then president Donald Trump raged that she should "work on her Anger Management problem." In response, Thunberg tweaked her Twitter bio to include "a teenager working on her anger management problem."

In a piece that described the relative ease with which the Parkland teens disarmed the conservative internet to call for gun reform, writer Charlie Warzel notes that their sparrers in the media sphere had miscalculated in attacking them. Pundits and blowhards had chosen adversaries who were "born onto the internet" and "capable of waging an information war" with a command of the craft far superior to theirs.

Warzel observes that survivors of gun violence used "platforms like Twitter to call out and put pressure on politicians," addressing their critics not with bland, workshopped statements but with sparkling and clever insults, and real-time responses to misinformation. Their panache didn't spare the students online harassment, but it did make their adversaries sputter. Who had shown them how to talk like that?

It took researchers a long time to show the slightest interest in learning more about how girls communicate—to see their modes of interaction as something worth exploring. But in the 1990s, the Finnish professor Kaj Björkqvist started to delve into a particular facet of how girls relate to one another. His research upended a previous consensus. For a long time, scientists who studied aggressive behavior in schoolchildren identified and categorized it based on its overt manifestations—pushing at recess, hitting, throwing things. In that scheme, girls were just not as aggressive as their male counterparts. That conclusion ratified how all kinds of societies liked to think of them. As warm. As loving and protective. As kinder and more caring.

But girls are not nicer. The conversations Björkqvist had when he started interviewing actual middle school girls startled him. He asked them about their behavior. He wanted to understand their social hierarchies and their view of themselves and others. Researchers found that girls tend to stop exhibiting combative behavior at around four—around the same time that children start to internalize gender norms.

Social pressure squeezes out the hitting and punching. But that change did not mean that girls—as Björkqvist discovered—had stopped wanting to act on their aggression. It just required the development of new and more indirect modes of attack.

"Their superior social intelligence enabled them to wage complicated battles with other girls aimed at damaging relationships or reputations," a writer summarizing Björkqvist's research explains. In other words, girls learned to land more lasting blows. "Girls better understand how [others] feel," Björkqvist said in an interview in 2002. It made them dangerous. "[T]hey know better how to harm."

Björkqvist published his work on girlhood a decade before Instagram was invented. But his studies identified a unique and advanced form of warfare. In the face of girls' discipline and their relationships and their knack for sharing information within social circles, their opponents seemed to melt down. Social media has just sharpened their skills.

In a paper about the mechanisms of social progress, researchers affirm that social media, for all its flaws, allows users to build communities and share experiences on a much larger platform than traditional social networks do.

And despite the rank and disproportionate sexism and abuse that female users endure on the internet, their presence dominates.

In 2021, almost 60 percent of Instagram users were women. The platform helped Jamie Margolin find one of her Zero Hour cofounders; the two introduced themselves in DMs.

The gender breakdown is about the same on TikTok in the United States—just over 60 percent of users are female. The platform has become home to some of the most creative output in the pro-choice movement, as women use it to share exuberant explainers and laugh-out-loud political parodies. Alex Cueto, a clinic volunteer with the organization Charlotte for Choice, went viral for several video snippets filmed outside the clinics where she works. One blared the tune "Short, Short Man" over a clip of an anti-choice protester: "Eeny-weeny teeny-weeny shriveled little short, short man." It earned her over two million views.

Even Twitter has its purpose. It will never be the most attractive or widespread platform, but it connects people who need to reach one another. In 2016, a week after police shot and killed Philando Castile and Alton Sterling, two friends took to Twitter to announce plans for a sit-in. Eva Lewis, then seventeen, knew one of them from her old school. When she saw the posts, she offered to help. She had never planned a demonstration, but she had helped write press releases for friends who had protested the Chicago Public Schools a few months earlier. Another volunteer later joined. All four on the impromptu steering committee were Black girls.

"I said, we need a group chat," Lewis recalled. "I said, we need goals, we need a purpose. What we wanted was this to be a peaceable protest. We had a goal of no arrests, which seemed impossible, because I hadn't heard of a protest with no arrests—like this weekend was wild."

Over one thousand people descended on Millennium Park in Chicago for the silent sit-in—held when the sun was out so that children could come. When it was over, Lewis and the other three went to eat pizza. An interviewer later asked how she had prepared for the event. Lewis told her she sang gospel songs. Bernice Johnson would have beamed.

Historic events tend to have a medium of documentation associated with them. We remember the World Wars in great books and serif-font letters. The civil rights movement has been sequenced in thousands of photos. When the Twin Towers fell, millions of people watched their collapse on television. The Arab Spring was live streamed. The war in Ukraine aired on TikTok.

That evolution—that democratization—has been a mixed bag for the media. Local news has been eroded. A content creator is not a journalist. But the process has diversified the kinds of voices that reach the public. Women and girls have been written out of canonical narratives. Their letters have been tossed aside. The internet has shifted how we consume protest—and whom we see.

The cultural critic Jane Hu has assessed how the mechanics of protest have evolved. She describes this most recent era as the "'online' moment of social unrest," one in which "the struggle in the public square" is not captured and then streamed or tweeted, but is happening at the same time as "a takeover of the virtual one."

"Amid cell-phone footage of protests and toppling statues, the Internet has been further inundated with what we might call activist media," she writes. She cites the proliferation of links to bail-fund donations and retweets calling for people to match them. She recounts how email and phone call templates urge users to reach out to their elected officials. Fewer people seem to want or care to distinguish between one world and the other. There is less need to—the streams have crossed.

Girls are the proof. Activists like Lewis and Margolin have shown that Instagram and Twitter can be tools of connection and collaboration. High school students—used to drafting their papers in Google Docs—now workshop their mission statements in real time. TikTok videos educate a generation in the principles of abolition.

And then there is Darnella Frazier.

Frazier was seventeen when she witnessed the murder of George Floyd. She had been shopping with a cousin when she saw the scene unfold: a man writhing on the ground, the now former officer Derek Chauvin bearing down on him. She took out her phone. She pressed record. She posted the clip to Facebook a few hours later, having seen the police report that claimed a man had had a "medical incident" and died that afternoon. "Medical incident???" she wrote on Facebook, furious. "Watch outtt." He had been killed.

Protests lit up thousands of cities and towns. Demonstrations spread all over the world—in dozens of countries. The rallies and marches brought people together who had never joined a protest before. That summer, *Chicago Tribune* reached out to Eva Lewis to see what she had been up to since her 2016 sit-in. She was still a committed activist, now in her twenties. The pandemic had created new needs, which she wanted to meet. She was coordinating drop-offs of food for families who lacked access to fresh groceries. She crowdfunded rental assistance. People sent her videos of demonstrations, and she reposted them on social media. She wanted people to see activists at work. She wanted to make sure that those in law enforcement knew she and her peers were watching. "I'm just sharing as much as I can," she said.

Social media was awash in the videos that Jane Hu describes—activists streaming into downtown districts, police reacting with force, leaders shouting into bullhorns, people calling out names and hearing them called back.

Zee Thomas was at home in Nashville thumbing through her feed when she composed a tweet of her own. She wanted to lead a protest—at least if her mom said she was allowed. Thomas connected with five other girls in less than a week and soon led ten thousand people in a march to call attention to police violence. All six organizers were between the ages of fourteen and sixteen. It was the first protest that Thomas—a self-described introvert—had ever attended.

There were others. Two teenage girls connected on Instagram to lead a Black Lives Matter protest across the Golden Gate Bridge. The march was organized in eighteen hours. In Chicago, a high school senior spent the week of her graduation campaigning to eliminate the police presence in local public schools. Her mother discovered her daughter's involvement when she saw her face on the cover of the *Chicago Tribune* at Walgreens. A St. Louis teenager active with the Sunrise Movement programmed a teach-in for local high school and college students. She invited Cori Bush—then a candidate, now a member of the House of Representatives—to call in. Bush did. Girls rallied in front of courthouses and police stations. Girls shared protest flyers on Instagram. Some had been active in organized demonstrations before. Others were experiencing the thrill of protest for the first time.

Girls double tapped. Girls slid into DMs. Girls live streamed. Girls got exhausted and didn't pretend otherwise. Whose interests did it serve to make believe that girls were invincible? Thomas rejected the high-wire act that girls who have wanted to make progress have been told to perfect—that dance between using girlhood as a shield and turning it into a weapon.

In an interview, she was defiant: "We're allowed to be weak. We are teenagers, we're young women, and we're allowed to be emotional."

Months after the summer protests—and with the video Frazier had taken as a central piece of evidence—Derek Chauvin was convicted. Frazier testified at the trial. The incident still haunted her. She cried on the stand. Millions of people had seen her video. Far fewer had heard her voice. Frazier has not participated in interviews and has done almost no press, but she is still active on social media. In 2021, she posted a statement on Facebook to reflect on how much had happened since that horrible afternoon. The murder "changed how I viewed life," she wrote. "It made me realize how dangerous it is to be Black in America."

She had been honored with a Pulitzer Prize. She had turned eighteen. She had helped deliver some justice. Chauvin is serving over two decades in prison.

But Frazier did not feel special. People liked to talk about the girl who had been there. It was different to be her. To live as the person who had seen a Black man murdered.

She wanted to heal. She needed to cope with her trauma. Yet she wrote that she was proud of what she had done. If it weren't for her video and the social media apparatus that helped distribute it, "the world wouldn't have known the truth. I own that."

ADOLESCENCE IS COMPLICATED even under the most charmed of circumstances. Gen Z has not had the most charmed circumstances. The threat of climate disaster is inexorable. School massacres are a fact of American life. The outbreak of the coronavirus pandemic upended not just the usual rites like prom and graduation but the process of starting an independent life and finding meaningful work. Making new friends and dating have gotten harder. Loneliness is an epidemic too. Gen Z had never been much impressed with its leaders. The bungled governmental response to a once-in-a-lifetime public health crisis does not seem to have inspired new confidence.

In 2022, the Harvard Youth Poll reported that over half of its respondents agree with the statement that politics have proven unable "to meet the challenges" of the present American moment. Still, the poll found no real reduction in Gen Z's intention to vote in future elections. Their generation was disappointed, but it refused to cede its influence. It has no choice but to engage.

Young people now are even more progressive than their millennial predecessors, which puts them at particular odds with the Republican officeholders who are determined to roll back several decades of social progress. Even Democrats who purport to stand with them on issues like abortion and immigration and LGBTQ+ rights have failed to prevent the fall of *Roe*, the constant threat to federal programs like DACA, and the introduction of hundreds of legislative proposals designed to target trans people.

Teens are put on this earth to question the decisions that people in power make. That is the superpower of adolescence. But for this latest generation, there is the sense that time is running out. Adults fall short, but now their foibles have world-altering consequences. The organization Gen-Z for Change was founded to stave off such destructive impulses. It draws on the skills of its leadership and leans on social media to get its points across. It has a progressive bent and a delicious set of guerrilla-warfare tactics.

In place of a traditional team photo on its website, the nonprofit uses a screenshot of a packed Zoom meeting—complete with awkward camera angles. It captures their work well: online, but on message. The Highlander Folk School was a succor for Parks. The work that Gen-Z for Change does is wi-fi enabled but no less of a haven. To wit: When a hotline was set up to receive tips about violators of a recent Texas anti-abortion law, volunteers with the nonprofit inundated it with Shrek porn. (The website crashed.) When the Supreme Court draft that indicated *Roe* would be overturned leaked in 2022, the organization took to TikTok to educate over a million people on the embattled state of reproductive choice.

One of Gen-Z for Change's fiercest political strategists is Olivia Julianna, who raised over two million dollars at nineteen for abortion care on the back of a Twitter throwdown with a Republican congressman who had tried to humiliate her. She traces the stunning success of that push to the groundwork she and other advocates laid months earlier, when the team tried to organize online around immigration reform. It didn't succeed, but it sold her on the potential of grassroots online activism with a sense of humor. "That helped us create the template," she said of the failed bid. "We had spreadsheets with journalist contacts, with other creators on TikTok and Twitter and Instagram. That helped set the precedent."

Julianna relies on the word "we" as less confident speakers use "um" or "like." It is a rhetorical habit that serves a purpose: to emphasize the collective. She has become the focus of profiles in national publications and can deliver a dependable sound bite. But she doesn't work alone. "I feel like I've been made out to be this character," she said. She is not a lone ranger or an avatar for a cause. She is an actual person—not "a means to an end."

"It has been a real adjustment period," she said. "I have been an organizer. I've been an activist. But this is so public facing." After the Twitter fracas, the transition was extreme and instant—from polite interest on the part of adults to intense expectation. People wanted to know what she was doing. Strangers scrutinized not just her looks but her level of contribution to the causes she has been championing since high school. Was she a real activist or was her work a stunt? How much did she know about the subjects she was being invited to discuss on national television?

Julianna has taken online classes instead of enrolling in traditional in-person college. She has been known to skimp on sleep even as she deals with diabetes and PCOS—two conditions that make her sensitive to stress. "Young women who are in these lines of work—we lose a lot because of the movements we care about," she said. She feels the pressure to accept overtures from media outlets and invitations to events. Declining would risk people thinking she doesn't care, that her work is superficial. "I don't think people realize there are other people who can be asked to do these things," she said. But CNN, MSNBC, *Business*

Insider, NPR—the media doesn't seem to want other people. It wants her: the girl from Twitter.

"You get branded as this activist who is doing these incredible things," she said. But she has seen that kind of goodwill evaporate fast. When she defies conventional wisdom or shares an unpopular opinion, she loses her street cred: "Then it's like, well, I'm just a kid."

Julianna advises candidates. She consults on Gen Z outreach and voter mobilization. She should want to get this part over with: to fast-forward to a time when she does not have to balance school and events. To when she can command even more respect.

Instead, she stews. She wonders whether she—a self-identified queer, disabled woman of color—will be able to pull off the transition to full adulthood. Whether she will be allowed to keep doing this work at this level and with this impact when her age doesn't make for such a good headline. "You're a young woman in these spaces. You feel like sometimes you have to take every offer that's presented to you because you don't know if you'll get another," she said. "You do worry, 'So what's my expiration date?'"

THE ORGANIZATION Run for Something supports progressives who want to run for local office and are still at the start of their careers. It has backed millennials and Gen Z candidates in down-ballot races nationwide. It has sent hundreds of them to seats of power in their communities. It endorsed Cassandra Levesque when she ran for the New Hampshire State House in 2018. She was nineteen.

Levesque had not planned to run for office. She had been thinking about becoming a photographer. She is soft spoken on the phone, with a quiet confidence. She had gotten interested in politics when she started to pursue the Gold Award, the ultimate badge of honor in the

Girl Scouts, of which she was a member. She decided she wanted to end child marriage in New Hampshire. She was seventeen, and the practice was legal for girls over thirteen—with parental consent and the approval of a local judge. She could remember what it had been like to be them. She pictured middle schoolers shopping for wedding dresses and then returning to bedrooms "with band posters and stuffed animals and Barbie dolls." It seemed insane.

She approached several state legislators in search of someone interested in picking up a bill. One informed her he was not about to overhaul an old law because of "a request from a minor doing a Girl Scout project." Levesque fumed. Then she upped the ante: She ran for the state legislature and won.

The average age of the people with whom Levesque served in her first term was sixty-six. Almost three quarters of them were male. The man who had rebuffed her was not there—he declined to run for re-election after their dustup.

Girls will claw and scratch for power, Julianna said. It is the old catfight trope, reclaimed. But Julianna also knows what the girls featured in this book do: that girls are often defenseless. That even begging and pleading and coalition building and targeted organizing and voter registration and volunteering and commanding the best-trained troops on the social media front lines can sometimes fail to overcome the undemocratic and illiberal tactics that conspire to keep people disempowered.

Restrictions on abortion access passed since the fall of *Roe* have compelled middle schoolers to contemplate motherhood. Book bans limit libraries and thus portals to more expansive and just worlds. Voter suppression efforts take root and spread. In 2021, one in five Gen Z adults identified as LGBTQ+, while school districts implemented policies aimed at making that population feel not just miserable but demonized.

So girls do as their forebears did and stand in front of crowded and sometimes hostile rooms to invoke that unique and revered treasure: their girlhood. How else did Anna Elizabeth Dickinson seize a platform? What allowed Mabel Ping-Hua Lee to lecture older white women and be greeted as a hero? How did girls like Barbara Johns claim the upper hand? Girlhood is the bargaining chip that girl activists can bring to the table. The ante, upped.

In 2021 alone, 150 bills targeting transgender children and adolescents were introduced nationwide. In 2022, the Human Rights Campaign recorded almost that same number of bills introduced in just four months. Elected officials in statehouses consider bills that ban trans children from seeking medical care for gender transitions, even with the support of their parents and doctors. Others seek to police which bathrooms are available to them. In Alabama, doctors can be sentenced to up to a decade in prison for prescribing medication to support gender transitions for patients under nineteen.

Young trans people are watching. Some research indicates that up to 85 percent have followed legislative sessions and listened as politicians questioned their identities. The Trevor Project has noted that as the attacks continue, mental health issues in affected communities rise. The percentage of trans children and teenagers who have reported contemplating suicide has increased to 52 percent.

There are a million opportunities for growing up to go wrong, and two in particular: You can be forced to grow up. You can be denied the right to do so. The United States has long imposed limits on girlhood. Who qualifies? Who is denied the privilege? That trend continues.

Libby Gonzales became a trans activist at seven when she testified at the Texas State Capitol in Austin. Her parents spoke for about six minutes. The debate: a bathroom bill. Gonzales told legislators it would be "so weird" if she were compelled to use a different bathroom. "Please keep me safe," she said.

Her first appearance was almost half her life ago. She has made dozens since then. Gonzales likes sewing and is a self-identified foodie. She loves video games and her dogs. Activism has never been one of her hobbies. It's more like a chore—something she keeps having to do. In 2021, Texas considered fifty-two bills targeting trans people, with an emphasis on trans kids. The state has threatened to investigate parents of children who receive gender-affirming medical care. Texas would like to label that treatment abuse. Gonzales travels to Austin with her parents to bear witness and fight back, and her mother knows that it makes them targets.

The prospect of showing up and addressing the public intimidates Gonzales less than it used to. "When I'm waiting to speak, I feel excited and nervous. But when I talk, I feel like I have to seem confident and like I am not scared to be there at all," she said. When we talk on the phone, she's twelve.

In April 2022, Gonzales and a friend practiced their testimonies as the clock inched nearer to midnight during a late-night legislative session. She took deep breaths. She rehearsed. She stood in her power poses. Advocates who backed the anti-trans bill found her and her friend and her little sister, who had come to support her. Grown men and women took pictures of them; salvation arrived in the form of then Texas House representative Jasmine Crockett, who offered the girls her office to hide in. When Gonzales remembers the experience, she is quiet. But she perks up when she recalls what Crockett did for her. "Now we're besties," she said.

The night in April that Gonzales described ended in a whimper. The testimonies were cut off at midnight. Gonzales never got to speak.

She had a chance to share more in the CNN Special Report "Deep in the Pockets of Texas," which explores the hand that two billionaires have had in shaping the bills that haunt her. She finds their crusade as baffling as it is frightening. She told reporters she had "no idea" what was so hard for people to understand: "I'm just a girl . . . living in Texas with amazing hair."

There are more visible trans women in the media, in the worlds of fashion and entertainment and politics, than there were when Gonzales got her start as an activist. More women living full and rich lives. More trans women doctors and state legislators. It's a relief to have a role model.

When she speaks at events, Hayden Valentina Bisset tries to focus on the delight and happiness she has found in being trans. She's sixteen and knows that kids are in the audience. "Just seeing someone older makes it like, 'Oh, I can do it. I will be there. It will all make sense,'" she said. "I love knowing other girls could be looking up to me. It makes me think of when I was in that space. It's just a powerful time for trans girls in particular. You're blossoming."

Gonzales will go to high school. She will turn eighteen and then nineteen, and her medical choices will no longer be subject to state oversight. How much will she have to sacrifice in the process?

Girls have raised their voices for centuries. Modern technologies have amplified them. The internet lets a whisper roar. Harriet Hanson could have done a lot with a microphone. But something has to come after the podium.

Cassandra Levesque is old enough now to let her work speak for her. Whether she can continue to be heard in the statehouse will depend on her constituents. She now answers to them. At the start of 2022, she was still fighting to raise the minimum marriage age in

New Hampshire. It has inched up from thirteen to sixteen, thanks to her work. She would like to see it raised to eighteen. In an interview with *Politico*, she said that the conditions of childhood had changed and its parameters needed to as well. She wanted kids to have the space "to be able to grow up" at their own pace. To take big leaps and to experiment. As she had. She wanted to see that time honored.

When Levesque first ran for office, she knew her age was part of the reason that her race had drawn so much attention. It never bothered her. When she won the election, it seemed to her like she could now earn the interest—"like I was starting something," she said.

What a thrill. To still be at the beginning.

CONCLUSION

S tories of remarkable girls abound now. We greet them with far less incredulousness and a little more awe. But we still have our theories. In newspapers and magazines, reporters punctuate stories about girls with descriptive asides about their smallness—about their oversize sweatshirts or cutoff jean shorts, about their flip and bracing frankness.

Sometimes writers fantasize about what it would mean to have them in charge. Smart girls. Girls who are capable and eager to do good. Elect them president!

But sometimes a note of condescension sneaks in. It sounds like: "Let's not get ahead of ourselves, girls." It sounds like: "Let's keep the training wheels on, shall we?"

I met the activist Marley Dias when she was in middle school. She had just launched #1000BlackGirlBooks, an initiative that set out to collect books with Black girls as protagonists. Celebrities tweeted about it. Donations poured in.

I read in an interview that she wanted to be a magazine editor when she grew up, so I invited her to come join me at *Elle*, where I worked at the time. We came up with the idea for a digital zine and spent weeks brainstorming stories and writing headlines. She was the boss. It was a glorious time at work. It reminded me what it was like to be eleven or twelve or fifteen—to be a girl just starting to flex her power. The seeds of this book were planted then.

That summer was almost a decade ago. In the time since, Dias and I have texted and emailed and had lunch and sent each other memes. I am so aware that I now seem old to her. She and I have talked a lot about what made her so effective back then—how she developed such ironclad convictions. She has met First Ladies and Oscar winners. She executive-produced a Netflix series. She did lose an election to serve in student government—the kind of adolescent disappointment that can befall even a world-renowned activist. She turned eighteen while I put the finishing touches on this book. What will she want to do next? Who will the world let her be?

When do these beloved girls—the ones we mark for praise or for exploitation or as "mature for their age"—become women? When does one of them—as Jamie Margolin put it—stop being so cute? Is it when she graduates high school? When she graduates college? When her age at last does not end in "-teen"? When she can drink? When she can rent a car?

How long is a girl useful?

Girls have made transformative social movements possible in America. With their boldness and with their decisive action, and also with their cherubic faces. Girls have laid miles of groundwork. Seldom have their efforts been accorded even a partial measure of credit.

The critic Sarah Nicole Prickett has traced the rise and fall and relentless rise of the teen. She writes that adolescents have been "idolized and sacrificed" since researchers coined a term to group them and thus established their existence. For girls in particular, that whiplash can be ferocious. Whether the attention that comes with it is lavish or invasive or both, it can be complicated to grow out of it.

Girlhood does not and cannot last. The activists whose stories I tell here aged out of it and out of some of the characteristics with which that phase is associated—idealism, blind determination, black-and-white principles, enthusiasm and compassion, an ever-replenishing reservoir of hope, the wherewithal to pull all-nighters. Friendships that had once been so nourishing fractured. The bonds that high school and college made possible—the kind forged before children and partners—had to stretch and adapt.

Some became women who were determined to establish a new relationship to organizing, armed with more experience and qualities that teens are not quite as well known for. Heather Booth—née Tobis—has self-identified as an activist since she was a little kid. She is still one all these decades later—now with a basement apartment that she lets other, newer organizers use as a home base. She is, to use her own term, *obsessed* with the question of what makes some women drop out of activism or feel as though it has less to offer them after adolescence. Belonging to a network of grassroots organizers has helped her remain involved, she told me when I interviewed her. So did gaining perspective—not something she expects of the girls she mentors. "That comes later," she said, with a laugh.

Some girls could never recapture the sense of omnipotence that their adolescence gave them. Some didn't want to.

Anna Elizabeth Dickinson died furious.

Mabel Ping-Hua Lee could have taken her talents to several

continents. Her friends were baffled when she decided to put them to use in a small Baptist church in Chinatown. She told them she was content. At sixteen, she had led ten thousand women in a call for their freedom. In adulthood, she chose something closer to solitude—and for an unmarried woman, perhaps another kind of freedom.

Diane Nash—who had once been so bold as to recruit teenage girls to embark on a treacherous ride through the Deep South—married James Bevel in 1961. The two were a civil rights power couple in their twenties, despite Bevel's erratic and sometimes narcissistic behavior. Their union marked the end of not just her girlhood but her tenure as a leader. Bevel rose to greater prominence. His career ended in disgrace after he was tried for and convicted of incest in 2008. Nash receded, although she was awarded the Presidential Medal of Freedom in 2022. When President Biden presented it to her, he noted that she had asked him to mention the "hundreds of thousands of patriotic Americans who sacrificed so much" for the cause. "She asked me to make sure to add that," he said, "because she didn't want to take all the credit herself."

In an interview decades after she led her school in a transformative walkout in Mississippi, Brenda Travis wondered whether her childhood action had been worth it. "I'm not sure that we were that effective," she said. What had the movement achieved? McComb seemed more broken to her now. She had marched for her people, but it felt to her that her people had splintered. She was disappointed that more progress had not been made, built on top of her own. The man interviewing her asked whether she would still do what she had done at sixteen—risk it all—if she knew what would happen next.

"I would still participate," she said. "I'm a movement person. So how can I get around that?"

Bernice Johnson was another movement person who could not get around that. She married Cordell Reagon in 1963. Johnson Reagon later founded an all-Black female a cappella ensemble. She earned her PhD. She became a scholar in residence at Stanford. Growing up did not hold her back.

In an interview, she recounted how activism had found her. In 1956, she read an article about a woman named Autherine Lucy, who had become the first Black student to enroll at the University of Alabama. The school had not known she was Black when she was admitted. After administrators realized their mistake, her acceptance was rescinded. She sued, with Thurgood Marshall representing her in court. The case was brutal. She won, although she was barred from the school's cafeterias and dorms. Hecklers tailed her. White female students put on a skit in blackface. Within the week, she was suspended "for her own protection." She was expelled not long after. The school accused her of defaming it in legal documents.

"I was eleven or twelve, pulling for this woman," Johnson Reagon recalled. She had felt determined—even galvanized. But Marshall and his legal team believed the expulsion would stick. Johnson Reagon's hero got married and settled down. "I thought we were just beginning to fight," she said. "I was real upset, because it felt like when she got married, she got tired. . . . I did not want her to be tired . . . and I didn't want her to rest. I wanted her to go back."

Johnson Reagon could still recall that impatience. She had been so sure of what she would have done if she had been the one. She developed more compassion when she got older. There were limits on what people could give of themselves.

Even the movement—often canonized as a total rupture with the generations that had come before it—had ancestors. Johnson Reagon had once been a girl shaking her head at her elders. She came to see their sacrifices. She and her peers had not taken some "unbelievable leap," as she put it. "It is . . . a continuance."

In 1988, the University of Alabama lifted the ban that had barred Autherine Lucy Foster from campus. She enrolled and completed her master's degree alongside her daughter, who earned her bachelor's degree at the same time. The two women graduated together in 1992.

Alice de Rivera married and became Alice Haines. She studied to be a doctor and has dedicated her career to helping her patients. Her girlhood activism lives on in that work. So what if she never wanted to do a few rounds on the speaking circuit? She chose happiness. She was proud to have once been the girl who raised hell. She is quieter now but no less devoted to her principles. That is good enough.

"We spend a lot of time thinking about Malalas and Greta Thunbergs—both people I admire," said the poet Amanda Gorman, who was named the first National Youth Poet Laureate at nineteen and earned instant acclaim after President Biden tapped her to compose the poem performed at his inauguration in 2021. Gorman could see how the emphasis on people like her and Thunberg had given others permission to let themselves off the hook. She didn't believe that was how progress was supposed to work. She is no savior.

Girls have pushed this nation and forced it to be better. Their example has inspired millions of people to protest and vote and demand action on climate change. It has spurred several national reckonings and an overhaul of dress codes.

We look to girls to stoke something in us—to make us feel mad or sad or inspired. We point to them and applaud. But we seldom accept our marching orders from them. We teach them—one slight after another—not to expect much power as adults. So much so that a recent paper found that the older girls get, the likelier it is that they will associate men with leadership.

The fashion critic Robin Givhan once noted that "to be girlish is to be powerful because power is redefined." She wrote that about Vice

President Kamala Harris—the first woman and woman of color to serve in the role. Harris had run for office wearing Converse sneakers. She had taken her infectious giggle and penchant for jeans on the trail. "Henceforth, gravitas is no longer measured in octaves," Givhan wrote.

What will it be measured in instead? We wait to find out.

We insist we are excited for the world new generations will build for us. We mean it as encouragement, but it is just as much an abdication. Adults have delivered the line more than once. So far, no new world. The sociologist Hava Rachel Gordon cites research that has called on people to reconsider the role adolescents have in democratic life. Young people should be considered "political agents in their own right," she writes, rather than "citizens-in-the-making." Tending to our—crumbling!—civic institutions needs to be reframed not as a responsibility left for adults but as an "ongoing and joint process between generations."

Girls have ideas and proposals and convictions. We have patted ourselves on the back for inviting them to speak to us—the microphone goosenecked down to their mouths. But we have not ceded power to them.

Perhaps Clarissa Williams was thinking about that refusal to step aside or to act in the interest of the generation on whom so much has forever depended when she addressed an audience of her peers at a demonstration in 1966. She was seventeen and determined to tear down the obstacles that stood in her path. She had her ambitions. She had her hopes. But she needed more.

She was old enough to know that even the most rapturous applause could not force laws to be rewritten. She needed more than a gold star.

"Friends, we do not have a dream, we do *not* have a dream," she said, "we have a plan."

ACKNOWLEDGMENTS

This book tells the stories of girls who seized their moment. I am first and foremost thankful to them—for refusing to accept the world as it is. You shouldn't have to do this alone. And also: We are so grateful.

In what feels like another lifetime, I met the agent Kim Witherspoon. I soon realized I had encountered the one person whose cult I would join without hesitation. Kim: Your superlative judgment, counsel, and support made this book possible. At Inkwell Management, I also want to thank Maria Whelan, who seems to know to offer words of encouragement when I need them most.

I am grateful to the wonderful people at Viking. You've made me feel so taken care of and not at all insane for the frequent emails. On that last point, thanks to Paloma Ruiz for shepherding this manuscript from draft to publication, and to Kathryn Ricigliano, Tricia Conley, Diandra Alvarado, Tess Espinoza, Nicole Celli, Jane Cavolina, Claire Vaccaro, Meighan Cavanaugh, Lynn Buckley, Julia Rickard, and Chantal Canales for making it look so good. Confetti! Adoration! A parade of gratitude for Emily Wunderlich. You championed this book from the beginning and saw in it what I did. Your commitment to these girls pushed me to do them justice.

In the process of researching and writing, I drew on the expertise of dozens of scholars, historians, librarians, and activists. I am indebted to all of them. Thanks to those who shared their personal memories of transformative—and sometimes traumatic—movement work, including but not limited to: Joan Cobbs, Doris Crenshaw, Susan Wilbur Wamsley, Heather Booth, Alice Haines, Mary Beth Tinker, Jamie Margolin, Naomi Wadler, Olivia Julianna, Libby Gonzales, Hayden Valentina Bisset, Cassandra Levesque, and Marley Dias.

What good fortune it was to have asked Jessica Grose whether she knew a fact-checker who would be kind and thorough in equal measure. Indeed, she did. Hilary McClellen: It has been a gift to work together. Your care and diligence refined this book and made it stronger.

I am so thankful to Leah Chernikoff, who believed in me when I was not much older than the girls in these pages and who continues to be a sounding board and an incredible friend. Thanks too to editors who've given me space to write and explore: Chloe Schama, Samantha Barry, Stellene Volandes, Adam Rathe, and Julia Rubin, in particular.

Reynold Levy, is it possible that I was an actual teenager when you hired me for that job? I guess so. Richard Shebairo, your regular assurances that I'm doing fine and it's all going to be OK help me sleep better at night. You are both princes.

Thanks to Julia Rubin and Estelle Tang for the generous and meticulous feedback. Special gratitude to Estelle, who agreed to "write" with me once a week while I labored over the proposal for what would become this project. The best part of our sessions tended to arrive thirty or forty minutes in, when we decided we had accomplished more than enough for the evening and could get another drink. To the Marlton Hotel and Primo's, we note and appreciate the tolerance of our computer screens and modest orders.

Where would I be without the friends who've known me since I hid in the bathroom so I wouldn't have to run the presidential mile? I never want to find out. Rachel, the little girls who walked around Lake Waubeeka plotting their futures would be so proud. There is no me without you. Davida, thank you for introducing me to *Horrible Histories*—the first nonfiction book I ever loved.

Group chats are a privilege. I am honored to be a part of each one. Thanks to the people in them and to the friends who've sustained me with good cheer, perfect gossip, links to RealReal scores, Bravo news updates, and memes I miss, including Ilana, Michelle, Anne, and Aminatou, among others.

Mom, when people express shock over how often we speak (at least twice before noon, minimum), I feel bad for them that such utter paradise is outside the bounds of their imagination. Dream bigger! Thanks for checking this manuscript for the equivalent of "cerulean." Thank you for the haircut rescue missions and *Middlemarch*. I feel so fortunate that we have identical taste in fiction. The next time we cross the Atlantic Ocean, let's remember to pack several more novels.

Dad, I hate when writers describe things as "indescribable," but I suspect I will never find the words to express what it means to have such an ambitious, brilliant, loving father. I'm glad I don't have to. Thanks for telling me I was a "fucking genius" even though I never understood high school calculus. Thanks for trusting me. You've modeled what it looks like to be devoted to great art without sacrificing an inner life. I am taking notes. Let it be written in print and recorded for all time: You are as good a father as Nana was a mother.

To Annie, an acknowledgment is the bare minimum. How about I take a megaphone and shout it from the rooftops? You made me who I am. Thank you for helping to raise me and for knowing sooner than I did that I would be a writer. Thanks for telling me Jason was a keeper. He knew it and I did too: Your approval was essential.

Josh and Doria, it's nice to let me tell the same stories again and again without protest. I appreciate it so much. Josh, thanks for celebrating even the smallest milestones and for living in Los Angeles, which meant I had someone to talk to while I walked home from parties (and libraries) in the wee morning hours on the East Coast.

Thanks to Marvin, who turned me into a dog person in about thirty minutes.

Last, to Jason Hellerstein: Thanks for surprising me. With that text. With such unwavering devotion. Your careful edits on each successive draft of this book have made it so much better. One in particular saved me from a misguided musical reference so embarrassing that we can never speak of it again. Thanks for the cards and for washing all the dishes. Thanks for loving me and growing up with me. You are the best decision I will ever make.

NOTES

vii **"I love to see"**: Maya Angelou, *Conversations with Maya Angelou*, ed. Jeffrey M. Elliot (Jackson: University Press of Mississippi, 1989), 161.

vii **"How can you say"**: Cameron Crowe, "Harry Styles' New Direction," *Rolling Stone*, April 18, 2017.

INTRODUCTION

xi **In 2017, I wrote**: Mattie Kahn, "All the Light They Cannot See," *Elle*, June 2017.

xi **In a show of political spin**: Kahn, "All the Light They Cannot See."

xii **The congresswoman wanted**: Kahn, "All the Light They Cannot See."

xiii **brave and headstrong**: "Sybil Ludington," American Battlefield Trust, https://www
.battlefields.org/learn/biographies/sybil-ludington.

xiii **She was immortalized**: "Sybil Ludington," Women on Stamps: Part I, Smithsonian National Postal Museum, https://postalmuseum.si.edu/exhibition/women-on-stamps
-part-1-forming-the-nation-revolutionary-fighters/sybil-ludington.

xiii **"Ludington remained obscured"**: "Sybil Ludington," American Battlefield Trust.

xiv **New work had cast doubt**: Paula D. Hunt, "Sybil Ludington, the Female Paul Revere: The Making of a Revolutionary War Heroine," *New England Quarterly* 88, no. 2 (2015): 188–89.

xiv **A paper published**: Hunt, "Sybil Ludington, the Female Paul Revere," 188–94.

xiv **Ludington's descendants provided**: Hunt, "Sybil Ludington, the Female Paul Revere," 190, 196.

xiv **points to Ludington's exclusion:** Hunt, "Sybil Ludington, the Female Paul Revere," 194.

xvi **"It's as if she never":** Interview with Carol Berkin, July 23, 2021.

xix **"We don't need":** Mattie Kahn, "The World According to Greta," *Glamour,* October 22, 2019, https://www.glamour.com/story/women-of-the-year-2019-greta-thunberg.

xxii **calls it "premature knowing":** Nazera Sadiq Wright, *Black Girlhood in the Nineteenth Century* (Urbana: University of Illinois Press, 2016): 60–92.

CHAPTER ONE: MATERIAL GIRLS: DREAMERS AND SCHEMERS AT THE DAWN OF A LABOR MOVEMENT

1 **Hanson estimated that:** Harriet H. Robinson, *Loom and Spindle: Or Life Among the Early Mill Girls with a Sketch of "The Lowell Offering" and Some of Its Contributors* (Boston: Thomas Y. Crowell & Company, 1898), 83–84.

2 **When the appointed hour:** William Moran, *The Belles of New England: The Women of the Textile Mills and the Families Whose Wealth They Wove* (New York: Thomas Dunne Books, 2002), 31.

2 **One participant delivered:** Robinson, *Loom and Spindle,* 83.

2 **"Oh! Isn't it":** Robinson, *Loom and Spindle,* 84.

2 **It would be decades before:** Jonathan Grossman, "The Coal Strike of 1902: Turning Point in U.S. Policy," United States Department of Labor, https://www.dol.gov/general /aboutdol/history/coalstrike; "Woolworth to Shut Its Detroit Stores," *New York Times,* March 1, 1937, https://www.nytimes.com/1937/03/01/archives/woolworth-to-shut-its -detroit-stores-area-chief-says-all-40-with.html.

2 **In Massachusetts, women lost:** Dianne Avery and Alfred S. Konefsky, "The Daughters of Job: Property Rights and Women's Lives in Mid-Nineteenth-Century Massachusetts," *Law and History Review* 10, no. 2 (1992): 326.

3 **Their mastermind was:** Moran, *The Belles of New England,* 14.

3 **When he returned:** Moran, *The Belles of New England,* 15.

3 **Over time, Lowell's partners:** Moran, *The Belles of New England,* 15.

3 **The influx was so rapid:** Chad Montrie, "'I Think Less of the Factory Than of My Native Dell': Labor, Nature, and the Lowell 'Mill Girls,'" *Environmental History* 9, no. 2 (2004): 282.

4 **The salaries could amount:** Hannah Josephson, *The Golden Threads: New England's Mill Girls and Magnates* (New York: Duell, Sloan and Pearce, 1949), 6.

4 **Their income paid:** Sylvia Jenkins Cook, "'Oh Dear! How the Factory Girls Do Rig Up': Lowell's Self-Fashioning Workingwomen," *New England Quarterly* 83, no. 2 (2010): 220.

4 **Now the daughters:** Josephson, *The Golden Threads,* 22–24.

4 **When the novelist:** Anthony Trollope, *North America* (New York: Harper & Brothers Publishers, 1862), 274.

5 **Lowell envisioned the job:** Moran, *The Belles of New England,* 15.

5 **But he couldn't hold:** Josephson, *The Golden Threads,* 22.

5 **His habit of designating:** Moran, *The Belles of New England,* 52.

5 **Girls were a problem:** Josephson, *The Golden Threads,* 23.

5 **Housemothers were hired:** Josephson, *The Golden Threads,* 23–24.

6   **Nichols graduated in 1854:** Moran, *The Belles of New England*, 8–9.

6   **If parents now see:** John Demos and Virginia Demos, "Adolescence in Historical Perspective," *Journal of Marriage and Family* 31, no. 4 (1969): 633.

6   **Books aimed at older:** Demos and Demos, "Adolescence in Historical Perspective," 634.

6   **These books, with titles like:** Demos and Demos, "Adolescence in Historical Perspective," 633–34.

7   **Lowell's technological innovations:** Josephson, *The Golden Threads*, 6.

7   **The writer James Fenimore Cooper:** Moran, *The Belles of New England*, 12.

7   **In June 1833:** "Andrew Jackson in New England," *Proceedings of the Massachusetts Historical Society* 56 (1922–1923): 253.

7   **In the crowd, someone marveled:** "Andrew Jackson in New England," *Proceedings of the Massachusetts Historical Society*, 234.

7   **He compares them:** Moran, *The Belles of New England*, 8.

7   **William Moran writes:** Moran, *The Belles of New England*, 12.

8   **The "determinist narratives":** Lori Merish, *Archives of Labor: Working-Class Women and Literary Culture in the Antebellum United States* (Durham, NC: Duke University Press, 2017), 97–98.

8   **The risk of their defilement:** Moran, *The Belles of New England*, 8.

8   **The workers had retained:** Charles Dickens, *American Notes for General Circulation* (1842; repr., New York: Penguin Books, 2000), 77. See also George Frederick Kenngott, *The Record of a City: A Social Survey of Lowell, Massachusetts* (New York: Macmillan Company, 1912), 14.

8   **And like Dickens:** Moran, *The Belles of New England*, 15.

9   **Broadsides advertised jobs:** "75 Young Women 15 to 35 Years of Age, Wanted to Work in the Cotton Mills," c. 1870, Baker Old Class Collection, Baker Library, Harvard Business School, Harvard University.

9   **Hanson started in the Lowell:** Robinson, *Loom and Spindle*, 159.

9   **At first, she worked:** Claudia Bushman, *"A Good Poor Man's Wife": Being a Chronicle of Harriet Hanson Robinson and Her Family in Nineteenth-Century New England* (Hanover, NH: University Press of New England, 1998), 14.

9   **In her book, she describes:** Bushman, *"A Good Poor Man's Wife": Being a Chronicle of Harriet Hanson Robinson*, 9.

9   **That meant "unrelenting household labor":** Bushman, *"A Good Poor Man's Wife": Being a Chronicle of Harriet Hanson Robinson*, 13–14.

9   **Those leftover minutes:** Robinson, *Loom and Spindle*, 30.

10 **He identifies three:** Julie Husband, "'The White Slave of the North': Lowell Mill Women and the Reproduction of 'Free' Labor," *Legacy* 16, no. 1 (1999): 18.

10 **Their work, their cash:** Husband, "'The White Slave of the North,'" 18.

10 **Being denied it was:** Husband, "'The White Slave of the North,'" 19–20.

11 **Fears about shopping-obsessed:** T. H. Breen, *The Marketplace of Revolution: How Consumer Politics Shaped American Independence* (Oxford: Oxford University Press, 2004), 173.

11 **Boots and shoes:** Moran, *Belles of New England*, 11.

12 **Season tickets were issued:** Josephson, *The Golden Threads*, 86.

12 **Hanson writes in her memoir:** Robinson, *Loom and Spindle*, 42–43.

12   **Without the work:** Robinson, *Loom and Spindle*, 65–66.

12   **A Harvard professor:** Doug Stewart, "Proud to Be a Mill Girl," *American Heritage*, Spring 2012, https://www.americanheritage.com/proud-be-mill-girl.

12   **Affluent women kicked off:** Sylvia Jenkins Cook, "'Oh Dear! How the Factory Girls Do Rig Up': Lowell's Self-Fashioning Workingwomen," *New England Quarterly* 83, no. 2 (2010): 220.

12   **one worker articulated:** Cook, "'Oh Dear! How the Factory Girls Do Rig Up,'" 241.

13   **Curfew was not:** Josephson, *The Golden Threads*, 75–76.

13   **People died in the mills:** Moran, *The Belles of New England*, 22–23.

13   **Girls boarded up to:** Josephson, *The Golden Threads*, 69.

13   **It also meant that:** Josephson, *The Golden Threads*, 23.

13   **Turnover was a constant:** Josephson, *The Golden Threads*, 236–37.

13   **With the mushrooming:** Thomas Dublin, *Women at Work: The Transformation of Work and Community in Lowell, Massachusetts, 1826–1860* (New York: Columbia University Press, 1993), 100.

13   **A unilateral withdrawal:** Josephson, *The Golden Threads*, 230.

14   **In 1829, sixty weavers:** Josephson, *The Golden Threads*, 231.

14   **Faced with an incandescent workforce:** Thomas Dublin, "Women, Work, and Protest in the Early Lowell Mills: 'The Oppressing Hand of Avarice Would Enslave Us,'" *Labor History* 16 (1975): 100.

14   **The *Boston Post*:** "Turn-Out at Lowell," *The Boston Evening Transcript*, February 17, 1834.

14   **Enough withdrew their savings:** Dublin, "Women, Work, and Protest in the Early Lowell Mills," 107.

14   **That same weekend:** "Union Is Power," *Vermont Courier*, February 28, 1834.

14   **The factories had no trouble:** Dublin, "Women, Work, and Protest in the Early Lowell Mills," 110.

14   **The action this time:** Robinson, *Loom and Spindle*, 84.

15   **"Not one of them":** Robinson, *Loom and Spindle*, 83–86.

15   **"As I looked back":** Robinson, *Loom and Spindle*, 85.

15   **Hanson was eleven:** Josephson, *The Golden Threads*, 237–38.

15   **The new organization:** Josephson, *The Golden Threads*, 238.

15   **It insisted that:** "Constitution of the Lowell Factory Girls Association," in *Feminist Manifestos: A Global Documentary Reader*, ed. Penny A. Weiss (New York: New York University Press, 2018), 54–55.

16   **Since books were forbidden:** Josephson, *The Golden Threads*, 87.

16   **Another memorized the Bible:** Allan MacDonald, "Lowell: A Commercial Utopia," *New England Quarterly* 10, no. 1 (1937): 47.

16   **Once the two publications:** MacDonald, "Lowell: A Commercial Utopia," 48.

16   ***A New England Girlhood*:** Lucy Larcom, *A New England Girlhood: Outlined from Memory* (New York: Houghton Mifflin Company, 1889), 212.

16   **Larcom wrote that:** Larcom, *A New England Girlhood*, 211.

16   **Later, another worker-led:** Moran, *The Belles of New England*, 41.

17   ***The Offering* found:** Moran, *The Belles of New England*, 40.

17   **The preacher William Ellery Channing:** Josephson, *The Golden Threads*, 188.

17   **Larcom started as:** Chaim M. Rosenberg, *Child Labor in America: A History* (Jefferson, NC: McFarland & Company, 2013), 16.

17 **She was, like Hanson:** Josephson, *The Golden Threads*, 64.

17 **Larcom was eleven:** Rosenberg, *Child Labor in America*, 76.

17 **She was twenty-one:** Rosenberg, *Child Labor in America*, 16.

17 **Of course, she wrote:** Josephson, *The Golden Threads*, 89.

17 **"Other nations can look":** MacDonald, "Lowell: A Commercial Utopia," 49.

18 **The historian Sylvia Jenkins Cook:** Cook, "'Oh Dear! How the Factory Girls Do Rig Up!'" 229.

18 **'the beauties of nature':** Cook, "'Oh Dear! How the Factory Girls Do Rig Up!'" 234.

18 **What could she add:** Cook, "'Oh Dear! How the Factory Girls Do Rig Up!'" 234.

18 **Another contributor composed:** Cook, "'Oh Dear! How the Factory Girls Do Rig Up!'" 234.

18 **Their responses included:** Cook, "'Oh Dear! How the Factory Girls Do Rig Up!'" 236.

18 **The idea of adolescence:** Crista DeLuzio, *Female Adolescence in American Scientific Thought, 1830–1930* (Baltimore: Johns Hopkins University Press, 2007), 90–91.

19 **Hanson is frank:** Robinson, *Loom and Spindle*, 82–86.

19 **Hanson's mother was fired:** Robinson, *Loom and Spindle*, 82–86.

19 **The newspaper added:** Moran, *The Belles of New England*, 28–29.

19 **After the 1836 walkout:** Moran, *The Belles of New England*, 31.

20 **The writer frames:** "Lowell—Its Aspects—Manufacturers—Conditions of Labor—Reforms," *New-York Daily Tribune*, May 14, 1846.

20 **In 1847, the same newspaper:** "New-Hampshire Ten-Hour Law," *New-York Daily Tribune*, August 11, 1847.

21 **The public picture:** Merish, *Archives of Labor*, 77–78.

21 **Larcom later questioned:** Lucy Larcom, *Idyl of Work* (Boston: James R. Osgood and Company, 1875), available from the University of Michigan Humanities at https://quod.lib.umich.edu/a/amverse/BAD5902.0001.001/1:14?rgn=div1;view=fulltext.

21 **In *The Voice*:** Moran, *The Belles of New England*, 41.

21 **A poem submitted:** Moran, *The Belles of New England*, 42.

22 **That number was reduced:** MacDonald, "Lowell: A Commercial Utopia," 60.

22 **The "old guard":** Robinson, *Loom and Spindle*, 82–86.

22 **"fought a dignified campaign":** Josephson, *The Golden Threads*, 227.

22 **The reformer association:** Moran, *The Belles of New England*, 44.

23 **When someone was sick:** Benita Eisler, *The Lowell Offering: Writings by New England Women (1840–1845)* (New York: W. W. Norton & Company), 44.

23 **attributed the formation:** Dublin, "Women, Work, and Protest in the Early Lowell Mills," 31.

23 **"It did not take long":** Philip S. Foner, *The Factory Girls* (Urbana: University of Illinois Press, 1977), xxii.

24 **The girls looked like:** Robinson, *Loom and Spindle*, 65–66.

24 **Charged with "but one":** Moran, *The Belles of New England*, 22.

24 **became an ardent:** "Harriet Hanson Robinson," National Park Service, https://www.nps.gov/lowe/learn/historyculture/robinson.htm.

24 **Abba Ann Goddard:** Moran, *The Belles of New England*, 45.

25 **"provided its contributors":** C. David Heymann, "Like Living Machines," *New York Times*, January 29, 1978.

26 **Per one report:** Moran, *The Belles of New England*, 22–23.

26 **five of them:** "141 Men and Girls Die in Waist Factory Fire; Trapped High Up in Washington Place Building; Street Strewn with Bodies; Piles of Dead Inside," *New York Times*, March 26, 1911.

26 **she had been given:** Robinson, *Loom and Spindle*, 73.

27 **"I felt that I belonged":** Lucy Larcom, "A New England Girlhood," in *Written by Herself: Autobiographies of American Women: An Anthology*, ed. Jill Ker Conway (New York: Vintage, 1992), 324.

CHAPTER TWO: THE MOUTH ON THAT GIRL: ANNA ELIZABETH DICKINSON AND A NATION AT WAR

29 **the fifth child:** J. Matthew Gallman, *America's Joan of Arc: The Life of Anna Elizabeth Dickinson* (Oxford: Oxford University Press, 2006), 9.

29 **She scored a clerk's position:** Gallman, *America's Joan of Arc*, 17.

29 **She became the first woman:** "Anna Elizabeth Dickinson," photograph by Mathew B. Brady, National Portrait Gallery, https://npg.si.edu/object/npg_NPG.87.290.

29 **She was so popular:** Interview with Kate Lemay, April 1, 2021.

30 **The word "precocious":** Gallman, *America's Joan of Arc*, 9.

30 **his speech was so vehement:** Judith Anderson, "Anna Dickinson, Antislavery Radical," *Pennsylvania History: A Journal of Mid-Atlantic Studies* 3, no. 3 (1936): 149.

30 **In a moment of desperation:** Gallman, *America's Joan of Arc*, 9.

30 **She told Tarbell:** Anna Elizabeth Dickinson, Anna E. Dickinson Papers: General Correspondence, 1859–1911; Ida M. Tarbell, 1910, Manuscript/Mixed Material, Library of Congress, https://www.loc.gov/item/mss184240238.

30 **Frederick Douglass and Robert Purvis:** Gallman, *America's Joan of Arc*, 10.

30 **It was notable:** Ashley Council, "Ringing Liberty's Bell," *Pennsylvania History* 87, no. 3 (2020): 496–97.

31 **Her first published:** Gallman, *America's Joan of Arc*, 10–11.

31 **Or did its citizens:** Anna Elizabeth Dickinson, "Southern Outrage," *Liberator*, February 22, 1856, 32.

31 **"How long will":** Dickinson, "Southern Outrage," 32.

31 **She signed the letter:** Dickinson, "Southern Outrage," 32.

32 **That conviction gave:** Gallman, *America's Joan of Arc*, 12.

32 **Others submitted letters:** Gallman, *America's Joan of Arc*, 14.

33 **Jacobs must have known:** Franny Nudelman, "Harriet Jacobs and the Sentimental Politics of Female Suffering," *ELH* 59, no. 4 (1992): 957.

33 **"The truth can never":** Harriet A. Jacobs, "Letter from a Fugitive Slave: Slaves Sold under Peculiar Circumstances," *New-York Daily Tribune*, June 21, 1853, 6, https://docsouth.unc.edu/fpn/jacobs/support16.html.

33 **Public speaking became:** Gallman, *America's Joan of Arc*, 13.

33 **Sojourner Truth, the preacher:** Gallman, *America's Joan of Arc*, 14.

34 **She declined:** Gallman, *America's Joan of Arc*, 16.

34 **"In Heaven's name, sir":** Gallman, *America's Joan of Arc*, 16.

34 **"However erratic, enthusiastic":** Gallman, *America's Joan of Arc*, 17.

34 **"Her greatest oratorical":** James Harvey Young, "Anna Elizabeth and the Civil War: For and Against Lincoln," *Mississippi Valley Historical Review* 31, no. 1 (1944): 62.

35 **But revolutions in communication:** Manisha Sinha, *The Slave's Cause: A History of Abolition* (New Haven, CT: Yale University Press, 2016), 228.

35 **Sinha calls their strategies:** Sinha, *The Slave's Cause*, 228.

35 **A carpenter hid him:** Sinha, *The Slave's Cause*, 234.

35 **She was in a sense:** Anderson, "Anna Dickinson, Antislavery Radical," 152.

35 **The recent battle:** Anderson, "Anna Dickinson, Antislavery Radical," 152.

36 **Fellow abolitionists—men in particular:** Gallman, *America's Joan of Arc*, 45.

36 **she wrote home:** Gallman, *America's Joan of Arc*, 22.

36 **Her audience arrived:** Young, "Anna Elizabeth Dickinson and the Civil War," 62.

36 **In a lookback:** Anderson, "Anna Dickinson, Antislavery Radical," 154.

36 **When she lectured:** Anderson, "Anna Dickinson, Antislavery Radical," 154.

37 **"It must be a great trial":** Gallman, *America's Joan of Arc*, 23.

37 **heralded her arrival:** Young, "Anna Elizabeth Dickinson and the Civil War," 65.

37 **"perfect mistress of her art":** Gallman, *America's Joan of Arc*, 27

37 **The abolitionist Wendell Phillips:** Young, "Anna Elizabeth Dickinson and the Civil War," 65.

37 **Outlets that sided:** Young, "Anna Elizabeth Dickinson and the Civil War," 65.

38 **she received a hand-delivered:** Young, "Anna Elizabeth Dickinson and the Civil War," 68.

38 **"red-lipped, slim-waisted":** Gallman, *America's Joan of Arc*, 3.

38 **Or was she so inflamed:** Gallman, *America's Joan of Arc*, 3.

38 **When she did:** Young, "Anna Elizabeth Dickinson and the Civil War," 69.

39 **One newspaper claims:** Gallman, *America's Joan of Arc*, 38.

39 **"She was the young elephant":** Gallman, *America's Joan of Arc*, 23.

39 **She was charged:** Susan Visvanathan, "Representing Joan of Arc," *India International Centre Quarterly* 24, no. 4 (1997): 22–25.

40 **The scholar Françoise Meltzer:** Françoise Meltzer, *For Fear of the Fire: Joan of Arc and the Limits of Subjectivity* (Chicago: University of Chicago Press, 2001), 203.

40 **The speaking circuit declined:** Gallman, *America's Joan of Arc*, 136.

40 **In 1876, she premiered:** Gallman, *America's Joan of Arc*, 145.

40 **In 1893, the editors:** Frances Elizabeth Willard and Mary Ashton Rice Livermore, *A Woman of the Century: Fourteen Hundred-Seventy Biographical Sketches Accompanied by Portraits of Leading American Women in All Walks of Life* (Buffalo, NY: Charles Wells Moulton, 1893), 246, https://archive.org/details/bub_gb_zXEEAAAAYAAJ/page/241/mode/2up.

40 **One historian notes:** Gallman, *America's Joan of Arc*, 211.

41 **to describe her short hair:** Gallman, *America's Joan of Arc*, 175.

41 **"You want to sit down":** Gallman, *America's Joan of Arc*, 175.

41 **She drank more:** Gallman, *America's Joan of Arc*, 177.

41 **suffragist Susan B. Anthony:** Ann D. Gordon, review of *America's Joan of Arc: The Life of Anna Elizabeth Dickinson*, by J. Matthew Gallman, *Pennsylvania Magazine of History and Biography* 131, no. 3 (2007): 329.

41 **None panned out:** Gallman, *America's Joan of Arc*, 178–80.

42 **She never spoke to:** Gallman, *America's Joan of Arc*, 181.

42 **In 1898, she won two:** Gallman, *America's Joan of Arc*, 198.

42 **Lucretia Mott spent:** Debra Michals, "Lucretia Mott," National Women's History Museum, 2017, https://www.womenshistory.org/education-resources/biographies/lucretia-mott.

42 **The Grimké sisters were:** Kerri Lee Alexander, "Sarah Moore Grimké," National Women's History Museum, 2018, https://www.womenshistory.org/education-resources/biographies/sarah-moore-grimke.

42 **A thousand people attended:** Nell Irvin Painter, *Sojourner Truth: A Life, A Symbol* (New York: W. W. Norton & Company, 1996), 255.

42 **Both cite a quote:** Anna Elizabeth Dickinson: 1842–1932, historical marker erected on June 2, 2001, Goshen, New York, https://www.hmdb.org/m.asp?m=25762.

CHAPTER THREE: SEE ME:
A GIRL'S BATTLE FOR WOMEN'S SUFFRAGE

43 **The march was one:** Cathleen D. Cahill, *Recasting the Vote: How Women of Color Transformed the Suffrage Movement* (Chapel Hill: University of North Carolina, 2020), 25.

43 **Lee was still:** Cahill, *Recasting the Vote*, 31.

44 **It went on to outline:** J. Matthew Gallman, *America's Joan of Arc: The Life of Anna Elizabeth Dickinson* (Oxford: Oxford University Press, 2006), 12.

44 **Frederick Douglass was:** Ellen Carol DuBois, *Suffrage: Women's Long Battle for the Vote* (New York: Simon & Schuster, 2020), 11.

44 **Charlotte Woodward, later:** For biographical information, see: Kat Eschner, "Only One Woman Who Was at the Seneca Falls Women's Rights Convention Lived to See Women Win the Vote," *Smithsonian*, July 19, 2017, https://www.smithsonianmag.com/smart-news/only-one-woman-who-was-seneca-falls-lived-see-women-win-vote-180964044/. Note: Charlotte Woodward's married name is sometimes spelled "Pierce" and sometimes recorded as "Peirce." In most contemporaneous writings, including in a death notice published in *The Philadelphia Inquirer* on March 16, 1924, it is spelled "Peirce." See also: Bill Hunt, "Signer #37: Charlotte Woodward, 'The Last Survivor,'" 100 Signers Project, July 2, 2021, https://www.100signersproject.com/signer-profiles/signer-37-charlotte-woodward-the-last-survivor. Hunt, creator of the 100 Signers Project, includes photocopies of census records that indicate the couple indeed spelled it "Peirce."

44 **Her parents relied on:** Rheta Childe Dorr, "The Eternal Question," *Collier's National Weekly*, October 30, 1920, 6.

44 **Her parents—and parents like them:** Dorr, "The Eternal Question," 6.

45 **Peirce told her interviewer:** Dorr, "The Eternal Question," 6.

45 **She died in 1924:** "Obituary: Mrs. Charlotte L. Peirce," *The Philadelphia Inquirer*, March 16, 1924, 17.

45 **"It is no loss":** Lisa Tetrault, *The Myth of Seneca Falls: Memory and the Women's Suffrage Movement, 1848–1989* (Chapel Hill: University of North Carolina Press, 2014), 1.

46 **When white women:** DuBois, *Suffrage*, 74–75.

46 **When some took their bid:** DuBois, *Suffrage*, 151.

46 **Between 1890 and 1896:** "Teach a Girl to Lead: Women's Suffrage in the U.S. by State," Center for American Women and Politics, August 2014, https://tag.rutgers.edu/wp-content/uploads/2014/05/suffrage-by-state.pdf.

46 **CESL reorganized as:** DuBois, *Suffrage*, 170.

47 **These organizers shrugged:** DuBois, *Suffrage*, 171.

47 **Students and recent grads "treated":** DuBois, *Suffrage*, 171.

47 **Over a decade after:** "Teach a Girl to Lead."

47 **"The agony is":** DuBois, *Suffrage*, 173.

47 **campaign for the California:** Philip S. Foner, *Women and the American Labor Movement* (New York: Free Press, 1982), 126–27.

47 **In November 1909:** Tony Michels, "Uprising of 20,000 (1909)," *Shalvi/Hyman Encyclopedia of Jewish Women*, December 31, 1999, Jewish Women's Archive, https://jwa.org /encyclopedia/article/uprising-of-20000-1909.

48 **"I have listened":** Foner, *Women and the American Labor Movement*, 137.

48 **The strike kicked off:** Zoe Greenberg, "Overlooked No More: Clara Lemlich Shavelson, Crusading Leader of Labor Rights," *New York Times*, August 1, 2018, https:// www.nytimes.com/2018/08/01/obituaries/overlooked-clara-lemlich-shavelson.html.

48 **One union leader:** Foner, *Women and the American Labor Movement*, 139.

49 **How else were women:** Foner, *Women and the American Labor Movement*, 141.

49 **"There was no doubt":** "Federation Women Fight over By-Laws," *New York Times*, December 3, 1909.

49 **College students collected funds:** Foner, *Women and the American Labor Movement*, 143.

49 **Rose Perr, a teenager:** Foner, *Women and the American Labor Movement*, 145.

50 **When the strikers protested:** Nancy Schrom Dye, *As Equals and as Sisters: Feminism, the Labor Movement, and the Women's Trade Union League of New York* (Columbia: University of Missouri Press, 1980), 132.

50 **Leonora O'Reilly, the garment worker:** DuBois, *Suffrage*, 175–80.

51 **And still, state government:** DuBois, *Suffrage*, 180.

51 **girls could pull it off:** DuBois, *Suffrage*, 180.

51 **It helped that Blatch:** Cahill, *Recasting the Vote*, 33.

52 **The event started:** Ellen Carol DuBois, *Harriot Stanton Blatch and the Winning of Woman Suffrage* (New Haven, CT: Yale University Press, 1999), 141.

52 **But he conceded:** "Parade of the Women," *New York Times*, May 6, 1911, https://times machine.nytimes.com/timesmachine/1911/05/06/105026491.html?pageNumber=12.

52 **"No cause," he wrote:** "Parade of the Women."

52 **"The enemy must be":** DuBois, *Harriot Stanton Blatch*, 141.

53 **She was "clad":** "Chinese Girl Wants Vote: Miss Lee, Ready to Enter Barnard, to Ride in Suffrage Parade," *New-York Tribune*, April 13, 1912.

53 **a lot of Chinese girls:** Cahill, *Recasting the Vote*, 33–35.

53 **How was it possible:** Cahill, *Recasting the Vote*, 26–28.

53 **In *The Oregonian*:** "Chinese Women Dine with White," *Oregonian*, April 12, 1912.

54 **Mabel was given:** Cahill, *Recasting the Vote*, 32.

54 **Chinese nationalist leaders:** Hua Liang, "Fighting for a New Life: Social and Patriotic Activism of Chinese American Women in New York City, 1900–1945," *Journal of American Ethnic History* 17, no. 2 (1988): 24–25.

54 **Lee had become:** Liang, "Fighting for a New Life," 25.

54 **She invoked her:** Cahill, *Recasting the Vote*, 32.

54 **Lee, who would later:** Veronica Chambers et al., "Meet the Brave but Overlooked Women of Color Who Fought for the Vote," *New York Times*, August 19, 2020.

55 **"Is that not natural"**: "Chinese Women to Parade for Woman Suffrage," *New York Times*, April 14, 1912.

55 ***The New York Times* blared**: "Vast Suffrage Host Is on Parade To-Day," *New York Times*, May 4, 1912.

55 **Despite their historically poor treatment**: "Vast Suffrage Host Is on Parade To-Day."

56 **She marched with**: DuBois, *Suffrage*, 190–93.

56 **Several women who marched**: Cahill, *Recasting the Vote*, 35.

56 **One reporter considered**: DuBois, *Harriot Stanton Blatch*, 142.

57 **In 1914, an attendee**: T. V. Soong, "Eastern Conference at Amherst, Mass.," *The Chinese Students' Monthly* 10, no. 1 (October 1914): 32.

57 **Lee could boost**: Cahill, *Recasting the Vote*, 148.

57 **Week after week, she**: Cahill, *Recasting the Vote*, 150.

57 **She was part of a**: Jon Savage, *Teenagers: The Prehistory of Youth Culture: 1875–1945* (New York: Penguin Books, 2008), 208.

57 **Between 1919 and 1922 alone**: Savage, *Teenagers*, 208.

57 **Soldiers who had just**: Thomas D. Snyder, ed., *120 Years of American Education: A Statistical Portrait* (Washington, D.C.: Center for Education Statistics, 1993), 82–84.

58 **Anna Kong made a splash**: Cahill, *Recasting the Vote*, 152.

58 **The "welfare of China"**: Mabel Ping-Hua Lee, "China's Submerged Half," transcript of speech delivered at the Suffrage Shop of the Women's Political Union, New York, 1915, https://timtsengdotnet.files.wordpress.com/2013/12/mabel-lee-speech-china_s -submerged.pdf.

58 **If the Union**: Lee, "China's Submerged Half."

58 **in 1915, Lee was**: Cahill, *Recasting the Vote*, 154.

59 **Soong smeared her**: Cahill, *Recasting the Vote*, 160.

59 **New York enfranchised**: "Teach a Girl to Lead."

59 **After the race**: Cahill, *Recasting the Vote*, 160.

59 **In one of the editorials**: Mabel Ping-Hua Lee, "Meaning of Women's Suffrage," *The Chinese Students' Monthly* 9, no. 7 (May 1914): 528.

60 **She graduated in 1921**: Cahill, *Recasting the Vote*, 181.

60 **To travel to Europe**: Cahill, *Recasting the Vote*, 274.

60 **She died in 1965**: Cahill, *Recasting the Vote*, 277.

60 **The First Chinese Baptist Church**: Cahill, *Recasting the Vote*, 277.

CHAPTER FOUR: BAD GIRLS:
TROUBLEMAKERS AND THE CIVIL RIGHTS MOVEMENT

63 **Oliver Brown walked**: DeNeen L. Brown, "The Determined Father Who Took Linda Brown by the Hand and Made History," *Washington Post*, March 27, 2018.

64 **It's her last name**: Brown, "The Determined Father Who Took Linda Brown by the Hand and Made History."

64 **When Chief Justice Earl Warren**: *Brown v. Board of Education*, 347 U.S. 483 (1954), https://supreme.justia.com/cases/federal/us/347/483/.

64 **"What a wonderful world"**: Arnold Rampersad, *Ralph Ellison: A Biography* (New York: Vintage Books, 2007), 298.

64 **"In each of the cases"**: *Brown v. Board of Education*.

65 **He "consigns parents":** Justin Driver, *The Schoolhouse Gate: Public Education, the Supreme Court, and the Battle for the American Mind* (New York: Vintage Books, 2018), 249.

65 **She made her peace:** Richard Kluger, *Simple Justice: The History of* Brown v. Board of Education *and Black America's Struggle for Equality* (1975; repr., New York: Vintage Books, 2004), 454.

65 **Her paternal grandmother:** Kluger, *Simple Justice*, 455.

65 **Her uncle, Vernon:** Kluger, *Simple Justice*, 455.

66 **Vernon Johns was a pastor:** Lynne Olson, *Freedom's Daughters: The Unsung Heroines of the Civil Rights Movement from 1830 to 1970* (New York: Scribner, 2001), 81.

66 **He identified what he called:** Kluger, *Simple Justice*, 455.

66 **He railed against white:** Bernard K. Duffy and Richard W. Leeman, *The Will of a People: A Critical Anthology of Great African American Speeches* (Carbondale, IL: Southern University Press, 2012), 252.

66 **His hot-tempered sermons:** Duffy and Leeman, *The Will of a People*, 242.

66 **She couldn't be quiet:** Interview with Joan Cobbs, May 3, 2021.

66 **When she first moved:** Kluger, *Simple Justice*, 454–55.

66 **Their textbooks were tattered:** Joan Cobbs interview.

67 **At Moton, the standards:** Olson, *Freedom's Daughters*, 80.

67 **"I told her how sick":** Kluger, *Simple Justice*, 468.

67 **Davenport threw the question:** Joan Cobbs interview.

67 **That prompt proved:** Kluger, *Simple Justice*, 468.

67 **But Johns invoked:** Kluger, *Simple Justice*, 468.

67 **"We knew we had":** Rebecca de Schweinitz, *If We Could Change the World: Young People and America's Long Struggle for Racial Equality* (Chapel Hill: University of North Carolina Press, 2011), 220.

68 **First, she dismissed:** Kluger, *Simple Justice*, 469.

68 **"Out," she shouted:** Olson, *Freedom's Daughters*, 81.

68 **Her sister, Joan:** Joan Cobbs interview.

68 **With that, she led:** Olson, *Freedom's Daughters*, 81.

68 **Two girls signed it:** Kluger, *Simple Justice*, 471.

69 **"It seemed like reaching":** Kluger, *Simple Justice*, 471.

69 **He worried it was:** Kluger, *Simple Justice*, 477.

69 **A week after the representatives:** Kluger, *Simple Justice*, 477.

70 **But as a movement person:** de Schweinitz, *If We Could Change the World*, 221.

70 **"It came to me":** Olson, *Freedom's Daughters*, 82.

71 **The parents of Farmville:** Olson, *Freedom's Daughters*, 82.

71 **"Give me the doll":** Kenneth B. Clark, *Prejudice and Your Child* (Middletown, CT: Wesleyan University Press, 1963), 23.

71 **Most Black children:** Clark, *Prejudice and Your Child*, 23.

71 **The Clarks' work:** *Brown v. Board of Education*.

71 **In parsing the effects:** "A Revealing Experiment: *Brown v. Board* and 'The Doll Test,'" NAACP Legal Defense and Educational Fund, https://www.naacpldf.org/brown-vs-board/significance-doll-test/.

72 **She said to her grandmother:** Kluger, *Simple Justice*, 472.

72 **She wore a pristine:** David Margolick, "Through a Lens, Darkly," *Vanity Fair*, September 24, 2007, https://www.vanityfair.com/news/2007/09/littlerock200709.

72 **He federalized the Arkansas:** Margolick, "Through a Lens, Darkly."

73 **A pamphlet circulated:** de Schweinitz, *If We Could Change the World*, 125.

73 **A father called on:** de Schweinitz, *If We Could Change the World*, 125.

73 **"I just couldn't":** "Before Rosa Parks, a Teenager Defied Segregation on an Alabama Bus," *All Things Considered*, NPR, March 2, 2015, https://www.npr.org/sections /codeswitch/2015/02/27/389563788/before-rosa-parks-a-teenager-defied-segregation -on-an-alabama-bus.

74 **It was sedate:** Phillip Hoose, *Claudette Colvin: Twice Toward Justice* (New York: Square Fish, 2009), 12.

74 **"A 'No Trespassing'":** Hoose, *Claudette Colvin*, 12.

74 **The one riddle:** Hoose, *Claudette Colvin*, 12.

74 **Colvin remembered him:** Hoose, *Claudette Colvin*, 12.

75 **lest their hair:** Hoose, *Claudette Colvin*, 17.

75 **Her mother put:** Hoose, *Claudette Colvin*, 17.

75 **Her rage would:** Ellen Levine, *Freedom's Children: Young Civil Rights Activists Tell Their Own Stories* (1993; repr., New York: Puffin Books, 2000), 20.

76 **The omnipresent threat:** Olson, *Freedom's Daughters*, 202; de Schweinitz, *If We Could Change the World*, 312–25.

76 **In 1949, scholars:** de Schweinitz, *If We Could Change the World*, 209.

77 **"Whenever one of":** Hoose, *Claudette Colvin*, 12.

77 **In 1943, at an NAACP conference:** de Schweinitz, *If We Could Change the World*, 184.

77 **"For some reason":** Hoose, *Claudette Colvin*, 22.

78 **What good had placating:** de Schweinitz, *If We Could Change the World*, 215.

78 **"I wrote I was":** Levine, *Freedom's Children*, 20.

78 **"Everybody said, 'Oh, Claudette!'":** Levine, *Freedom's Children*, 21.

79 **"I kept wearing it":** Levine, *Freedom's Children*, 22.

79 **Both were men:** Hoose, *Claudette Colvin*, 29.

79 **"I was done talking":** Hoose, *Claudette Colvin*, 29.

80 **"She doesn't have to":** Levine, *Freedom's Children*, 23.

80 **The driver pointed:** Hoose, *Claudette Colvin*, 34.

80 **The police report filed:** Arrest report for Claudette Colvin, March 2, 1955, Martin Luther King, Jr. Research and Education Institute, Online King Records Access (OKRA) database, http://okra.stanford.edu/transcription/document_images/undecided/550302 -001.pdf.

81 **"It was the worst sound":** Hoose, *Claudette Colvin*, 36.

81 **In another interview:** Levine, *Freedom's Children*, 25.

81 **"Bless her heart":** Olson, *Freedom's Daughters*, 93.

81 **Leaders and activists:** Olson, *Freedom's Daughters*, 92.

82 **"The wonderful thing":** Hoose, *Claudette Colvin*, 39.

82 **"I think they knew":** Hoose, *Claudette Colvin*, 42.

82 **"I was looking":** Hoose, *Claudette Colvin*, 45.

82 **The *Alabama Journal*:** "Negro Girl Found Guilty of Segregation Violation," *Alabama Journal*, March 19, 1955.

83 **"Doubts crept in":** Hoose, *Claudette Colvin*, 52.

83 **"If the white press":** Gary Younge, "She Would Not Be Moved," *Guardian*, December 15, 2000, https://www.theguardian.com/theguardian/2000/dec/16/weekend7.weekend12.

83 **her "agonized sobs":** Jo Ann Gibson Robinson, *The Montgomery Bus Boycott and the Women Who Started It* (Knoxville: University of Tennessee Press, 1987), 42.

83 **"Nowadays, you'd call it":** Younge, "She Would Not Be Moved."

84 **"Well, who wouldn't be":** Hoose, *Claudette Colvin*, 49.

84 **Someone who looked:** "Before Rosa Parks, a Teenager Defied Segregation on an Alabama Bus."

84 **She told the driver:** Stewart Burns, ed., *Daybreak of Freedom* (Chapel Hill: University of North Carolina Press, 1997), 6.

85 **Smith's father had paid:** Olivia B. Waxman, "'I Was Not Going to Stand.' Rosa Parks Predecessors Recall Their History-Making Acts of Resistance," *Time*, March 2, 2020, https://time.com/5786220/claudette-colvin-mary-louise-smith/.

85 **She lived in a frame house:** Hoose, *Claudette Colvin*, 60.

85 **Robinson had drafted:** Olson, *Freedom's Daughters*, 93.

CHAPTER FIVE: LOST LEADERS:
THE MOVEMENT'S INVISIBLE GIRLS

87 **She was thinking about:** Jeanne Theoharis, *A More Beautiful and Terrible History: The Uses and Misuses of Civil Rights History* (Boston: Beacon Press, 2018), 192.

88 **The protest would start:** Lynne Olson, *Freedom's Daughters: The Unsung Heroines of the Civil Rights Movement from 1830 to 1970* (New York: Scribner, 2001), 111.

88 **She made thirty-five thousand:** Olson, *Freedom's Daughters*, 112.

88 **Parks's friend Johnnie:** Olson, *Freedom's Daughters*, 114.

88 **When Parks arrived:** Rosa Parks and Jim Haskins, *Rosa Parks: My Story* (New York: Puffin Books, 1992), 133.

88 **Homes and cars:** Olson, *Freedom's Daughters*, 117.

88 **Desegregation seemed inconceivable:** Olson, *Freedom's Daughters*, 116.

89 **Another advocated for hiring:** Stewart Burns, ed., *Daybreak of Freedom* (Chapel Hill: University of North Carolina Press, 1997), 98.

89 **No one did:** Olson, *Freedom's Daughters*, 123.

89 **Two of them were teenage:** Phillip Hoose, *Claudette Colvin: Twice Toward Justice* (New York: Square Fish, 2009), 85.

90 **if he dared:** Parks and Haskins, *Rosa Parks*, 30.

90 **"I had a feeling":** Interview with Doris Crenshaw, June 9, 2021.

90 **Colvin, who joined:** Jeanne Theoharis and Say Burgin, "Pitting Rosa Parks Against Claudette Colvin Distorts History," *Washington Post*, October 19, 2022, https://www.washingtonpost.com/made-by-history/2022/10/19/rosa-parks-documentary/.

90 **The workshop introduced:** Olson, *Freedom's Daughters*, 106–7.

91 **when her two-week:** Theoharis, *A More Beautiful and Terrible History*, 192.

91 **When she went home:** Theoharis, *A More Beautiful and Terrible History*, 192.

92 **Colvin—attuned as:** Jeanne Theoharis, *The Rebellious Life of Mrs. Rosa Parks* (Boston: Beacon Press, 2013), 58.

92 **passing around handouts:** Theoharis, *A More Beautiful and Terrible History*, 192.

92 **The historian Jeanne Theoharis:** Interview with Jeanne Theoharis, May 12, 2021.

92 **Parks did not become:** "Local NAACP Rolls Up Big Membership," *Los Angeles Sentinel,* April 12, 1956.

93 **Wasn't that the point:** Theoharis, *The Rebellious Life of Mrs. Rosa Parks,* 58.

93 **"We had the same":** Ellen Levine, *Freedom's Children: Young Civil Rights Activists Tell Their Own Stories* (1993; repr., New York: Puffin Books, 2000), 26.

93 **She was denied:** Hoose, *Claudette Colvin,* 67.

94 **She used the time:** Hoose, *Claudette Colvin,* 70–71.

95 **"I had one last speech":** Hoose, *Claudette Colvin,* 85.

95 **Instead, she had an infant:** Hoose, *Claudette Colvin,* 89.

95 **He wasn't responsible:** Willy S. Leventhal, ed., *The Children Coming On: A Retrospective of the Montgomery Bus Boycott and the Oral Histories of Boycott Participants* (Montgomery, AL: River City Publishing, 1998), 156–58.

95 **Colvin was under oath:** Burns, *Daybreak of Freedom,* 77.

96 **"We sat there":** Hoose, *Claudette Colvin,* 88.

96 **Before Colvin went to sleep:** Hoose, *Claudette Colvin,* 101.

97 **"I didn't hear from":** Hoose, *Claudette Colvin,* 105.

97 **"There was all sorts":** Jeanne Theoharis interview.

98 **Neither were the other women:** Olson, *Freedom's Daughters,* 125–26.

98 **"Let Rosa be the one":** Brooks Barnes, "From Footnote to Fame in Civil Rights History," *New York Times,* November 25, 2009, https://www.nytimes.com/2009/11/26/books/26colvin.html.

99 **She did not return:** Susan Reyburn, "The Private Cost of Public Heroism: On Rosa Parks' Life in Detroit," *Lit Hub,* January 28, 2020, https://lithub.com/the-private-cost-of-public-heroism-on-rosa-parks-life-in-detroit/.

99 **observed with considerable ire:** Martin Luther King, Jr., *The Papers of Martin Luther King, Jr., Volume IV: Symbol of the Movement: January 1957–December 1958,* ed. Clayborne Carson et al. (Berkeley: University of California Press, 2000), 144n3.

100 **The "adultification" of Black girls:** Mihir Zaveri, "Body Camera Footage Shows Arrest by Orlando Police of 6-Year-Old at School," *New York Times,* February 27, 2020, https://www.nytimes.com/2020/02/27/us/orlando-6-year-old-arrested.html.

100 **teachers use words:** Monique W. Morris, *Pushout: The Criminalization of Black Girls in Schools* (New York: New Press, 2016), 11.

100 **It's a trend that:** Morris, *Pushout,* 2.

101 **"Here I have come":** Student Nonviolent Coordinating Committee, *Freedom School Poetry* (New York: Packers Press, 1966), 14.

102 **It was in visiting schools:** Theoharis, *A More Beautiful and Terrible History,* 148.

102 **"Too often teachers":** Theoharis, *A More Beautiful and Terrible History,* 149–50.

102 **The protests left behind:** Theoharis, *A More Beautiful and Terrible History,* 153.

103 **"Things were hard":** Interview with Joan Cobbs, May 3, 2021.

103 **"something that was tragic":** Joan Cobbs interview.

103 **"One day someone might":** Levine, *Freedom's Children,* 26.

103 **In a rare interview:** Barnes, "From Footnote to Fame in Civil Rights History."

103 **"I'm glad I did it":** Levine, *Freedom's Children,* 26.

104 **"It's every kind":** Joan Cobbs, interview.

CHAPTER SIX: CLIQUES: FEMALE FRIENDSHIP AND FREEDOM

108 **Oh, he could still:** Howard Zinn, "Finishing School for Pickets," *Nation*, August 6, 1960, https://www.thenation.com/article/archive/finishing-school-pickets/.

108 **the week of Valentine's:** David Halberstam, *The Children* (New York: Fawcett Books, 1998), 3.

108 **Then she felt:** Halberstam, *The Children*, 6.

109 **grounded in love:** Lynne Olson, *Freedom's Daughters: The Unsung Heroines of the Civil Rights Movement from 1830 to 1970* (New York: Scribner, 2001), 155.

109 **The protest would be held:** Olson, *Freedom's Daughters*, 156.

109 **The journalist David Halberstam:** Halberstam, *The Children*, 4.

109 **come up with an excuse:** Halberstam, *The Children*, 4.

109 **Nash steeled herself:** Halberstam, *The Children*, 10.

109 **She and her friends:** Diane Nash, "Address to the National Catholic Conference for Interracial Justice," transcript of speech delivered in Detroit, Michigan, August 25, 1961, https://awpc.cattcenter.iastate.edu/2019/08/09/address-to-the-national-catholic-conference-for-interracial-justice-august-25-1961/.

110 **"The Chaucer classes":** Fred Powledge, *Free at Last? The Civil Rights Movement and the People Who Made It* (New York: Little, Brown and Company, 1990), 252.

110 **The Freedom Ride:** Diane McWhorter, "The Enduring Courage of the Freedom Riders," *Journal of Blacks in Higher Education*, 61 (2008): 66.

110 **He was the cofounder:** McWhorter, "The Enduring Courage of the Freedom Riders," 67.

111 **The rides were designed:** McWhorter, "The Enduring Courage of the Freedom Riders," 67.

111 **Lewis was attacked:** Halberstam, *The Children*, 256.

111 **When rescue at last:** Halberstam, *The Children*, 264.

112 **No sooner were the groups:** Halberstam, *The Children*, 264.

112 **Nash collected almost:** Halberstam, *The Children*, 280.

113 **Susan, nineteen, would go:** Interview with Susan Wilbur Wamsley, July 8, 2021.

113 **was waving them in:** Taylor Branch, *Parting the Waters: America in the King Years, 1954–63* (New York: Simon & Schuster, 1988), 448.

114 **She could still recall:** Susan Wilbur Wamsley interview.

114 **He had his luggage:** Olson, *Freedom's Daughters*, 189.

115 **Smith was squeezed:** Olson, *Freedom's Daughters*, 194.

115 **"There were a lot":** Pete Seeger and Bob Reiser, *Everybody Says Freedom* (New York: W. W. Norton & Company, 1989), 65.

116 **But it made no:** Brenda Travis with John Obee, *Mississippi's Exiled Daughter: How My Civil Rights Baptism Under Fire Shaped My Life* (Montgomery, AL: NewSouth Books, 2018), 36.

116 **"I decided that I":** Olson, *Freedom's Daughters*, 203.

116 **"To me, it was":** Elizabeth Anne Payne et al., ed., *Mississippi Women: Their Histories, Their Lives,* vol. 2 (Athens: University of Georgia Press, 2010), 252.

116 **Emmett Till had been:** Harvey Parson, "Brenda Travis Took a Stand and Was Ordered to Leave State at 17 or Forfeit Her Freedom," *Mississippi Today*, August

17, 2018, https://mississippitoday.org/2018/08/17/brenda-travis-took-a-stand-and-was
-ordered-to-leave-state-at-17-or-forfeit-her-freedom/.

116 **the brutalization of Black men:** "A History of Racial Injustice Calendar," Equal
Justice Initiative, https://shop.eji.org/collections/books-calendars/products/a-history
-of-racial-injustice-calendar-2022. See "Black Woman Lynched by White Mob in Tennessee after They Couldn't Find Her Brother," March 15, 1901; "Mary Turner, Pregnant, Lynched in Georgia for Publicly Criticizing Husband's Lynching," May 19, 1918.

116 **Divens knew she deserved:** Olson, *Freedom's Daughters*, 203.

116 **In Moses, she:** Olson, *Freedom's Daughters*, 203.

117 **She knew on an emotional:** Travis and Obee, *Mississippi's Exiled Daughter*, 36.

117 **She knew it could:** Travis and Obee, *Mississippi's Exiled Daughter*, 37.

118 **Their arrival was:** Olson, *Freedom's Daughters*, 206.

118 **Who could put:** Travis and Obee, *Mississippi's Exiled Daughter*, 40.

118 **And though she was released:** Travis and Obee, *Mississippi's Exiled Daughter*, 44.

118 **"The kids ran out":** Olson, *Freedom's Daughters*, 207.

119 **That didn't appease:** David Ray, "Brave Times at Burglund High," *Jackson Free
Press*, February 19, 2014, https://www.jacksonfreepress.com/news/2014/feb/19/brave
-times-burglund-high/.

119 **it identified Bob Zellner:** "114 Negroes Arrested," *New York Times*, October 5, 1961,
https://timesmachine.nytimes.com/timesmachine/1961/10/05/101476447.html?
pageNumber=21.

119 **"For those of us":** Halberstam, *The Children*, 406.

120 **And for her service:** Travis and Obee, *Mississippi's Exiled Daughter*, 55.

120 **The witness was later:** Travis and Obee, *Mississippi's Exiled Daughter*, 44.

120 **Lee's heartbroken wife:** Halberstam, *The Children*, 409.

121 **"stood up and went against":** Olson, *Freedom's Daughters*, 210.

121 **"Here we are":** Olson, *Freedom's Daughters*, 210.

121 **For her book *Linked Lives*:** Lucy Rose Fischer, *Linked Lives: Adult Daughters and Their
Mothers* (New York: Harper & Row, 1987), 83.

121 **"a waste of time":** Fischer, *Linked Lives*, 81.

121 **"helplessness and dependence":** Wini Breines, *Young, White, and Miserable: Growing Up
Female in the Fifties* (Chicago: University of Chicago Press, 2001), 78.

122 **"more open and exciting":** Steven Mintz, *Huck's Raft: A History of American Childhood*
(Cambridge, MA: Harvard University Press, 2004), 285.

122 **"occupied a special and separate":** Viviana Zelizer, *Pricing the Priceless Child: The
Changing Social Value of Children* (1985; repr., Princeton, NJ: Princeton University Press,
1994), 209.

123 **The press sided:** Grace Palladino, *Teenagers: An American History* (New York: Basic
Books, 1996), 3.

123 **When the *Los Angeles Times*:** "Talking Girl in Film Show Gets Slapped," *Los Angeles
Times*, October 3, 1936, 9.

123 **Her complaint was dismissed:** Palladino, *Teenagers*, 3.

123 **The formal invention of the term:** Mintz, *Huck's Raft*, 252.

124 **"helped to create the idea":** Palladino, *Teenagers*, 5.

124 **It found them inhabiting:** "Teen-Age Girls: They Live in a Wonderful World of
Their Own," *Life*, December 1944, https://time.com/3639041/.

124 **"big and special market"**: "Teen-Age Girls."

124 **Production workers saw**: Palladino, *Teenagers*, 101.

125 **There were more cars**: Kelly Schrum, *Some Wore Bobby Sox: Emergence of Teenage Girls' Culture, 1920–1945* (New York: Palgrave Macmillan, 2004), 4.

125 **The number of households**: "Radio, TV Output Down in January," *New York Times*, February 26, 1951, 38.

125 **The critic Dwight Macdonald**: Dwight Macdonald, "A Caste, a Culture, a Market—II," *New Yorker*, November 21, 1958.

125 **Girls earned less**: Angela R. Record, "Born to Shop: Teenage Women and the Marketplace in the Postwar United States," in *Sex & Money: Feminism and Political Economy in the Media*, ed. Eileen R. Meehan and Ellen Riordan (Minneapolis: University of Minnesota, 2002), 183.

125 **In 1959, *Life* pegged**: Breines, *Young, White, and Miserable*, 92.

125 **Cosmetics rang up**: Breines, *Young, White, and Miserable*, 95.

126 **"sang about the pull"**: Susan J. Douglas, *Where the Girls Are* (New York: Times Books, 1994), 87.

126 **For Claudette Colvin**: Phillip Hoose, *Claudette Colvin: Twice Toward Justice* (New York: Square Fish, 2009), 17.

127 **For Diane Nash**: Olson, *Freedom's Daughters*, 154.

127 **She wet her pants**: Annette Jones White, "Expression of My Discontent," in *Hands on the Freedom Plow: Personal Accounts by Women in SNCC*, ed. Faith S. Holsaert et al. (Urbana: University of Illinois Press, 2012), 101.

127 ***Seventeen* didn't cast**: Jada Jackson, "*Seventeen*'s First Black Cover Model, Joyce Walker-Joseph, Is Still Breaking Barriers," *Oprah Daily*, n.d., https://www.oprahdaily.com/life/a36697337/joyce-walker-joseph-interview/.

127 **cultural products favored**: Breines, *Young, White, and Miserable*, 93.

128 **Adults complained about the fads**: Thomas Doherty, *Teenagers and Teenpics: The Juvenilization of American Movies in the 1950s* (Philadelphia: Temple University Press, 2002), 46.

128 **Racist parents were**: Rebecca de Schweinitz, *If We Could Change the World: Young People and America's Long Struggle for Racial Equality* (Chapel Hill: University of North Carolina Press, 2011), 126.

128 **White supremacists fretted**: de Schweinitz, *If We Could Change the World*, 126.

128 **The would-be harrowing**: Palladino, *Teenagers*, 88.

128 **"Although the goal"**: Susan Wilbur Wamsley interview.

129 **"We all recognized"**: Joyce Ladner, "Standing Up for Our Beliefs," in *Hands on the Freedom Plow*, 220.

129 **Instead, she said**: Ladner, "Standing Up for Our Beliefs," 221.

129 **When the dean**: Ladner, "Standing Up for Our Beliefs," 221.

130 **Johnson complained to friends**: Juan Williams, *Eye on the Prize* (1987; repr., New York: Penguin Books, 2013), 164.

130 **"When he *does* something"**: Jones White, "Expression of My Discontent," 103.

131 **The president fired**: Olson, *Freedom's Daughters*, 226.

131 **Five hundred people**: Olson, *Freedom's Daughters*, 227.

131 **"Yeah, sugar," he told her**: Joann Christian Mants, "We Turned This Upside-Down Country Right Side Up," in *Hands on the Freedom Plow*, 130.

132 **"That night in jail"**: Mants, "We Turned This Upside-Down Country Right Side Up," 131.

132 **"It was strange":** Mants, "We Turned This Upside-Down Country Right Side Up," 131.

132 **The dustup was called:** David Miller, "A Loss for Dr. King—New Negro Roundup: They Yield," *New York Herald Tribune*, December 19, 1961.

132 **The elite college:** Jones White, "Expression of My Discontent," 114–15.

133 **The finished tops:** Jones White, "Expression of My Discontent," 115.

133 **It allowed her:** Dick Cluster, "The Borning Struggle: An Interview with Bernice Johnson Reagon," Radical America 12 (November/December 1978): 21.

133 **Joann Christian integrated:** Mants, "We Turned This Upside-Down Country Right Side Up," 137.

133 **"She would call me":** Olson, *Freedom's Daughters*, 245.

134 **"No one picks my friends":** Mants, "We Turned This Upside-Down Country Right Side Up," 139.

134 **In cities like Chicago:** Palladino, *Teenagers*, 88.

134 **These are not the problems:** "The U.S. Student Population Is More Diverse, but Schools Are Still Highly Segregated," *Morning Edition*, NPR, July 14, 2022, https://www.npr.org/2022/07/14/1111060299/school-segregation-report.

135 **friends with white students:** Olson, *Freedom's Daughters*, 295, 371.

135 **the concept of relatedness:** Jean Smith Young, "Do Whatever You Are Big Enough to Do," in *Hands on the Freedom Plow*, 249.

135 **"This posture of":** Young, "Do Whatever You Are Big Enough to Do," 249.

135 **Young came to believe:** Young, "Do Whatever You Are Big Enough to Do," 249.

CHAPTER SEVEN: TALKING BODIES:
SEX AND SINGLE GIRLS IN SECOND-WAVE FEMINISM

137 **Some estimates put:** Elisabeth Stevens, "When Abortion Was Illegal: A 1966 *Post* Series Revealed How Women Got Them Anyway," *Washington Post*, June 9, 2019, https://www.washingtonpost.com/history/2019/06/09/when-abortion-was-illegal-post-series-revealed-how-women-got-them-anyway/.

138 **The chemicals she'd ingested:** Stevens, "When Abortion Was Illegal."

138 **some would die:** Stevens, "When Abortion Was Illegal."

138 **Heather Tobis picked up:** Clara Bingham, "Code Names and Secret Lives: How a Radical Underground Network Helped Women Get Abortions before They Were Legal," *Vanity Fair*, April 17, 2019, https://www.vanityfair.com/style/2019/04/jane-network-abortion-feature.

139 **Goodman and Schwerner were white:** Lynne Olson, *Freedom's Daughters: The Unsung Heroines of the Civil Rights Movement from 1830 to 1970* (New York: Scribner, 2001), 300.

139 **"You're killing your mother!":** Olson, *Freedom's Daughters*, 300.

139 **Did she need a leader:** Olson, *Freedom's Daughters*, 352.

140 **She felt free:** Bingham, "Code Names and Secret Lives."

140 **"someone else called":** Interview with Heather Booth, July 20, 2021.

140 **"We negotiated on price":** Heather Booth interview.

140 **"Pregnant? Don't Want to Be?":** "Before 'Roe v. Wade,' The Women of 'Jane' Provided Abortions for the Women of Chicago," *All Things Considered*, NPR, January 19, 2018, https://www.npr.org/2018/01/19/578620266/before-roe-v-wade-the-women-of-jane-provided-abortions-for-the-women-of-chicago.

141 **The attendant noticed:** Ann Fessler, *The Girls Who Went Away: The Hidden History of Women Who Surrendered Children for Adoption in the Decades before* Roe v. Wade (New York: Penguin Books, 2006), 50.

142 **The staffer who saw:** Heather Booth interview.

142 **A still-green journalist:** Gloria Steinem, "The Moral Disarmament of Betty Coed," *Esquire*, September 1, 1962, https://classic.esquire.com/article/1983/6/1/the-moral-disarmament-of-betty-coed.

142 **It was her first:** Elisabeth Bumiller, "Gloria Steinem, the Everyday Rebel," *Washington Post*, October 12, 1983, https://www.washingtonpost.com/archive/lifestyle/1983/10/12/gloria-steinem-the-everyday-rebel/164d44d2-3f21-49a9-9d62-c12408446409/.

142 **The piece delves into:** Steinem, "The Moral Disarmament of Betty Coed."

143 **"The names of such doctors":** Steinem, "The Moral Disarmament of Betty Coed."

143 **"preoccupied with sex":** Steinem, "The Moral Disarmament of Betty Coed."

143 **The danger was:** Steinem, "The Moral Disarmament of Betty Coed."

143 **The landmark book identifies:** Betty Friedan, *The Feminine Mystique* (1963; repr., New York: W. W. Norton & Company, 2001), 57.

144 **It was grounded in conversations:** Friedan, *The Feminine Mystique*, 534.

144 **transformed into a mother:** Rachel Shteir, "Why We Can't Stop Talking About Betty Friedan," *New York Times*, February 3, 2021, https://www.nytimes.com/2021/02/03/us/betty-friedan-feminism-legacy.html.

144 **In 1966, Friedan seemed:** Shteir, "Why We Can't Stop Talking About Betty Friedan."

145 **Newer histories have elevated:** Benita Roth, *Separate Roads to Feminism: Black, Chicana, and White Feminist Movements in America's Second Wave* (Cambridge: Cambridge University Press, 2004), 2–3.

145 **Revolt against the social order:** Gael Graham, *Young Activists: American High School Students in the Age of Protest* (DeKalb: Northern Illinois University Press, 2006), 164.

146 **"They are really thinking":** Kelley Massoni, *Fashioning Teenagers: A Cultural History of* Seventeen *Magazine* (2010; repr., New York: Routledge, 2016), 38.

146 *Seventeen* **launched in 1944:** Massoni, *Fashioning Teenagers*, 27.

146 **An editorial in its first:** Massoni, *Fashioning Teenagers*, 49.

146 **When someone wrote in:** Grace Palladino, *Teenagers: An American History* (New York: Basic Books, 1996), 91.

147 **Cooking and cleaning were:** Palladino, *Teenagers*, 65.

147 **In the second half of:** Kelly Schrum, "'Teena Means Business': Teenage Girls' Culture and *Seventeen* Magazine," in *Delinquents and Debutantes: Twentieth-Century American Girls' Cultures*, ed. Sherrie A. Inness (New York: New York University Press, 1998), 139.

147 **The magazine christened:** Massoni, *Fashioning Teenagers*, 94.

147 **The text in one flyer:** "Seventeen . . . The First Eight Months," April 15, 1945, box 18, folder 5, Estelle Ellis Papers, Archives Center, National Museum of American History, Washington, D.C., https://transcription.si.edu/view/23310/NMAH-AC0423-0000034-02.

147 **"You are the bosses":** Alexis Chaney, "Swooning, Screaming, Crying: How Teenage Girls Have Driven 60 Years of Pop Music," *Vox*, January 28, 2016, https://www.vox.com/2016/1/28/10815492/teenage-girls-screaming.

147 **Girls were the shop clerks:** Barbara Ehrenreich et al., "Beatlemania: Girls Just Want to Have Fun," in *The Adoring Audience: Fan Culture and Popular Media*, ed. Lisa A. Lewis (London: Routledge, 1992), 94.

148 **After that, a blank:** Wini Breines, *Young, White, and Miserable: Growing Up Female in the Fifties* (Chicago: University of Chicago Press, 2001), 106–7.

148 **Girls study and receive:** Breines, *Young, White, and Miserable*, 107.

148 **Douvan and Adelson's research:** Breines, *Young, White, and Miserable*, 107.

149 **Beatlemania had come:** Ehrenreich et al., "Beatlemania," 84.

149 **What made the Beatles:** Ehrenreich et al., "Beatlemania," 85.

149 **When the music arrived:** Ehrenreich et al., "Beatlemania," 85.

149 **compared the scene to:** Jon Savage, "The Columbus Day Riot: Frank Sinatra Is Pop's First Star," *Guardian*, June 10, 2011, https://www.theguardian.com/music/2011/jun/11/frank-sinatra-pop-star.

149 **Elvis mesmerized girls:** Jack Gould, "Lack of Responsibility Is Shown by TV in Exploiting Teen-Agers," *New York Times*, September 16, 1956, https://archive.nytimes.com/www.nytimes.com/partners/aol/special/elvis/early-elvis3.html.

149 **Their restlessness perhaps foretold:** Breines, *Young, White, and Miserable*, 129.

150 **Beatlemania gave girls permission:** Ehrenreich et al., "Beatlemania," 85.

150 **"It was the first":** Ehrenreich et al., "Beatlemania," 85.

150 **when the *Chicago Tribune* profiled:** Paul Galloway, "A Woman Born to Be Riled," *Chicago Tribune*, February 14, 1985, https://www.chicagotribune.com/news/ct-xpm-1985-02-14-8501090494-story.html.

150 **She had inequalities:** Galloway, "A Woman Born to Be Riled."

151 **Still, the document landed:** Olson, *Freedom's Daughters*, 333–34.

151 **It placed the odds:** Casey Hayden and Mary King, "Sex and Caste: A Kind of Memo," in *Dear Sisters: Dispatches from the Women's Liberation Movement*, ed. Rosalyn Baxandall and Linda Gordon (New York: Basic Books, 2001), 22.

151 **an astonishing 70 percent:** Olson, *Freedom's Daughters*, 354.

152 **She marched in support:** Carrie Golus, "Organizing Principle," *University of Chicago Magazine*, Winter 2019, https://mag.uchicago.edu/law-policy-society/organizing-principle.

152 **She founded a center:** Heather Booth interview.

152 **That is the feeling:** Heather Booth interview.

153 **In 1927, she backed:** Alexis McGill Johnson, "I'm the Head of Planned Parenthood. We're Done Making Excuses for Our Founder," *New York Times*, April 17, 2021, https://www.nytimes.com/2021/04/17/opinion/planned-parenthood-margaret-sanger.html.

153 **Programs limited the number:** Nicole Lynn Lewis, *Pregnant Girl: A Story of Teen Motherhood, College, and Creating a Better Future for Young Families* (Boston: Beacon Press, 2021), 86.

153 **he was the product:** Lewis, *Pregnant Girl*, 86.

153 **And like Riddick:** Stacey Naggiar, "Victims of Forced Sterilization to Receive $10 Million from North Carolina," NBC News, July 25, 2013, https://www.nbcnews.com/nightly-news/victims-forced-sterilization-receive-10-million-north-carolina-flna6c10753957.

153 **"seems the bonds":** Kera Lovell, "Girls Are Equal Too: Education, Body Politics, and the Making of Teenage Feminism," *Gender Issues* 33, no. 2 (2016): 80.

154 **In 1965, that number:** Frank E. Furstenberg, Jr., "Teenage Childbearing as a Public Issue and Private Concern," *Annual Review of Sociology* 29 (2003): 25.

155 **Just over one hundred:** Julie Solow Stein, "Youthful Transgressions: Teenagers, Sexuality, and the Contested Path to Adulthood in Postwar America," (PhD diss., University of California, Berkeley, 2013), 109.

155 **It cited "moral unfitness":** "2 Unwed Mothers Get Chance to Finish School," *Chicago Daily Defender,* July 12, 1969, 13.

155 **the law protected:** "2 Unwed Mothers Get Chance to Finish School."

155 **"a girl has one child":** *Clydie Marie Perry v. Grenada Municipal Separate School District,* 300 F. Supp. 748 (N.D. Miss. 1969), https://law.justia.com/cases/federal/district-courts/FSupp /300/748/1820850/.

155 **"reopened the door":** Carl Rowan, "Quiet Mississippi Decision Important for U.S. Poor," *Toledo Blade,* July 16, 1969, 26.

156 **when it became undeniable:** Stein, "Youthful Transgressions," 110.

156 **Unwed mothers were not:** Stein, "Youthful Transgressions," 110.

156 **when the school board:** Melissa Murray, "Sex and the Schoolhouse," review of *The Schoolhouse Gate: Public Education, the Supreme Court, and the Battle for the American Mind* by Justin Driver, *Harvard Law Review* 132, no. 5 (2019): 1470.

156 **her marital status:** Edwin Kiester Jr., "What's Happening in the Rest of the Country," *Chicago Tribune,* September 10, 1972.

156 **The judge in:** *Ordway v. Hargraves,* 323 F. Supp. 1155 (D. Mass. 1971), https://law.justia .com/cases/federal/district-courts/FSupp/323/1155/1572587/.

157 **She gave birth:** Stein, "Youthful Transgressions," 110.

157 **Soon Title IX:** Stein, "Youthful Transgressions," 111.

157 **the ACLU settled:** "ACLU Settles Kentucky Case of Pregnant Teens Denied Entry to Honor Society," ACLU, October 22, 1999, https://www.aclu.org/press-releases/aclu -settles-kentucky-case-pregnant-teens-denied-entry-honor-society.

157 **New York Civil Liberties Union:** "NYCLU Gives Schools Chancellor Levy an 'F' for Failing to Stop Discrimination Against Pregnant and Parenting Girls," ACLU of New York, March 24, 2002, https://www.nyclu.org/en/press-releases/nyclu-gives -schools-chancellor-levy-f-failing-stop-discrimination-against-pregnant.

158 **It made the call:** Arek Sarkissian, "Florida Court Says Teen Isn't Mature Enough to Get an Abortion," *Politico,* August 16, 2022, https://www.politico.com/news/2022/08/16 /parentless-teen-cant-have-an-abortion-under-state-parental-consent-law-00052211.

158 **"Must we sit":** Diane Devlin, "The Plight of the Gay Student," *Off Our Backs* 1, no. 6 (1970): 11.

159 **That revelation became:** Susan J. Douglas, *Where the Girls Are* (New York: Times Books, 1994), 97.

159 **"What we have here":** Douglas, *Where the Girls Are,* 97.

160 **"most of us had never":** Susan Brownmiller, "Sisterhood Is Powerful," *New York Times,* March 15, 1970, https://www.nytimes.com/1970/03/15/archives/sisterhood-is-powerful -a-member-of-the-womens-liberation-movement.html.

160 **The eventual book:** Robin Morgan, ed., *Sisterhood Is Powerful: An Anthology of Writings from the Women's Liberation Movement* (New York: Vintage Books, 1970), 374.

160 **"Getting together and rapping":** Morgan, *Sisterhood Is Powerful,* 374.

160 **"We've all been fucked over"**: Morgan, *Sisterhood Is Powerful*, 374.

161 **the high school faction**: Lovell, "Girls Are Equal Too," 89.

161 **Some girls went further**: Lovell, "Girls Are Equal Too," 82.

161 **sex education ranked**: Lovell, "Girls Are Equal Too," 81.

162 **a volunteer held**: "Liberation Conference," Emmanuel College, *The Emmanuel Focus* 21, no. 11, May 9, 1969, https://www.ourbodiesourselvestoday.org/wp-content /uploads/2020/02/Emmanuel-Focus-5-9-1969.pdf.

162 **A resource group**: Deck, "How It Came to Be."

163 **Even Booth, who had**: Heather Booth interview.

163 **"I was shocked!"**: Heather Booth interview.

163 **A sisterhood, gathered around**: Bingham, "Code Names and Secret Lives."

163 **The group purchased**: Bingham, "Code Names and Secret Lives."

163 **"It was the beginning"**: Bingham, "Code Names and Secret Lives."

164 **Each was booked**: Bingham, "Code Names and Secret Lives."

164 **New ones have been**: Jamie Ducharme, "New Abortion Clinics Are Opening Near Borders and Airports to Stretch Access as Far as It Will Go," *Time*, June 9, 2022, https://time.com/6185519/abortion-clinics-travel-state-borders/.

164 **Not all girls are**: "Gen Z Marchers Praying for an End to US Abortion," BBC, January 22, 2022, https://www.bbc.com/news/av/world-us-canada-60088680.

164 **But an astonishing number**: Ed Kilgore, "Gen Z May Break the Deadlock Over Abortion Rights," *New York Magazine*, June 1, 2022, https://nymag.com/intelligencer /2022/06/gen-z-may-break-the-deadlock-over-abortion-rights.html.

164 **A 2022 poll**: "Americans' View on Whether, and in What Circumstances, Abortion Should Be Legal," Pew Research Center, May 6, 2022, https://www.pewresearch.org /religion/2022/05/06/americans-views-on-whether-and-in-what-circumstances -abortion-should-be-legal/.

164 **When Senate Bill 8**: Haley Reyes, "'Shame on You': 16-Year-Old in Texas Refuses to Be Silent About Her Reproductive Rights," *Ms. Magazine*, February 16, 2022, https:// msmagazine.com/2022/02/16/teenager-texas-abortion-reproductive-rights/.

164 **she was bitter**: Shriya Bhattacharya, "Gen Z Is Preparing to Fight for Reproductive Justice in a Future without *Roe v. Wade*," Prism Reports, May 24, 2022, https://prism-reports.org/2022/05/24/gen-z-fight-for-reproductive-justice-post-roe-v-wade/.

165 **"We need to be thinking"**: Bhattacharya, "Gen Z Is Preparing to Fight for Reproductive Justice in a Future without *Roe v. Wade*."

CHAPTER EIGHT: GOOD GIRLS:
CRUSADERS IN MINISKIRTS AND THE RIGHT TO AN EDUCATION

167 **The pair met**: Laurie Gwen Shapiro, "How a Thirteen-Year-Old Girl Smashed the Gender Divide in American High Schools," *New Yorker*, January 26, 2019, https://www .newyorker.com/culture/culture-desk/how-a-thirteen-year-old-girl-smashed-the -gender-divide-in-american-high-schools.

167 **She was the daughter**: Interview with Alice Haines, August 21, 2021.

168 **She invited de Rivera**: Shapiro, "How a Thirteen-Year-Old Girl Smashed the Gender Divide."

168 **The NECLC had backed:** Shapiro, "How a Thirteen-Year-Old Girl Smashed the Gender Divide."

168 **But if she wanted to:** Shapiro, "How a Thirteen-Year-Old Girl Smashed the Gender Divide."

168 **So Ripston approached:** "One Tough Case," Berkeley Law, March 1, 2009, https://www.law.berkeley.edu/article/one-tough-case/.

168 **De Rivera took her notes:** Shapiro, "How a Thirteen-Year-Old Girl Smashed the Gender Divide."

168 **The most famous enthusiasts:** Charlotte E. Biester, "Catharine Beecher's Views of Home Economics," *History of Education Journal* 3, no. 3 (1952): 88.

169 **Men went to school:** Biester, "Catharine Beecher's Views of Home Economics," 88.

169 **She was prepared to work:** Biester, "Catharine Beecher's Views of Home Economics," 89.

169 **It had to expand:** Biester, "Catharine Beecher's Views of Home Economics," 88–89.

169 **"proper education of a man":** Catharine Beecher, *A Treatise on Domestic Economy* (1841; repr., New York: Harper & Brothers, 1848), 37.

170 **In the struggle:** Susan J. Douglas, *Where the Girls Are* (New York: Times Books, 1994), 22.

170 **In 1966, when Yale:** Jerome Karabel, *The Chosen: The Hidden History of Admission and Exclusion at Harvard, Yale, and Princeton* (Boston: Houghton Mifflin, 2005), 417.

170 **Kingman Brewster, then Yale's president:** Karabel, *The Chosen,* 417.

171 **Too much exposure:** Nancy Weiss Malkiel, "'Keep the Damned Women Out': The Struggle for Coeducation in the Ivy League, the Seven Sisters, Oxford, and Cambridge," *Proceedings of the American Philosophical Society* 161, no. 1 (2017): 32.

171 **"What is all this nonsense":** Malkiel, "'Keep the Damned Women Out,'" 33.

171 **Their response pointed:** Katelyn X. Li, "When Harvard Met Radcliffe," *Harvard Crimson,* May 27, 2019, https://www.thecrimson.com/article/2019/5/27/harvard-radcliffe-1969/. See also: Pamela Ferdin, "Radcliffe to Merge with Harvard, Become a Center for Advanced Study," *Washington Post,* April 21, 1999.

171 **In 1970, a Dartmouth alum:** Malkiel, "'Keep the Damned Women Out,'" 32.

172 **She and de Rivera filed:** Shapiro, "How a Thirteen-Year-Old Girl Smashed the Gender Divide."

172 **News of the case:** "Girl Challenges Stuyvesant High's All-Boy Policy," *New York Times,* January 21, 1969.

172 **"I wasn't prepared":** Alice Haines interview.

172 **She was a kid:** Alice Haines interview.

172 **the Manhattan Supreme Court:** "Girl Challenges Stuyvesant High's All-Boy Policy."

172 **"with a lot of chutzpah":** Alice Haines interview.

172 **A student reporter wanted:** Shapiro, "How a Thirteen-Year-Old Girl Smashed the Gender Divide."

173 **"the school thing":** Shapiro, "How a Thirteen-Year-Old Girl Smashed the Gender Divide."

173 **Over one photo:** Shapiro, "How a Thirteen-Year-Old Girl Smashed the Gender Divide."

173 **The two, a pair:** Shapiro, "How a Thirteen-Year-Old Girl Smashed the Gender Divide."

173 **In anticipation of her arrival:** Alice Haines interview.

173 **"getting the support":** Shapiro, "How a Thirteen-Year-Old Girl Smashed the Gender Divide."

173 **"I had all this attention":** Alice Haines interview.

173 **"I feel like":** Alice Haines interview.

174 **Piel also quoted:** Shapiro, "How a Thirteen-Year-Old Girl Smashed the Gender Divide."

174 **Black people were not:** Lynne Olson, *Freedom's Daughters: The Unsung Heroines of the Civil Rights Movement from 1830 to 1970* (New York: Scribner, 2001), 55.

174 **his work on civil rights:** Shapiro, "How a Thirteen-Year-Old Girl Smashed the Gender Divide."

175 **"It was a cultural precedent":** Shapiro, "How a Thirteen-Year-Old Girl Smashed the Gender Divide."

175 **The reporter would witness:** Ashley Fetters, "The First of the 'Yale Women,'" *The Atlantic*, September 22, 2019, https://www.theatlantic.com/education/archive/2019/09/first-undergraduate-women-yale/598216/.

175 **230 female high school seniors:** Fetters, "The First of the 'Yale Women.'"

175 **the same note of caution:** Fetters, "The First of the 'Yale Women.'"

176 **Professors started to call:** Harriet H. Coffin, "Women of Yale," *New York Times*, July 15, 1971.

176 **The gender imbalance meant:** Coffin, "Women of Yale."

176 **Coping meant making:** Coffin, "Women of Yale."

176 *Time* **ran a major:** Ruth Brine, "The New Feminists: Revolt Against Sexism," *Time*, November 21, 1969.

177 **So-called militant feminism:** Brine, "The New Feminists."

177 **"The radical women":** Brine, "The New Feminists."

178 **their testimonies drove the school:** Kera Lovell, "Girls Are Equal Too: Education, Body Politics, and the Making of Teenage Feminism," *Gender Issues* 33, no. 2 (2016): 84.

178 **Lowell High School:** Lovell, "Girls Are Equal Too," 85.

178 **The cafeteria work was deemed:** Eleanor Blau, "Brooklyn High School Blends Class Work and Jobs," *New York Times*, March 14, 1971.

178 **Lovell has argued:** Lovell, "Girls Are Equal Too," 86.

179 **Bayh refuted the notion:** Robert Blaemire, *Birch Bayh: Making a Difference* (Bloomington: Indiana University Press, 2019), 209.

179 **That kind of thinking:** Adam Clymer, "Birch Bayh, 91, Dies; Senator Drove Title IX and 2 Amendments," *New York Times*, March 14, 2019.

179 **"I really want to play":** Lovell, "Girls Are Equal Too," 86.

179 **But while legislative stipulations:** *Women's Educational Equity Act of 1973: Hearings Before the Subcommittee on Education of the Committee on Labor and Public Welfare*, U.S. Congress Senate, 93rd Cong., 1st sess., 1973, 38.

180 **Problems that focused:** *Women's Educational Equity Act of 1973*, 47.

180 **Sandler told her audience:** *Women's Educational Equity Act of 1973*, 48.

180 **Imagine how horrified:** Francesca Donner and Emma Goldberg, "In 25 Years, the Pay Gap Has Shrunk by Just 8 Cents," *New York Times*, March 24, 2021.

180 **Girls now do:** Carolyn Jones, "Girls Draw Even with Boys in High School STEM Classes, but Still Lag in College and Careers," EdSource, March 12, 2017, https://edsource.org/2017/girls-now-outnumber-boys-in-high-school-stem-but-still-lag-in-college-and-career/578444.

181 **The factor that does seem:** Kim A. Weeden et al. "Pipeline Dreams: Occupational Plans and Gender Differences in STEM Major Persistence and Completion," *Sociology of Education* 93, no. 4 (2020): 301.

181 **Natalia Thompson wrote:** Natalia Thompson, "Confessions of a Teenage Feminist," *Off Our Backs* 37, no. 4 (2007): 37.

181 **"it's less about feminism":** Thompson, "Confessions of a Teenage Feminist," 40.

182 **The Virginia Military Institute:** Mike Allen, "Defiant V.M.I. to Admit Women, but Will Not Ease the Rules for Them," *New York Times*, September 22, 1996, https://www.nytimes.com/1996/09/22/us/defiant-vmi-to-admit-women-but-will-not-ease-rules-for-them.html.

182 **"There is unfinished business":** William C. Rhoden, "Black and White Women Far from Equal under Title IX," *New York Times*, June 10, 2012, https://www.nytimes.com/2012/06/11/sports/title-ix-has-not-given-black-female-athletes-equal-opportunity.html.

183 **the magazine interviewed:** Claudia Wallis, "Women Face the '90s," *Time*, December 4, 1989, https://content.time.com/time/subscriber/article/0,33009,959163,00.html.

183 **She moved on:** Alice Haines interview.

184 **When the women moved in:** Fetters, "The First of the 'Yale Women.'"

184 **Black students total:** "Stuyvesant High School Enrollment (2020–2021)," New York State Education Department, 2020, https://data.nysed.gov/enrollment.php?year=2020&instid=800000046741.

184 **She escaped the pressure:** Alice Haines interview.

184 **She sticks to:** Alice Haines interview.

184 **it awarded her:** Alice Haines interview.

CHAPTER NINE: LOOK AT ME NOW: TINKER, TAILOR, AND THE AESTHETICS OF A MOVEMENT

186 **She answered herself:** Vanessa Friedman, "The Naked Truth," *Financial Times*, April 25, 2014, https://www.ft.com/content/5f9643e6-c639-11e3-ba0e-00144feabdc0#axzz30BeErll3.

186 **Suffragists wore white:** Emily Crockett, "Hillary Clinton Wore White—a Symbol of Women's Suffrage—to Trump's Inauguration," *Vox*, January 20, 2017, https://www.vox.com/identities/2017/1/20/14336204/hillary-clinton-trump-inauguration-wearing-white-suffragists.

186 **Antiwar protesters wore:** Betty Luther Hillman, *Dressing for the Culture Wars: Style and the Politics of Self-Presentation in the 1960s and 1970s* (Lincoln: University of Nebraska Press, 2015), 2–4.

186 **In a meditation:** Carli Velocci, "Why Protesters Love Costumes," *Racked*, March 2, 2018, https://www.racked.com/2018/3/2/17042504/protest-costumes.

186   **can offer refuge:** Velocci, "Why Protesters Love Costumes."

187   **In Zuccotti Park:** Edward Lovett, "How Did Guy Fawkes Become a Symbol of Oc-cupy Wall Street?," *ABC News*, November 5, 2011, https://abcnews.go.com/blogs /headlines/2011/11/how-did-guy-fawkes-become-a-symbol-of-occupy-wall-street.

187   **In a quiet demonstration:** Justin Driver, *The Schoolhouse Gate: Public Education, the Supreme Court, and the Battle for the American Mind* (New York: Pantheon Books, 2018), 73–74.

187   **a Quaker activist:** Michael E. Ruane, "Vietnam Critic's End Was the Start of Fam-ily's Pain," *Washington Post*, November 1, 2015, https://www.washingtonpost.com/local /vietnam-critics-end-was-the-start-of-familys-pain/2015/11/01/b50e1d54-7cdf -11e5-b575-d8dcfedb4ea1_story.html.

187   **At the Tinkers' school:** Driver, *The Schoolhouse Gate*, 73–74.

188   **The trio declined:** Driver, *The Schoolhouse Gate*, 73–74.

188   **In the 7–2 decision:** *Tinker v. Des Moines*, 393 U.S. 503 (1969), https://supreme.justia .com/cases/federal/us/393/503/.

188   **The girls—with their parents:** Driver, *The Schoolhouse Gate*, 62.

188   **He situated it:** Driver, *The Schoolhouse Gate*, 63–64.

188   **If children were not allowed:** *West Virginia State Board of Education v. Barnette*, 319 U.S. 624 (1943), https://supreme.justia.com/cases/federal/us/319/624/#tab-opinion -1937809.

189   **the legal scholar Justin Driver:** Driver, *The Schoolhouse Gate*, 72.

189   **the prevailing opinion:** *Tinker v. Des Moines*.

189   **Tinker herself marvels:** Interview with Mary Beth Tinker, August 25, 2021.

193   **used to deliver:** "John Tinker Describes the Inspiration to Protest the Vietnam War," Iowa Pathways, PBS, Johnston, Iowa, February 21, 2019, https://www.iowapbs. org/iowapathways/artifact/1424/john-tinker-describes-inspiration-protest -vietnam-war.

193   **"an admonition to school officials":** "The Armband Case," *Des Moines Register*, Feb-ruary 27, 1969, 8.

194   ***The Boston Globe* writes:** "Rights for Students," *Boston Globe*, February 27, 1969, 27.

194   ***The New York Times* declares:** "Armbands Yes, Miniskirts No," *New York Times*, Febru-ary 26, 1969, https://www.nytimes.com/1969/02/26/archives/armbands-yes-miniskirts-no .html.

194   **The reporter outlines:** "Armbands Yes, Miniskirts No."

194   **The justices who signed:** "Armbands Yes, Miniskirts No."

195   **The historian Deirdre Clemente:** Deirdre Clemente, *Dress Casual: How College Stu-dents Redefined American Style* (Chapel Hill: University of North Carolina Press, 2014), 9.

195   **The clothes themselves:** Hillman, *Dressing for the Culture Wars*, 43.

195   **"People wear clothes":** Interview with Deirdre Clemente, August 27, 2021.

196   **The historian Stephanie Shaw:** Stephanie J. Shaw, *What a Woman Ought to Be and to Do: Black Professional Women Workers During the Jim Crow Era* (Chicago: University of Chi-cago Press, 1996), 24.

196   **When Angelina Weld Grimké:** Shaw, *What a Woman Ought to Be and to Do*, 24.

197   **Miriam Matthews, later a:** Shaw, *What a Woman Ought to Be and to Do*, 24.

197   **That meant targeting:** Tanisha C. Ford, *Liberated Threads: Black Women, Style, and the Global Politics of Soul* (Chapel Hill: University of North Carolina Press, 2015), 69.

NOTES

198 **watched a white man:** Anne Moody, *Coming of Age in Mississippi: The Classic Autobiography of Growing Up Poor and Black in the Rural South* (New York: Random House, 2011), 290–91.

198 **The sit-in ended:** Moody, *Coming of Age in Mississippi*, 291.

198 **She wanted to get:** Moody, *Coming of Age in Mississippi*, 291.

198 **salons functioned as:** Ford, *Liberated Threads*, 73.

198 **restore themselves:** Ford, *Liberated Threads*, 74.

198 **one humiliation stood out:** Cynthia Griggs Fleming, *Soon We Will Not Cry: The Liberation of Ruby Doris Smith Robinson* (Oxford: Rowman & Littlefield Publishers, 1998), 77.

198 **Debbie Amis Bell remembered:** Ford, *Liberated Threads*, 76.

199 **SNCC volunteers had:** Gloria Jean Wade-Gayles: *Pushed Back to Strength: A Black Woman's Journey Home* (Boston: Beacon Press, 1993), 155–57.

199 **When she saw other:** Wade-Gayles: *Pushed Back to Strength*, 155–57.

199 **Another Swarthmore student:** Ford, *Liberated Threads*, 79.

200 **"outward manifestation that":** Ford, *Liberated Threads*, 79.

200 **It took her entire:** Barbara Ransby, *Ella Baker and the Black Freedom Movement: A Radical Democratic Vision* (Chapel Hill: University of North Carolina Press, 2003), 60.

201 **"forms of embodied activism":** Ford, *Liberated Threads*, 87.

201 **girls were penalized:** Kera Lovell, "Girls Are Equal Too: Education, Body Politics, and the Making of Teenage Feminism," *Gender Issues* 33, no. 2 (2016): 77.

202 **"I read all the literature":** Robin Morgan, ed., *Sisterhood Is Powerful: An Anthology of Writings from the Women's Liberation Movement* (New York: Vintage Books, 1970), 363.

202 **she concludes she was:** Morgan, *Sisterhood Is Powerful*, 364.

202 **her presence:** Morgan, *Sisterhood Is Powerful*, 364–65.

203 **squeezed into sequins:** "Untitled News Story about High School Girl Sassing a Mayor," in *Dear Sisters: Dispatches from the Women's Liberation Movement*, ed. Rosalyn Baxandall and Linda Gordon (New York: Basic Books, 2001), 188.

203 **"He didn't say anything":** "Untitled News Story about High School Girl Sassing a Mayor."

203 **"Zoe didn't seem to mind":** "Untitled News Story about High School Girl Sassing a Mayor."

204 **"being preoccupied with clothes":** Hillman, *Dressing for the Culture Wars*, 67.

204 **Abercrombie caved and pulled:** Brandee J. Tecson, "Abercrombie Pulls T-Shirts After Teen Girls Launch Boycott," MTV News, November 7, 2005, http://www.mtv.com/news/1513153/abercrombie-pulls-t-shirts-after-teen-girls-launch-boycott/.

205 **"The colorful scene":** Laurel Wamsley and Vanessa Romo, "With Speeches and Bright Dresses, Quinceañeras Protest Texas Sanctuary City Ban," NPR, July 19, 2017, https://www.npr.org/sections/thetwo-way/2017/07/19/538112799/with-speeches-and-bright-dresses-quincea-eras-protest-texas-sanctuary-city-ban.

205 **"In Latino culture":** Wamsley and Romo, "With Speeches and Bright Dresses, Quinceañeras Protest Texas Sanctuary City Ban."

206 **One of its cheerleaders:** Nicole Carroll, "Cristina Jiménez Moreta Helped Get DACA, Now She Helps Young Immigrants Find Their Voice," *USA Today*, August 20, 2020, https://www.usatoday.com/in-depth/life/women-of-the-century/2020/08/20/cristina-jimenez-moreta-advocates-daca-undocumented-youth-human-rights/5535786002/.

207 **Juarez told a reporter:** Amber Jamieson, "Teens Wore Quinceañera Dresses to Protest Texas' Immigration Law," *BuzzFeed*, July 20, 2017, https://www.buzzfeednews.com/article/amberjamieson/these-teens-wore-quinceanera-dresses-to-protest-an.

207 **In an indication:** Austin Considine, "Saying 'No' to Picture Perfect," *New York Times*, May 16, 2012, https://www.nytimes.com/2012/05/17/fashion/saying-no-to-picture-perfect.html.

208 **The feminist scholar Rosalind Gill:** Leslie A. Hahner and Scott J. Varda, "Modesty and Feminisms: Conversations on Aesthetics and Resistance," *Feminist Formations* 24, no. 3 (2012): 26.

208 **Twitter users have turned:** @ChronicCookieee, Twitter post, April 7, 2021, 3:33 a.m., https://twitter.com/ChronicCookieee/status/1379698734863314948; @tinderdistrict, Twitter post, March 23, 2021, 3:10 p.m., https://twitter.com/tinderdistrict/status/1374438403979153408; @_memesvalididi, Twitter post, June 22, 2021, 7:56 a.m., https://twitter.com/_memesvalididi/status/1407306476872355846.

208 **conservative politicians belittled:** Nicola Dall'Asen, "Why You Shouldn't Wear Oil-Based Beauty Products While Protesting," *Allure*, June 3, 2020, https://www.allure.com/story/beauty-products-not-to-wear-when-protesting.

208 **In a primer:** Kandist Mallett, "What to Know before Heading to a Protest," *Teen Vogue*, May 29, 2020, https://www.teenvogue.com/story/how-to-prepare-protest.

209 **"The heart of this case":** Mary Beth Tinker interview.

CHAPTER TEN: IN HER FEELINGS:
GIRLHOOD AT THE END OF THE WORLD

211 **"I do not think":** Michael G. Long, *Kids on the March: 15 Stories of Speaking Out, Protesting, and Fighting for Justice* (New York: Workman Publishing, 2021), 131.

212 **"the world situation":** Long, *Kids on the March*, 131.

212 **Without a pledge:** Long, *Kids on the March*, 131.

212 **Almost half of respondents:** Robert T. Schatz and Susan T. Fiske, "International Reactions to the Threat of Nuclear War: The Rise and Fall of Concern in the Eighties," *Political Psychology* 13, no. 1 (1992): 2.

212 **Some research pointed:** Schatz and Fiske, "International Reactions to the Threat of Nuclear War," 5.

212 **"We just had":** Tom Slayton, "Wondering If They'll Be Alive in 20 Years Led Children on Campaign Against Nuclear Arms," *Rutland Daily Herald*, August 2, 1981, 7. Note: In initial press coverage, Hannah Rabin (full name Susan Hannah Rabin) was referred to as Susan Rabin. She was later quoted as Hannah Rabin. To be consistent, this book refers to her as Hannah Rabin.

213 **she outlined her plan:** Long, *Kids on the March*, 132.

213 **an ominous note:** Guido Grünewald, *Children's Campaign for Nuclear Disarmament* (Geneva: International Peace Bureau, 1985), 40.

213 **For people around the world:** Elaine Tyler May, *Homeward Bound: American Families in the Cold War Era* (1988; repr., New York: Basic Books, 2009), 8–10.

213 **At a conference on:** "Dr. Spock Urges Parents to Allay Cold-War Tensions," *York Daily Record*, March 16, 1964, 12.

214 **a nurse at Bellevue:** Philip Benjamin, "2 Girls Convicted in Atom Sitdown," *New*

York Times, April 6, 1962, https://timesmachine.nytimes.com/timesmachine/1962/04/06/89854595.html?pageNumber=4.

214 **In 1966, another:** "Girl Pacifist, Held 68 Days, Is Released after Apology," *New York Times*, September 29, 1966, https://timesmachine.nytimes.com/timesmachine/1966/09/29/82513761.html?pageNumber=52.

214 **In 1982, a paper:** Milton Schwebel, "Effects of the Nuclear War Threat on Children and Teenagers: Implications for Professionals," *American Journal of Orthopsychiatry* 52, no. 4 (1982): 608.

214 **a Canadian paper:** S. J. Kiraly, "Psychological Effects of the Threat of Nuclear War," *Canadian Family Physician* 32 (1986): 170.

214 **The paper's lead author:** T. Solantaus et al., "The Threat of War in the Minds of 12-18-Year-Olds in Finland," *Lancet* 323, no. 8380 (1984): 784.

215 **Girls were instructed:** Leslie J. Miller, "Children's Hot Cold War," *New York Times*, June 12, 1982, https://www.nytimes.com/1982/06/12/opinion/childrens-hot-cold-war.html.

215 **It was a miserable period:** Miller, "Children's Hot Cold War."

215 **After the last letter:** Janet Domowitz, "Vermont Youths Declare War on Nuclear Weapons," *Christian Science Monitor*, March 18, 1982, https://www.csmonitor.com/1982/0318/031803.html.

215 **It congratulated their efforts:** Domowitz, "Vermont Youths Declare War on Nuclear Weapons."

216 **"While some may consider":** Domowitz, "Vermont Youths Declare War on Nuclear Weapons."

216 **"it's life or death":** Domowitz, "Vermont Youths Declare War on Nuclear Weapons."

216 **Monique Grodzki, fourteen:** Cynthia B. Marquand, "Children's Peace Committee Helps Educate Peers About World Issues," *Christian Science Monitor*, March 28, 1983, https://www.csmonitor.com/1983/0328/032834.html

216 **In San Francisco, Children:** Marquand, "Children's Peace Committee Helps Educate Peers About World Issues."

216 **"[W]e're little children":** Olive Evans, "Handling Children's Nuclear War Fears," *New York Times*, May 27, 1982, https://www.nytimes.com/1982/05/27/garden/handling-children-s-nuclear-war-fears.html.

216 **Two of the other:** Evans, "Handling Children's Nuclear War Fears."

217 **The prophetesses sold:** Thomas A. Robinson and Lanette D. Ruff, *Out of the Mouths of Babes: Girl Evangelists in the Flapper Era* (New York: Oxford University Press, 2012), 3–4.

217 **The organization's logo:** "What Is Extinction Rebellion and What Does It Want?," BBC News, April 14, 2022, https://www.bbc.com/news/uk-48607989.

218 **"The familiar cliché":** Eric Markusen, "Education and the Threat of Nuclear War," *Educational Perspectives* 21, no. 3 (1982): 32.

219 **"The work is sometimes":** Suzanne McIntire, *Speeches in World History* (New York: Infobase Publishing, 2009), 501.

219 **Between 2007 and 2015:** Maggie Fox, "Suicides in Teen Girls Hit 40-Year High," NBC News, August 3, 2017, https://www.nbcnews.com/health/health-news/suicides-teen-girls-hit-40-year-high-n789351.

219 **a full 70 percent:** Juliana Menasce Horowitz and Nikki Graf, "Most U.S. Teens See Anxiety and Depression as a Major Problem Among Their Peers," Pew Research Cen-

ter, February 20, 2019, https://www.pewresearch.org/social-trends/2019/02/20/most
-u-s-teens-see-anxiety-and-depression-as-a-major-problem-among-their-peers/.

219 **In an internal presentation:** Georgia Wells et al., "Facebook Knows Instagram Is
Toxic for Teen Girls, Company Documents Show," *Wall Street Journal*, September 14,
2021, https://www.wsj.com/articles/facebook-knows-instagram-is-toxic-for-teen-girls
-company-documents-show-11631620739.

220 **"For us, the destruction":** Sharon Pruitt-Young, "Young People Are Anxious About
Climate Change and Say Governments Are Failing Them," NPR, September 14, 2021,
https://www.npr.org/2021/09/14/1037023551/climate-change-children-young
-adults-anxious-worried-study.

220 **"I kept thinking":** Jonathan Watts, "Greta Thunberg, Schoolgirl Climate Change
Warrior: 'Some People Can Let Things Go. I Can't,'" *Guardian*, March 11, 2019, https://
www.theguardian.com/world/2019/mar/11/greta-thunberg-schoolgirl
-climate-change-warrior-some-people-can-let-things-go-i-cant.

221 **to be out there:** Watts, "Greta Thunberg, Schoolgirl Climate Change Warrior."

221 **soon after published:** Sarah Goody, "Climate Change Activism Improved My Mental
Health," *Teen Vogue*, April 10, 2020, https://www.teenvogue.com/story/climate-change
-activism-improved-my-mental-health.

221 **"Rather than hopelessness":** Goody, "Climate Change Activism Improved My Mental Health."

221 **The group started out:** Saul Elbein, "The Youth Group That Launched a Movement
at Standing Rock," *New York Times Magazine*, January 31, 2017, https://www.nytimes
.com/2017/01/31/magazine/the-youth-group-that-launched-a-movement-at-standing
-rock.html.

222 **Her siblings had:** Elbein, "The Youth Group That Launched a Movement at Standing
Rock."

223 **She decided to get involved:** Interview with Jamie Margolin, August 26, 2021.

223 **When she was eighteen:** Brooke Jarvis, "The Teenagers at the End of the World," *New
York Times Magazine*, July 21, 2020, https://www.nytimes.com/interactive/2020/07/21
/magazine/teenage-activist-climate-change.html.

223 **The more she did:** Jarvis, "The Teenagers at the End of the World."

224 **a fast-forwarded version:** Jamie Margolin interview.

224 **Who knew what:** Jamie Margolin interview.

224 **It energized her:** Jamie Margolin interview.

224 **"That was a bad place":** Jamie Margolin interview.

224 **"There's no guaranteed tomorrow":** Jarvis, "The Teenagers at the End of the World."

225 **She viewed herself:** Jamie Margolin interview.

225 **"When people ask me":** Jamie Margolin interview.

226 **"I've been motivated":** Jamie Margolin interview.

226 **Naomi Wadler was eleven:** Susan Baer, "What It's Like to Become the Voice of Your
Generation—at Age 12," *Washingtonian*, August 11, 2019, https://www.washingtonian
.com/2019/08/11/naomi-wadler-march-for-our-lives-voice-of-generation/.

227 **In the month between:** "'39 Days': How Parkland Shooting Survivors Turned Grief
into Action," CBS News, March 24, 2018, https://www.cbsnews.com/news/march-for
-our-lives-39-days-how-parkland-students-turned-grief-into-action/.

227 **"represent the African American women"**: Lisa Marie Segarra, "Naomi Wadler, 11, Captures Nation's Heart with Powerful Speech about Violence Against Black Women," *Time*, March 24, 2018, https://time.com/5214363/naomi-wadler-march-for-our-lives -speech-black-women/.

227 **She had come to declare**: Segarra, "Naomi Wadler, 11, Captures Nation's Heart with Powerful Speech about Violence Against Black Women."

228 **"balancing the demands"**: Baer, "What It's Like to Become the Voice of Your Generation—at Age 12."

228 **It seemed to dawn**: Baer, "What It's Like to Become the Voice of Your Generation—at Age 12."

228 **does not believe in minting**: Jane Kramer, "Road Warrior," *New Yorker*, October 12, 2015, https://www.newyorker.com/magazine/2015/10/19/road-warrior-profiles-jane-kramer.

228 **She has not let them**: Valerie Jarrett, "Yes, Dolores Can: The 90-Year-Old Activist on Speaking Up, Raising Hell, and Doing the Work," *Glamour*, October 13, 2020, https:// www.glamour.com/story/dolores-huerta-women-of-the-year-2020.

229 **"The headlines tend"**: Jamie Margolin interview.

230 **She was done**: Jamie Margolin interview.

230 **"People listened because"**: Interview with Naomi Wadler, August 17, 2021.

230 **At the walkout**: Baer, "What It's Like to Become the Voice of Your Generation—at Age 12."

230 **More people know**: Naomi Wadler interview.

230 **"so much more equipped"**: Naomi Wadler interview.

231 **She breaks down**: Emily Bent, "This Is Not Another Girl-Power Story: Reading Emma González as a Public Feminist Intellectual," *Signs* 45, no. 4 (2020): 795.

231 **Girl-power feminism**: Bent, "This Is Not Another Girl-Power Story."

231 **That posture "gives"**: Bent, "This Is Not Another Girl-Power Story."

231 **Its scripts and conventions**: Lyn Mikel Brown, *Powered by Girl: A Field Guide for Supporting Youth Activists* (Boston: Beacon Press, 2016), 19.

232 **her speaking time**: Ralph Ellis, "Parkland Student Survivor Throws Up on Stage, Then Finishes Her Speech," CNN, March 24, 2018, https://www.cnn.com/2018/03 /24/us/march-threw-up-on-stage/index.html.

232 **She and fifteen other children**: Anna North, "Young Female Activists Like Greta Thunberg Have the World's Attention," *Vox*, December 11, 2019, https://www.vox.com /2019/12/11/21010936/greta-thunberg-time-magazine-cover-person-year.

232 **It is one of several**: Lesley Clark, "First 'Kids' Climate Trial Will Be Heard in Montana," *Scientific American*, October 5, 2022, https://www.scientificamerican.com /article/first-kids-climate-trial-will-be-heard-in-montana.

232 **She did not want**: North, "Young Female Activists Like Greta Thunberg Have the World's Attention."

232 **"How dare you!"**: Aylin Woodward, "Greta Thunberg Addressed World Leaders Through Tears: 'How Dare You! You Have Stolen My Dreams and My Childhood With Your Empty Words.'" *Business Insider*, September 23, 2019, https://www.business insider.com/greta-thunberg-tearful-speech-un-climate-action-summit-2019-9.

233 **"those phrases are all"**: North, "Young Female Activists Like Greta Thunberg Have the World's Attention."

233 **"I've given many"**: "Greta Thunberg UN Climate Change Conference Speech Transcript," Rev, December 11, 2019, https://www.rev.com/blog/transcripts/greta-thunberg-un-climate-change-conference-speech-transcript.

233 **"that girls can shoulder"**: Bent, "This Is Not Another Girl-Power Story."

233 **Thunberg has been subjected**: North, "Young Female Activists Like Greta Thunberg Have the World's Attention."

233 **Margolin has been condescended to**: Jamie Margolin interview.

233 **"I'm still working"**: Naomi Wadler interview.

234 **At last someone**: Charlotte Alter et al., "2019 Person of the Year: Greta Thunberg," December 11, 2019, https://time.com/person-of-the-year-2019-greta-thunberg/.

234 **It galled her**: Samantha Hunt, "What Is a Teenage Girl?," *New York Times*, January 22, 2021, https://www.nytimes.com/2021/01/22/opinion/kamala-harris-girls.html.

234 **In the piece, Hunt invokes**: Hunt, "What Is a Teenage Girl?"

234 **love has been deemed**: Hunt, "What Is a Teenage Girl?"

235 **"burned ourselves out"**: Jamie Margolin interview.

235 **"I started to feel like"**: Naomi Wadler interview.

236 **a new environmental impact review**: Lisa Friedman, "Standing Rock Sioux Tribe Wins a Victory in Dakota Access Pipeline Case," *New York Times*, March 25, 2020, https://www.nytimes.com/2020/03/25/climate/dakota-access-pipeline-sioux.html.

236 **The environmental review**: Lawrence Hurley, "Dakota Access Pipeline Suffers U.S. Supreme Court Setback," Reuters, February 22, 2022, https://www.reuters.com/business/energy/us-supreme-court-turns-away-dakota-pipeline-operators-appeal-2022-02-22/.

236 **It had given people**: Matthew Green, "The Youth Activists Behind the Standing Rock Resistance," KQED, May 23, 2017, https://www.kqed.org/lowdown/27023/the-youth-of-standing-rock.

236 **"With this generation"**: Green, "The Youth Activists Behind the Standing Rock Resistance."

CHAPTER ELEVEN: STREAM OF CONSCIOUSNESS: HOW GIRLS USE THEIR VOICES

238 **Joe Biden and Kamala Harris**: Angela Nelson, "Young Voters Were Crucial to Biden's Win," Tufts Now, November 12, 2020, https://now.tufts.edu/2020/11/12/young-voters-were-crucial-bidens-win.

238 **Youth turnout had clocked**: Hannah Miao, "Young Voters Are Poised to Be a Decisive Factor Even as Coronavirus Creates Obstacles," CNBC, October 27, 2020, https://www.cnbc.com/2020/10/26/2020-election-young-voters-could-be-a-decisive-force-despite-coronavirus.html.

238 **Voter registration efforts**: B. J. Rudell, "Will Young Voters Be the Difference Makers in 2020," *The Hill*, September 24, 2019, https://thehill.com/opinion/campaign/462837-will-young-voters-be-the-difference-makers-in-2020/.

238 **When then candidate Joe Biden**: Errin Haines, "Biden Campaign Hopes to Reach Young Voters Through MTV Video Music Awards," The 19th, August 30, 2020,

https://19thnews.org/2020/08/biden-campaign-hopes-to-reach-young-voters-through-mtv-video-music-awards/.

238 **After the pandemic:** Tabitha Mueller, "Gen Z, Millennial Vote Organizers Hope to Channel Youth Energy into Historic Turnout," *Nevada Independent*, October 30, 2020, https://thenevadaindependent.com/article/gen-z-millennial-vote-organizers-hope-to-channel-youth-energy-into-historic-turnout.

238 **When voters went:** Barbara Rodriguez, "The Country Needs Poll Workers. Young Women Are Stepping Up," The 19th, October 21, 2020, https://19thnews.org/2020/10/poll-workers-young-women-stepping-up/.

239 **What she christened:** Rodriguez, "The Country Needs Poll Workers."

239 **"It's Gen Z reaching out":** Rodriguez, "The Country Needs Poll Workers."

239 **Turnout for people:** Lili Pike, "Why So Many Young People Showed Up on Election Day," *Vox*, November 7, 2020, https://www.vox.com/2020/11/7/21552248/youth-vote-2020-georgia-biden-covid-19-racism-climate-change.

239 **Young people helped:** Raisa Bruner, "'Civic Engagement Doesn't Have to Be Corny.' How Georgia Pulled Off Unprecedented Voter Turnout," *Time*, November 6, 2020, https://time.com/5908483/georgia-youth-vote/; Mariah Espada, "'We've Seen a Youthquake.' How Youth of Color Backed Joe Biden in Battleground States," *Time*, November 10, 2020, https://time.com/5910291/weve-seen-a-youthquake-how-youth-of-color-backed-joe-biden-in-battleground-states/.

239 **Polling data suggests:** "Black Youth Play Major Role in Democratic Victories in Georgia Runoffs," Center for Information & Research on Civic Learning and Engagement (CIRCLE) at Tufts, January 7, 2021, https://circle.tufts.edu/latest-research/black-youth-play-major-role-democratic-victories-georgia-runoffs.

239 **In 2018, CIRCLE found:** "The Gun Violence Prevention Movement Fueled Youth Engagement in 2018," CIRCLE at Tufts, February 15, 2019, https://circle.tufts.edu/latest-research/gun-violence-prevention-movement-fueled-youth-engagement-2018-election.

239 **In its own postmortem:** Evan Weber and Varshini Prakash, "Sunrise Movement's General Election Impact," Sunrise Movement, October 31, 2020, updated November 6, 2020, https://www.sunrisemovement.org/press-releases/sunrise-movements-general-election-impact/.

240 **The constitutional amendment:** Thomas F. Schaller, "50 Years Ago, the U.S. Ratified the 26th Amendment; Don't Expect It to Ratify Another—Ever," *Baltimore Sun*, June 30, 2021, https://www.baltimoresun.com/opinion/op-ed/bs-ed-op-0701-last-amendment-eve-20210630-ucn5ctsxbjbbljiq5kdjqnbad4-story.html.

240 **The appeal was instead:** Rebecca de Schweinitz, "The Proper Age for Suffrage: Vote 18 and the Politics of Age from World War II to the Age of Aquarius," in *Age in America: The Colonial Era to the Present*, ed. Corinne T. Field and Nicholas L. Syrett (New York: New York University Press, 2015), 209.

240 **It would help less:** de Schweinitz, "The Proper Age for Suffrage," 211.

241 **We "are quick":** de Schweinitz, "The Proper Age for Suffrage," 224.

241 **In Connecticut, a committee:** de Schweinitz, "The Proper Age for Suffrage," 220.

241 **Others framed the case:** de Schweinitz, "The Proper Age for Suffrage," 225.

241 **a Gallup poll found:** Jennifer Frost, "On Account of Age," *Australasian Journal of American Studies* 40, no. 2 (December 2021): 54.

242 **Its members were photographed:** Frost, "On Account of Age," 55.

242 **Writers who had:** Jennifer Frost, *"Let Us Vote!": Youth Voting Rights and the 26th Amendment* (New York: New York University Press, 2022), introduction.

242 **The NAACP decided:** Mae C. Quinn, "Black Women and Girls and the Twenty-Sixth Amendment: Constitutional Connections, Activist Intersections, and the First Wave Youth Suffrage Movement," *Seattle University Law Review* 43, no. 4 (2020): 1261.

242 **One movement fed:** Dash Coleman, "State Historical Marker to Commemorate Savannah Civil Rights Struggle," *Savannah Morning News*, September 21, 2016, https://www.savannahnow.com/news/2016-09-21/state-historical-marker-commemorate-savannah-civil-rights-struggle/13915450007.

242 **To demonstrate the wide support:** Manisha Claire, "How Young Activists Got 18-Year-Olds the Right to Vote in Record Time," *Smithsonian*, November 11, 2020, https://www.smithsonianmag.com/history/how-young-activists-got-18-year-olds-right-vote-record-time-180976261/.

242 **Quilloin obsessed over:** Emil Dansker, "NAACP Urges Support for Youth, Model Cities," *Dayton Daily News*, April 1, 1969, 2.

243 **In front of some:** Quinn, "Black Women and Girls and the Twenty-Sixth Amendment," 1269.

243 **"You have disarmed us":** Quinn, "Black Women and Girls and the Twenty-Sixth Amendment," 1269.

243 **The bill passed:** Vince Guerrieri, "How 13 Seconds Changed Kent State University Forever," *Smithsonian*, May 1, 2020, https://www.smithsonianmag.com/history/fifty-years-ago-kent-state-massacre-changed-university-forever-180974787/.

243 **The amendment was:** Claire, "How Young Activists Got 18-Year-Olds the Right to Vote in Record Time."

243 **Queen and Quilloin:** Quinn, "Black Women and Girls and the Twenty-Sixth Amendment," 1269.

243 **Their vote split:** Claire, "How Young Activists Got 18-Year-Olds the Right to Vote in Record Time."

244 **Voting wasn't just:** Rainesford Stauffer, "How Democrats Can Win the Youth Vote in November," *New York Times*, July 8, 2020, https://www.nytimes.com/2020/07/08/opinion/election-democrats-youth.html.

244 **It would allow teenagers:** Rick Sobey, "Elizabeth Warren Wants to Expand Youth Voting, Her Bill Would Require States to Have Pre-Registration for Those 16, 17 Years Old," *Boston Herald*, July 11, 2022, https://www.bostonherald.com/2022/07/11/elizabeth-warren-wants-to-expand-youth-voting-her-bill-would-require-states-to-have-pre-registration-for-those-16-17-years-old/.

245 **She curated musical selections:** Stauffer, "How Democrats Can Win the Youth Vote in November."

245 **"It's not just about elections":** Stauffer, "How Democrats Can Win the Youth Vote in November."

245 **In response, Thunberg:** "Greta Thunberg Changes Twitter Bio after Trump Dig," BBC, December 12, 2019, https://www.bbc.com/news/world-europe-50762373.

246 **Pundits and blowhards:** Charlie Warzel, "The Pro-Trump Media Has Met Its Match in

the Parkland Students," *BuzzFeed*, February 21, 2018, https://www.buzzfeednews.com/article/charliewarzel/parkland-school-shooting-survivors-crisis-actors-pro-trump.

246 **Warzel observes that:** Warzel, "The Pro-Trump Media Has Met Its Match in the Parkland Students."

246 **In that scheme:** Margaret Talbot, "Girls Just Want to Be Mean," *New York Times Magazine*, February 24, 2002, https://www.nytimes.com/2002/02/24/magazine/girls-just-want-to-be-mean.html.

247 **But that change did not:** Talbot, "Girls Just Want to Be Mean."

247 **"Their superior social intelligence":** Talbot, "Girls Just Want to Be Mean."

247 **"[T]hey know better":** Talbot, "Girls Just Want to Be Mean."

247 **the mechanisms of social progress:** Hedy Greijdanus et al., "The Psychology of Online Activism and Social Movements: Relations between Online and Offline Collective Action," *Current Opinion in Psychology* 35 (2020): 50–51.

247 **In 2021, almost 60 percent:** Alexis Lanza, "Young Women Are Using Instagram to Fight for the Future of the Planet," The 19th, November 25, 2020, https://19thnews.org/2020/11/young-women-climate-activists-instagram-future-planet/.

247 **The gender breakdown:** "Distribution of Monthly Active TikTok Users in the United States as of March 2021, by Gender," Statista, March 2021, https://www.statista.com/statistics/1095201/tiktok-users-gender-usa/.

248 **One blared the tune:** Jessica Grose, "The New Abortion Rights Advocates Are on TikTok," *New York Times*, December 10, 2020, https://www.nytimes.com/2020/12/10/style/abortion-rights-activists-tiktok.html.

248 **It earned her:** @alexthefeminist, TikTok post, August 27, 2020, https://www.tiktok.com/@princesskenny444/video/6865744033910639878?lang=en&is_copy_url=1&is_from_webapp=v1.

248 **"We had a goal":** Bettina Chang, "How Four Teenage Girls Organized This Week's Huge Silent Protest," *Chicago*, July 14, 2016, https://www.chicagomag.com/city-life/July-2016/Black-Lives-Matter-Chi-Youth-Sit-In-Rally/.

248 **Lewis told her:** Chang, "How Four Teenage Girls Organized This Week's Huge Silent Protest."

249 **"struggle in the public square":** Jane Hu, "The Second Act of Social-Media Activism," *New Yorker*, August 3, 2020, https://www.newyorker.com/culture/cultural-comment/the-second-act-of-social-media-activism.

249 **There is less need:** Hu, "The Second Act of Social-Media Activism."

249 **She had been shopping:** Elizabeth Alexander, "The Trayvon Generation," *New Yorker*, June 15, 2020, https://www.newyorker.com/magazine/2020/06/22/the-trayvon-generation.

250 **"I'm just sharing":** Nina Metz, "Eva Maria Lewis Has Found Her Voice as an Organizer, in On the Ground Chi," *Chicago Tribune*, June 5, 2020, https://www.chicagotribune.com/social-justice/ct-faces-of-fallout-george-floyd-eva-maria-lewis-0604-20200605-45uru2hte5fprnhbls4lurp25a-story.html.

250 **the first protest that Thomas:** Jessica Bennett, "These Teen Girls Are Fighting for a More Just Future," *New York Times*, July 3, 2020, https://www.nytimes.com/2020/06/26/style/teen-girls-black-lives-matter-activism.html.

251 **In Chicago, a high school:** Bennett, "These Teen Girls Are Fighting for a More Just Future."

251 **She invited Cori Bush:** Bennett, "These Teen Girls Are Fighting for a More Just Future."

251 **"We are teenagers":** Bennett, "These Teen Girls Are Fighting for a More Just Future."

251 **The murder "changed":** Giulia McDonnell Nieto del Rio, "Darnella Frazier, the Teenager Who Recorded George Floyd's Murder, Speaks Out," *New York Times*, May 25, 2021, https://www.nytimes.com/2021/05/25/us/darnella-frazier.html.

252 **If it weren't:** Nieto del Rio, "Darnella Frazier, the Teenager Who Recorded George Floyd's Murder, Speaks Out."

252 **The bungled governmental response:** Jessica Grose, "Gen Z Is Cynical. They've Earned It," *New York Times*, May 27, 2022, https://www.nytimes.com/2022/05/27/opinion/gen-z-uvalde-covid-climate.html.

253 **Still, the poll found:** "Harvard Youth Poll: Top Trends and Takeaways," Institute of Politics at the Harvard Kennedy School, April 25, 2022, https://iop.harvard.edu/youth-poll/spring-2022-harvard-youth-poll.

253 **That is the superpower:** Grose, "Gen Z Is Cynical. They've Earned It."

253 **It draws on the skills:** "About," Gen-Z for Change, https://genzforchange.org/about/.

253 **a traditional team photo:** "About," Gen-Z for Change, https://genzforchange.org/about/.

253 **When the Supreme Court:** Kalhan Rosenblatt, "A Gen Z Organization Is Enlisting People to Flood Anti-Abortion Websites Following Leak of Draft Opinion That Would Overturn Roe," NBC News, May 3, 2022, https://www.nbcnews.com/news/us-news/gen-z-organization-enlisting-people-flood-anti-abortion-websites-leak-rcna27117.

254 **"We had spreadsheets":** Interview with Olivia Julianna, August 22, 2022.

254 **"She is an actual":** Olivia Julianna interview.

255 **"I don't think people":** Olivia Julianna interview.

255 **When she defies:** Olivia Julianna interview.

255 **"You do worry":** Olivia Julianna interview.

256 **She pictured middle schoolers:** Interview with Cassandra Levesque, August 26, 2022.

256 **Then she upped:** Kate Taylor, "In New Class of Young Lawmakers, a Former Girl Scout Goes to the Statehouse," *New York Times*, https://www.nytimes.com/2018/11/13/us/young-candidates-elections.html.

256 **The man who had rebuffed:** Taylor, "In New Class of Young Lawmakers, a Former Girl Scout Goes to the Statehouse."

256 **In 2021, one in five:** Erin Doherty, "The Number of LGBTQ-Identifying Adults Is Soaring," Axios, February 19, 2022, https://www.axios.com/2022/02/17/lgbtq-generation-z-gallup.

257 **In Alabama, doctors:** Arthur Jones II and Aaron Navarro, "This Year on Pace to See Record Anti-Transgender Bills Passed by States, Says Human Rights Campaign," CBS News, April 22, 2022, https://www.cbsnews.com/news/2022-anti-transgender-legislation-record-human-rights-campaign/.

257 **The percentage of trans children:** Jones II and Navarro, "This Year on Pace to See Record Anti-Transgender Bills Passed by States."

258 **"Please keep me safe":** Alexa Ura, "Despite Losing Bathroom Bill Fight, a Texas Girl Gets Her Two Minutes," *Texas Tribune*, July 22, 2017, https://www.texastribune.org/2017/07/22/transgender-girl-gets-her-two-minutes-bathroom-bill/.

258 **In 2021, Texas considered:** Jo Yurcaba, "Texas Has Considered Dozens of Anti-Trans Bills. These Moms Have Helped Stop Them," NBC News, September 30, 2021,

https://www.nbcnews.com/nbc-out/out-politics-and-policy/texas-considered -dozens-anti-trans-bills-moms-helped-stop-rcna2355.

258 **Texas would like:** Andrew DeMillo, "Texas Investigations into Families with Trans Children Seeking Gender-Confirming Care Blocked," ABC News, June 13, 2022, https://abc13.com/texas-trans-child-abuse-aclu-lambda-legal-transgender -confirming-therapy/11945851/.

258 **Gonzales travels to Austin:** Interview with Rachel Gonzales, August 27, 2022.

258 **"When I'm waiting":** Interview with Libby Gonzales, August 27, 2022.

258 **"Now we're besties":** Libby Gonzales interview.

259 **She told reporters:** "Deep in the Pockets of Texas," CNN Special Report, July 24, 2022.

259 **"Just seeing someone older":** Interview with Hayden Valentina Bisset, August 25, 2022.

260 **She wanted kids:** Erick Trickey, "'Why Is Child Marriage Still Legal?': A Young Lawmaker Tackles a Hidden Problem," *Politico*, January 9, 2022, https://www.politico.com /news/magazine/2022/01/09/cassie-levesque-new-hampshire-child-marriage-52 4159.

260 **When she won:** Cassandra Levesque interview.

CONCLUSION

262 **It was a glorious:** Marley Dias, "ELLE.com Has a New Boss and She's 11 Years Old," Elle.com, September 19, 2016, https://www.elle.com/culture/career-politics/a38970 /marley-dias-editor-letter-marley-mag/.

263 **She writes that adolescents:** Sarah Nicole Prickett, "Jigsaw Youth," *Artforum*, March 14, 2014, https://www.artforum.com/film/sarah-nicole-prickett-on-matt-wolf-s-teenage -45709.

263 **"That comes later":** Interview with Heather Booth, July 20, 2021.

264 **His career ended:** "Incest Survivor Speaks Out," NPR, June 9, 2008, https://www .npr.org/templates/story/story.php?storyId=91308715.

264 **"She asked me":** Marianna Bacallao, "Diane Nash Says She Shares Her Presidential Medal of Freedom with Everyone Who 'Sacrificed So Much for the Cause,'" WPLN News, July 7, 2022, https://wpln.org/post/diane-nash-says-she-shares-her-presidential -medal-of-freedom-with-everyone-who-sacrificed-so-much-for-the-cause/.

264 **"I would still participate":** Brenda Travis, interview by Bruce Hartford, Civil Rights Movement Archive, February 2007, https://www.crmvet.org/nars/travisb.htm#btlbt.

265 **The school accused:** Elisabeth Griffith, *Formidable: American Women and the Fight for Equality: 1920–2020* (New York: Pegasus Books, 2022), 126.

265 **"I did not want":** Dick Cluster, "The Borning Struggle: An Interview with Bernice Johnson Reagon," Radical America 12 (November/December 1978): 11.

265 **some "unbelievable leap":** Bernice Johnson Reagon, "My Black Mothers and Sisters or On Beginning a Cultural Autobiography," *Feminist Studies* 8, no. 1 (1982): 94.

266 **The two women graduated:** Griffith, *Formidable*, 127; Richard Goldstein, "Autherine Lucy Foster, First Black Student at U. of Alabama, Dies at 92," *New York Times*, March 2, 2022, https://www.nytimes.com/2022/03/02/us/autherine-lucy-foster-dead.html.

266 **Her girlhood activism:** Interview with Alice Haines, August 21, 2021.

266 **She is no savior:** Clover Hope, "Poet Amanda Gorman Dreams of Becoming the President," *Wall Street Journal*, November 3, 2021, https://www.wsj.com/story/poet-amanda-gorman-dreams-of-becoming-the-president-2216ee71.

266 **a recent paper:** Barbara Rodriguez, "Girls Are Being Socialized to Lose Political Ambition—and It Starts Younger Than We Realized," The 19th, September 23, 2021, https://19thnews.org/2021/09/study-girls-socialized-lose-political-ambition-younger-age/.

266 **The fashion critic Robin Givhan:** Robin Givhan, "The Sound of a Shifting Power Structure," *Washington Post*, January 13, 2021, https://www.washingtonpost.com/nation/2021/01/13/power-structure-black-women-kamala-harris/.

267 **Tending to our:** Hava Rachel Gordon, "Gendered Paths to Teenage Political Participation: Parental Power, Civic Mobility, and Youth Activism," *Gender and Society* 22, no. 1 (2008): 32.

267 **"Friends, we do not":** Bernard Weinraub, "The Brilliancy of Black," *Esquire*, January 1, 1967.

BIBLIOGRAPHY

"'39 Days': How Parkland Shooting Survivors Turned Grief into Action." CBS News. March 24, 2018. https://www.cbsnews.com/news/march-for-our-lives-39-days-how-parkland -students-turned-grief-into-action/.

"114 Negroes Arrested." *New York Times.* October 5, 1961. https://timesmachine.nytimes .com/timesmachine/1961/10/05/101476447.html?pageNumber=21.

"141 Men and Girls Die in Waist Factory Fire; Trapped High Up in Washington Place Building; Street Strewn with Bodies; Piles of Dead Inside." *New York Times.* March 26, 1911, https://www.nytimes.com/1911/03/26/archives/141-men-and-girls-die-in-waist-factory -fire-trapped-high-up-in.html.

"2 Unwed Mothers Get Chance to Finish School." *Chicago Daily Defender.* July 12, 1969.

"A History of Racial Injustice Calendar." Equal Justice Initiative. https://shop.eji.org/collec tions/books-calendars/products/a-history-of-racial-injustice-calendar-2022.

"A Revealing Experiment: *Brown v. Board* and 'The Doll Test.'" NAACP Legal Defense and Educational Fund. https://www.naacpldf.org/brown-vs-board/significance-doll -test/.

"About." Gen-Z for Change. https://genzforchange.org/about/.

"ACLU Settles Kentucky Case of Pregnant Teens Denied Entry to Honor Society." ACLU. October 22, 1999. https://www.aclu.org/press-releases/aclu-settles-kentucky -case-pregnant-teens-denied-entry-honor-society.

"Americans' View on Whether, and in What Circumstances, Abortion Should Be Legal." Pew Research Center. May 6, 2022. https://www.pewresearch.org/religion/2022/05/06

/americans-views-on-whether-and-in-what-circumstances-abortion-should-be
-legal/.

"Andrew Jackson in New England." *Proceedings of the Massachusetts Historical Society* 56 (1922–
1923): 243–63.

"Anna Elizabeth Dickinson: 1842–1932." Historical Marker. June 2, 2001. Goshen, New
York. https://www.hmdb.org/m.aspm=25762.

"Armbands Yes, Miniskirts No." *New York Times.* February 26, 1969. https://www.nytimes
.com/1969/02/26/archives/armbands-yes-miniskirts-no.html.

"Before 'Roe v. Wade,' The Women of 'Jane' Provided Abortions for the Women of Chicago." *All Things Considered.* NPR. January 19, 2018. https://www.npr.org/2018/01
/19/578620266/before-roe-v-wade-the-women-of-jane-provided-abortions-for-the
-women-of-chicago.

"Before Rosa Parks, a Teenager Defied Segregation on an Alabama Bus." *All Things Considered.* NPR. March 2, 2015. https://www.npr.org/sections/codeswitch/2015/02/27/389563788
/before-rosa-parks-a-teenager-defied-segregation-on-an-alabama-bus.

"Black Youth Play Major Role in Democratic Victories in Georgia Runoffs." Center for Information & Research on Civic Learning and Engagement (CIRCLE) at Tufts. January
7, 2021. https://circle.tufts.edu/latest-research/black-youth-play-major-role-democratic
-victories-georgia-runoffs.

"Chinese Girl Wants Vote: Miss Lee, Ready to Enter Barnard, to Ride in Suffrage Parade."
New-York Tribune. April 13, 1912.

"Chinese Women Dine with White." *Oregonian.* April 12, 1912.

"Chinese Women to Parade for Woman Suffrage." *New York Times.* April 14, 1912.

"Constitution of the Lowell Factory Girls Association." In *Feminist Manifestos: A Global Documentary Reader,* edited by Penny A. Weiss, 53–55. New York: New York University Press,
2018.

"Deep in the Pockets of Texas." CNN Special Report. July 24, 2022.

"Distribution of Monthly Active TikTok Users in the United States as of March 2021, by
Gender." Statista. March 2021. https://www.statista.com/statistics/1095201/tiktok-users
-gender-usa/.

"Dr. Spock Urges Parents to Allay Cold-War Tensions." *York Daily Record.* March 16, 1964.

"Federation Women Fight over By-Laws." *New York Times.* December 3, 1909.

"Gen Z Marchers Praying for an End to US Abortion." BBC. January 22, 2022. https://www
.bbc.com/news/av/world-us-canada-60088680.

"Girl Challenges Stuyvesant High's All-Boy Policy." *New York Times.* January 21, 1969.

"Girl Pacifist, Held 68 Days, Is Released after Apology." *New York Times.* September
29, 1966. https://timesmachine.nytimes.com/timesmachine/1966/09/29/82513761.html?
pageNumber=52.

"Greta Thunberg Changes Twitter Bio after Trump Dig." BBC. December 12, 2019. https://
www.bbc.com/news/world-europe-50762373.

"Greta Thunberg UN Climate Change Conference Speech Transcript." Rev. December 11,
2019. https://www.rev.com/blog/transcripts/greta-thunberg-un-climate-change-conference-
speech-transcript.

"Harriet Hanson Robinson." National Park Service. https://www.nps.gov/lowe/learn/history
culture/robinson.htm.

"Harvard Youth Poll: Top Trends and Takeaways." Institute of Politics at the Harvard Kennedy School. April 25, 2022. https://iop.harvard.edu/youth-poll/spring-2022-harvard-youth-poll.

"Incest Survivor Speaks Out." NPR. June 9, 2008. https://www.npr.org/templates/story/story.php?storyId=91308715.

"John Tinker Describes the Inspiration to Protest the Vietnam War." Iowa Pathways. PBS. Johnston, Iowa. February 21, 2019. https://www.iowapbs.org/iowapathways/artifact/1424/john-tinker-describes-inspiration-protest-vietnam-war.

"Liberation Conference." *Emmanuel Focus*, May 1969. https://www.ourbodiesourselvestoday.org/wp-content/uploads/2020/02/Emmanuel-Focus-5-9-1969.pdf.

"Local NAACP Rolls Up Big Membership." *Los Angeles Sentinel*. April 12, 1956.

"Lowell—Its Aspects—Manufacturers—Conditions of Labor—Reforms." *New-York Daily Tribune*. May 14, 1846.

"Negro Girl Found Guilty of Segregation Violation." *Alabama Journal*. March 19, 1955.

"New-Hampshire Ten-Hour Law." *New-York Daily Tribune*. August 11, 1847.

"NYCLU Gives Schools Chancellor Levy an 'F' for Failing to Stop Discrimination Against Pregnant and Parenting Girls." ACLU of New York. March 24, 2002. https://www.nyclu.org/en/press-releases/nyclu-gives-schools-chancellor-levy-f-failing-stop-discrimination-against-pregnant.

"Obituary: Mrs. Charlotte L. Peirce." *Philadelphia Inquirer*. March 16, 1924.

"One Tough Case." Berkeley Law. March 1, 2009. https://www.law.berkeley.edu/article/one-tough-case/.

"Parade of the Women." *New York Times*. May 6, 1911. https://timesmachine.nytimes.com/timesmachine/1911/05/06/105026491.html?pageNumber=12.

"Radio, TV Output Down in January." *New York Times*. February 26, 1951.

"Rights for Students." *Boston Globe*. February 27, 1969.

"Stuyvesant High School Enrollment (2020–2021)." New York State Education Department. 2020. https://data.nysed.gov/enrollment.php?year=2020&instid=800000046741.

"Sybil Ludington: Women on Stamps: Part I." Smithsonian National Postal Museum. https://postalmuseum.si.edu/exhibition/women_on_stamps_part_1_forming_the_nation_revolutionary_fighters/sybil_ludington.

"Sybil Ludington." American Battlefield Trust. https://www.battlefields.org/learn/biographies/sybil_ludington.

"Talking Girl in Film Show Gets Slapped." *Los Angeles Times*. October 3, 1936.

"Teach a Girl to Lead: Women's Suffrage in the U.S. by State." Center for American Women and Politics. August 2014. https://tag.rutgers.edu/wp-content/uploads/2014/05/suffrage-by-state.pdf.

"Teen-Age Girls: They Live in a Wonderful World of Their Own." *Life*. December 1944. https://time.com/3639041/.

"The Armband Case." *Des Moines Register*. February 27, 1969.

"The Gun Violence Prevention Movement Fueled Youth Engagement in 2018." CIRCLE at Tufts. February 15, 2019. https://circle.tufts.edu/latest-research/gun-violence-prevention-movement-fueled-youth-engagement-2018-election.

"The U.S. Student Population Is More Diverse, but Schools Are Still Highly Segregated." *Morning Edition*. NPR. July 14, 2022. https://www.npr.org/2022/07/14/1111060299/school-segregation-report.

BIBLIOGRAPHY

"Turn-Out at Lowell." Boston Evening Transcript. February 17, 1834.

"Untitled News Story about High School Girl Sassing a Mayor." In *Dear Sisters: Dispatches from the Women's Liberation Movement*, edited by Rosalyn Baxandall and Linda Gordon. New York: Basic Books, 2001.

"Vast Suffrage Host Is on Parade To-Day." *New York Times*. May 4, 1912.

"What Is Extinction Rebellion and What Does It Want?" BBC. April 14, 2022. https://www .bbc.com/news/uk-48607989.

"Woolworth to Shut Its Detroit Stores." *New York Times*. March 1, 1937. https://www .nytimes.com/1937/03/01/archives/woolworth-to-shut-its-detroit-stores-area -chief-says-all-40-with.html.

A D I T I (@_memesvalididi). "ITEMS EVERY WOMAN SHOULD OWN . . ." Twitter post. June 22, 2021, 7:56 a.m. https://twitter.com/_memesvalididi/status/1407306476 872355846.

Alexander, Elizabeth. "The Trayvon Generation." *New Yorker*. June 15, 2020. https://www .newyorker.com/magazine/2020/06/22/the-trayvon-generation.

Alexander, Kerri Lee. "Sarah Moore Grimké." National Women's History Museum. 2018. https://www.womenshistory.org/education-resources/biographies/sarah-moore-grimke.

alexthefeminist (@alexthefeminist). TikTok post. August 27, 2020. https://www.tiktok .com/@princesskenny444/video/6865744033910639878?lang=en&is_copy_url=1&is _from_webapp=v1.

Allen, Mike. "Defiant V.M.I. to Admit Women, but Will Not Ease the Rules for Them." *New York Times*. September 22, 1996. https://www.nytimes.com/1996/09/22/us/defiant -vmi-to-admit-women-but-will-not-ease-rules-for-them.html.

Alter, Charlotte, Suyin Haynes, and Justin Worland. "2019 Person of the Year: Greta Thunberg." *Time*. December 11, 2019. https://time.com/person-of-the-year-2019-greta-thunberg/.

Anderson, Judith. "Anna Dickinson, Antislavery Radical." *Pennsylvania History: A Journal of Mid-Atlantic Studies* 3, no. 3 (1936): 147–63.

Angelou, Maya. *Conversations with Maya Angelou*. Edited by Jeffrey M. Elliot. Jackson: University Press of Mississippi, 1989.

Arrest report for Claudette Colvin. March 2, 1955. Martin Luther King, Jr. Research and Education Institute. Online King Records Access (OKRA) database. http://okra .stanford.edu/transcription/document_images/undecided/550302-001.pdf.

Avery, Dianne, and Alfred S. Konefsky. "The Daughters of Job: Property Rights and Women's Lives in Mid-Nineteenth-Century Massachusetts." *Law and History Review* 10, no. 2 (1992): 323–56.

Bacallao, Marianna. "Diane Nash Says She Shares Her Presidential Medal of Freedom with Everyone Who 'Sacrificed So Much for the Cause.'" WPLN News. July 7, 2022. https:// wpln.org/post/diane-nash-says-she-shares-her-presidential-medal-of-freedom-with -everyone-who-sacrificed-so-much-for-the-cause/.

Baer, Susan. "What It's Like to Become the Voice of Your Generation—at Age 12." *Washingtonian*. August 11, 2019. https://www.washingtonian.com/2019/08/11/naomi-wadler -march-for-our-lives-voice-of-generation/.

Baker Old Class Collection. Baker Library, Harvard Business School, Harvard University, Cambridge, MA.

Barnes, Brooks. "From Footnote to Fame in Civil Rights History." *New York Times*. November 25, 2009. https://www.nytimes.com/2009/11/26/books/26colvin.html.

Beecher, Catharine. *A Treatise on Domestic Economy.* 1841. Reprint, New York: Harper & Brothers, 1848.

Benjamin, Philip. "2 Girls Convicted in Atom Sitdown." *New York Times.* April 6, 1962. https://timesmachine.nytimes.com/timesmachine/1962/04/06/89854595.html?page Number=4.

Bennett, Jessica. "These Teen Girls Are Fighting for a More Just Future." *New York Times.* July 3, 2020. https://www.nytimes.com/2020/06/26/style/teen-girls-black-lives-matter -activism.html.

Bent, Emily. "This Is Not Another Girl-Power Story: Reading Emma González as a Public Feminist Intellectual." *Signs* 45, no. 4 (2020): 795–816.

Bhattacharya, Shriya. "Gen Z Is Preparing to Fight for Reproductive Justice in a Future without *Roe v. Wade.*" Prism Reports. May 24, 2022. https://prismreports.org/2022/05 /24/gen-z-fight-for-reproductive-justice-post-roe-v-wade/.

Biester, Charlotte E. "Catharine Beecher's Views of Home Economics." *History of Education Journal* 3, no. 3 (1952): 88–91.

Bingham, Clara. "Code Names and Secret Lives: How a Radical Underground Network Helped Women Get Abortions before They Were Legal." *Vanity Fair.* April 17, 2019. https://www.vanityfair.com/style/2019/04/jane-network-abortion-feature.

Blaemire, Robert. *Birch Bayh: Making a Difference.* Bloomington: Indiana University Press, 2019.

Blau, Eleanor. "Brooklyn High School Blends Class Work and Jobs." *New York Times.* March 14, 1971.

Brady, Mathew B. "Anna Elizabeth Dickinson." 1863. Albumen silver print. National Portrait Gallery, Washington, D.C. https://npg.si.edu/object/npg_NPG.87.290.

Branch, Taylor. *Parting the Waters: America in the King Years, 1954–63.* New York: Simon & Schuster, 1988.

Breen, T. H. *The Marketplace of Revolution: How Consumer Politics Shaped American Independence.* Oxford: Oxford University Press, 2004.

Breines, Wini. *Young, White, and Miserable: Growing Up Female in the Fifties.* Chicago: University of Chicago Press, 2001.

Brine, Ruth. "The New Feminists: Revolt Against Sexism." *Time.* November 21, 1969.

Brown, DeNeen L. "The Determined Father Who Took Linda Brown by the Hand and Made History." *Washington Post.* March 27, 2018.

Brown, Lyn Mikel. *Powered by Girl: A Field Guide for Supporting Youth Activists.* Boston: Beacon Press, 2016.

Brownmiller, Susan. "Sisterhood Is Powerful." *New York Times.* March 15, 1970. https://www .nytimes.com/1970/03/15/archives/sisterhood-is-powerful-a-member-of-the-womens -liberation-movement.html.

Bruner, Raisa. "'Civic Engagement Doesn't Have to Be Corny.' How Georgia Pulled Off Unprecedented Voter Turnout." *Time.* November 6, 2020. https://time.com/5908483 /georgia-youth-vote.

Bumiller, Elisabeth. "Gloria Steinem, the Everyday Rebel." *Washington Post.* October 12, 1983. https://www.washingtonpost.com/archive/lifestyle/1983/10/12/gloria-steinem-the -everyday-rebel/164d44d2-3f21-49a9-9d62-c12408446409/.

Burns, Stewart, ed. *Daybreak of Freedom.* Chapel Hill: University of North Carolina Press, 1997.

Bushman, Claudia. *"A Good Poor Man's Wife": Being a Chronicle of Harriet Hanson Robinson and Her Family in Nineteenth-Century New England.* Hanover, NH: University Press of New England, 1998.

Cahill, Cathleen D. *Recasting the Vote: How Women of Color Transformed the Suffrage Movement.* Chapel Hill: University of North Carolina, 2020.

Carroll, Nicole. "Cristina Jiménez Moreta Helped Get DACA, Now She Helps Young Immigrants Find Their Voice." *USA Today.* August 20, 2020. https://www.usatoday.com /in-depth/life/women-of-the-century/2020/08/20/cristina-jimenez-moreta -advocates-daca-undocumented-youth-human-rights/5535786002/.

Chambers, Veronica, Jennifer Schuessler, Amisha Padnani, Jennifer Harlan, Sandra E. Garcia, and Vivian Wang. "Meet the Brave but Overlooked Women of Color Who Fought for the Vote." *New York Times.* August 19, 2020. https://www.nytimes.com/2020/07/24 /books/finish-the-fight-excerpt.html.

Chaney, Alexis. "Swooning, Screaming, Crying: How Teenage Girls Have Driven 60 Years of Pop Music." *Vox.* January 28, 2016. https://www.vox.com/2016/1/28/10815492/teenage -girls-screaming.

Chang, Bettina. "How Four Teenage Girls Organized This Week's Huge Silent Protest." *Chicago.* July 14, 2016. https://www.chicagomag.com/city-life/July-2016/Black-Lives-Matter -Chi-Youth-Sit-In-Rally/.

ChronicCookieee (@ChronicCookieee). "You know when you need to go tampon shopping…" Twitter post. April 7, 2021, 3:33 a.m. https://twitter.com/ChronicCookieee/status/1379 698734863314948.

Claire, Manisha. "How Young Activists Got 18-Year-Olds the Right to Vote in Record Time." *Smithsonian.* November 11, 2020. https://www.smithsonianmag.com/history/how-young -activists-got-18-year-olds-right-vote-record-time-180976261/.

Clark, Kenneth B. *Prejudice and Your Child.* Middletown, CT: Wesleyan University Press, 1963.

Clark, Lesley. "First 'Kids' Climate Trial Will Be Heard in Montana." *Scientific American.* October 5, 2022. https://www.scientificamerican.com/article/first-kids-climate-trial-will -be-heard-in-montana/.

Clemente, Deirdre. *Dress Casual: How College Students Redefined American Style.* Chapel Hill: University of North Carolina Press, 2014.

Cluster, Dick. "The Borning Struggle: An Interview with Bernice Johnson Reagon." Radical America 12 (November/December 1978): 8–25.

Clymer, Adam. "Birch Bayh, 91, Dies; Senator Drove Title IX and 2 Amendments." *New York Times.* March 14, 2019.

Coffin, Harriet H. "Women of Yale." *New York Times.* July 15, 1971.

Coleman, Dash. "State Historical Marker to Commemorate Savannah Civil Rights Struggle." *Savannah Morning News.* September 21, 2016. https://www.savannahnow.com/news/ 2016-09-21/state-historical-marker-commemorate-savannah-civil-rights-struggle /13915450007.

Considine, Austin. "Saying 'No' to Picture Perfect." *New York Times.* May 16, 2012. https:// www.nytimes.com/2012/05/17/fashion/saying-no-to-picture-perfect.html.

Cook, Sylvia Jenkins. "'Oh Dear! How the Factory Girls Do Rig Up': Lowell's Self-Fashioning Workingwomen." *New England Quarterly* 83, no. 2 (2010): 219–49.

Council, Ashley. "Ringing Liberty's Bell." *Pennsylvania History* 87, no. 3 (2020): 494–531.

Crockett, Emily. "Hillary Clinton Wore White—a Symbol of Women's Suffrage—to Trump's Inauguration." *Vox.* January 20, 2017. https://www.vox.com/identities/2017/1/20/14336204/hillary-clinton-trump-inauguration-wearing-white-suffragists.

Crowe, Cameron. "Harry Styles' New Direction." *Rolling Stone.* April 18, 2017.

Dall'Asen, Nicola. "Why You Shouldn't Wear Oil-Based Beauty Products While Protesting." *Allure.* June 3, 2020. https://www.allure.com/story/beauty-products-not-to-wear-when -protesting.

Dansker, Emil. "NAACP Urges Support for Youth, Model Cities." *Dayton Daily News.* April 1, 1969.

de Schweinitz, Rebecca. "The Proper Age for Suffrage: Vote 18 and the Politics of Age from World War II to the Age of Aquarius." In *Age in America: The Colonial Era to the Present,* edited by Corinne T. Field and Nicholas L. Syrett. New York: New York University Press, 2015.

de Schweinitz, Rebecca. *If We Could Change the World: Young People and America's Long Struggle for Racial Equality.* Chapel Hill: University of North Carolina Press, 2011.

Deck, Barbara. "How It Came to Be: Remembering the 1969 Female Liberation Conference." Our Bodies Ourselves Today. https://www.ourbodiesourselvestoday.org/about-us/our -history/impact-influence/how-it-came-to-be-remembering-the-1969-female -liberation-conference/.

DeLuzio, Crista. *Female Adolescence in American Scientific Thought, 1830–1930.* Baltimore: Johns Hopkins University Press, 2007.

DeMillo, Andrew. "Texas Investigations into Families with Trans Children Seeking Gender-Confirming Care Blocked." ABC News. June 13, 2022. https://abc13.com/texas-trans -child-abuse-aclu-lambda-legal-transgender-confirming-therapy/11945851/.

Demos, John, and Virginia Demos. "Adolescence in Historical Perspective." *Journal of Marriage and Family* 31, no. 4 (1969): 632–38.

Devlin, Diane. "The Plight of the Gay Student." *Off Our Backs* 1, no. 6 (1970): 11.

Dias, Marley. "ELLE.com Has a New Boss and She's 11 Years Old." Elle.com. September 19, 2016. https://www.elle.com/culture/career-politics/a38970/marley-dias-editor-letter-marley-mag/.

Dickens, Charles. *American Notes for General Circulation.* 1842. Reprint, New York: Penguin Books, 2000.

Dickinson, Anna E. Papers. Library of Congress, Washington, D.C. https://www.loc.gov /item/mss184240238.

Dickinson, Anna Elizabeth. "Southern Outrage." *Liberator.* February 22, 1856.

Doherty, Erin. "The Number of LGBTQ-Identifying Adults Is Soaring." Axios. February 19, 2022. https://www.axios.com/2022/02/17/lgbtq-generation-z-gallup.

Doherty, Thomas. *Teenagers and Teenpics: The Juvenilization of American Movies in the 1950s.* Philadelphia: Temple University Press, 2002.

Domowitz, Janet. "Vermont Youths Declare War on Nuclear Weapons." *Christian Science Monitor.* March 18, 1982. https://www.csmonitor.com/1982/0318/031803.html.

Donner, Francesca, and Emma Goldberg. "In 25 Years, the Pay Gap Has Shrunk by Just 8 Cents." *New York Times.* March 24, 2021.

Dorr, Rheta Childe. "The Eternal Question." *Collier's National Weekly.* October 30, 1920.

Douglas, Susan J. *Where the Girls Are.* New York: Times Books, 1994.

Driver, Justin. *The Schoolhouse Gate: Public Education, the Supreme Court, and the Battle for the American Mind.* New York: Pantheon Books, 2018.

Dublin, Thomas. "Women, Work, and Protest in the Early Lowell Mills: 'The Oppressing Hand of Avarice Would Enslave Us.'" *Labor History* 16 (1975): 96–116.

Dublin, Thomas. *Women at Work: The Transformation of Work and Community in Lowell, Massachusetts, 1826–1860.* New York: Columbia University Press, 1993.

DuBois, Ellen Carol. *Harriot Stanton Blatch and the Winning of Woman Suffrage.* New Haven, CT: Yale University Press, 1999.

DuBois, Ellen Carol. *Suffrage: Women's Long Battle for the Vote.* New York: Simon & Schuster, 2020.

Ducharme, Jamie. "New Abortion Clinics Are Opening Near Borders and Airports to Stretch Access as Far as It Will Go." *Time.* June 9, 2022. https://time.com/6185519/abortion-clinics-travel-state-borders/.

Duffy, Bernard K., and Richard W. Leeman. *The Will of a People: A Critical Anthology of Great African American Speeches.* Carbondale, IL: Southern University Press, 2012.

Dye, Nancy Schrom. *As Equals and as Sisters: Feminism, the Labor Movement, and the Women's Trade Union League of New York.* Columbia: University of Missouri Press, 1980.

Ehrenreich, Barbara, Elizabeth Hess, and Gloria Jacobs. "Beatlemania: Girls Just Want to Have Fun." In *The Adoring Audience: Fan Culture and Popular Media,* edited by Lisa A. Lewis. London: Routledge, 1992.

Eisler, Benita. *The Lowell Offering: Writings by New England Women (1840–1845).* New York: W. W. Norton & Company, 1997.

Elbein, Saul. "The Youth Group That Launched a Movement at Standing Rock." *New York Times Magazine.* January 31, 2017. https://www.nytimes.com/2017/01/31/magazine/the-youth-group-that-launched-a-movement-at-standing-rock.html.

Ellis, Estelle. Papers. Archives Center, National Museum of American History, Washington, D.C.

Ellis, Ralph. "Parkland Student Survivor Throws Up on Stage, Then Finishes Her Speech." CNN. March 24, 2018. https://www.cnn.com/2018/03/24/us/march-threw-up-on-stage/index.html.

Eschner, Kat. "Only One Woman Who Was at the Seneca Falls Women's Rights Convention Lived to See Women Win the Vote." *Smithsonian.* July 19, 2017. https://www.smithsonianmag.com/smart-news/only-one-woman-who-was-seneca-falls-lived-see-women-win-vote-180964044/.

Espada, Mariah. "'We've Seen a Youthquake.' How Youth of Color Backed Joe Biden in Battleground States." *Time.* November 10, 2020. https://time.com/5910291/weve-seen-a-youthquake-how-youth-of-color-backed-joe-biden-in-battleground-states/.

Evans, Olive. "Handling Children's Nuclear War Fears." *New York Times.* May 27, 1982. https://www.nytimes.com/1982/05/27/garden/handling-children-s-nuclear-war-fears.html.

Fessler, Ann. *The Girls Who Went Away: The Hidden History of Women Who Surrendered Children for Adoption in the Decades Before Roe v. Wade.* New York: Penguin Books, 2006.

Fetters, Ashley. "The First of the 'Yale Women.'" *The Atlantic.* September 22, 2019. https://www.theatlantic.com/education/archive/2019/09/first-undergraduate-women-yale/598216/.

Fischer, Lucy Rose. *Linked Lives: Adult Daughters and Their Mothers.* New York: Harper & Row, 1987.

Fleming, Cynthia Griggs. *Soon We Will Not Cry: The Liberation of Ruby Doris Smith Robinson.* Oxford: Rowman & Littlefield Publishers, 1998.

Foner, Philip S. *The Factory Girls.* Urbana: University of Illinois Press, 1977.

Foner, Philip S. *Women and the American Labor Movement*. New York: Free Press, 1982.

Ford, Tanisha C. *Liberated Threads: Black Women, Style, and the Global Politics of Soul*. Chapel Hill: University of North Carolina Press, 2015.

Fox, Maggie. "Suicides in Teen Girls Hit 40-Year High." NBC News. August 3, 2017. https://www.nbcnews.com/health/health-news/suicides-teen-girls-hit-40-year-high-n789351.

Friedan, Betty. *The Feminine Mystique*. 1963. Reprint, New York: W. W. Norton & Company, 2001.

Friedman, Lisa. "Standing Rock Sioux Tribe Wins a Victory in Dakota Access Pipeline Case." *New York Times*. March 25, 2020. https://www.nytimes.com/2020/03/25/climate/dakota-access-pipeline-sioux.html.

Friedman, Vanessa. "The Naked Truth." *Financial Times*. April 25, 2014. https://www.ft.com/content/5f9643e6-c639-11e3-ba0e-00144feabdc0#axzz30BeErll3.

Frost, Jennifer. *"Let Us Vote!": Youth Voting Rights and the 26th Amendment*. New York: New York University Press, 2022.

Frost, Jennifer. "On Account of Age." *Australasian Journal of American Studies* 40, no. 2 (December 2021): 49–70.

Furstenberg, Frank E., Jr. "Teenage Childbearing as a Public Issue and Private Concern." *Annual Review of Sociology* 29 (2003): 23–39.

Gallman, J. Matthew. *America's Joan of Arc: The Life of Anna Elizabeth Dickinson*. Oxford: Oxford University Press, 2006.

Galloway, Paul. "A Woman Born to Be Riled." *Chicago Tribune*. February 14, 1985. https://www.chicagotribune.com/news/ct-xpm-1985-02-14-8501090494-story.html.

Givhan, Robin. "The Sound of a Shifting Power Structure." *Washington Post*. January 13, 2021. https://www.washingtonpost.com/nation/2021/01/13/power-structure-black-women-kamala-harris/.

Goldstein, Richard. "Autherine Lucy Foster, First Black Student at U. of Alabama, Dies at 92." *New York Times*. March 2, 2022. https://www.nytimes.com/2022/03/02/us/autherine-lucy-foster-dead.html.

Golus, Carrie. "Organizing Principle." *University of Chicago Magazine*. Winter 2019. https://mag.uchicago.edu/law-policy-society/organizing-principle.

Goody, Sarah. "Climate Change Activism Improved My Mental Health." *Teen Vogue*. April 10, 2020. https://www.teenvogue.com/story/climate-change-activism-improved-my-mental-health.

Gordon, Ann D. Review of *America's Joan of Arc: The Life of Anna Elizabeth Dickinson*, by J. Matthew Gallman. *Pennsylvania Magazine of History and Biography* 131, no. 3 (2007): 328–29.

Gordon, Hava Rachel. "Gendered Paths to Teenage Political Participation: Parental Power, Civic Mobility, and Youth Activism." *Gender and Society* 22, no. 1 (2008): 31–55.

Gould, Jack. "Lack of Responsibility Is Shown by TV in Exploiting Teen-Agers." *New York Times*. September 16, 1956. https://archive.nytimes.com/www.nytimes.com/partners/aol/special/elvis/early-elvis3.html.

Graham, Gael. *Young Activists: American High School Students in the Age of Protest*. DeKalb: Northern Illinois University Press, 2006.

Green, Matthew. "The Youth Activists Behind the Standing Rock Resistance." KQED. May 23, 2017. https://www.kqed.org/lowdown/27023/the-youth-of-standing-rock.

Greenberg, Zoe. "Overlooked No More: Clara Lemlich Shavelson, Crusading Leader of Labor Rights." *New York Times.* August 1, 2018. https://www.nytimes.com/2018/08/01/obituaries/overlooked-clara-lemlich-shavelson.html.

Griffith, Elisabeth. *Formidable: American Women and the Fight for Equality: 1920–2020.* New York: Pegasus Books, 2022.

Greijdanus, Hedy, Carlos A. de Matos Fernandes, Felicity Turner-Zwinkels, Ali Honari, Carla A. Roos, Hannes Rosenbusch, and Tom Postmes. "The Psychology of Online Activism and Social Movements: Relations between Online and Offline Collective Action." *Current Opinion in Psychology* 35 (2020): 49–54.

Grose, Jessica. "Gen Z Is Cynical. They've Earned It." *New York Times.* May 27, 2022. https://www.nytimes.com/2022/05/27/opinion/gen-z-uvalde-covid-climate.html.

Grose, Jessica. "The New Abortion Rights Advocates Are on TikTok." *New York Times.* December 10, 2020. https://www.nytimes.com/2020/12/10/style/abortion-rights-activists-tiktok.html.

Grossman, Jonathan. "The Coal Strike of 1902: Turning Point in U.S. Policy." United States Department of Labor. https://www.dol.gov/general/aboutdol/history/coalstrike.

Grünewald, Guido. *Children's Campaign for Nuclear Disarmament.* Geneva: International Peace Bureau, 1985.

Guerrieri, Vince. "How 13 Seconds Changed Kent State University Forever." *Smithsonian.* May 1, 2020. https://www.smithsonianmag.com/history/fifty-years-ago-kent-state-massacre-changed-university-forever-180974787/.

Hahner, Leslie A., and Scott J. Varda. "Modesty and Feminisms: Conversations on Aesthetics and Resistance." *Feminist Formations* 24, no. 3 (2012): 22–42.

Haines, Errin. "Biden Campaign Hopes to Reach Young Voters Through MTV Video Music Awards." The 19th. August 30, 2020. https://19thnews.org/2020/08/biden-campaign-hopes-to-reach-young-voters-through-mtv-video-music-awards/.

Halberstam, David. *The Children.* New York: Fawcett Books, 1998.

Hayden, Casey, and Mary King. "Sex and Caste: A Kind of Memo." In *Dear Sisters: Dispatches from the Women's Liberation Movement,* edited by Rosalyn Baxandall and Linda Gordon. New York: Basic Books, 2001.

Heymann, C. David. "Like Living Machines." *New York Times.* January 29, 1978.

Hillman, Betty Luther. *Dressing for the Culture Wars: Style and the Politics of Self-Presentation in the 1960s and 1970s.* Lincoln: University of Nebraska Press, 2015.

Hoose, Phillip. *Claudette Colvin: Twice Toward Justice.* New York: Square Fish, 2009.

Hope, Clover. "Poet Amanda Gorman Dreams of Becoming the President." *Wall Street Journal.* November 3, 2021. https://www.wsj.com/story/poet-amanda-gorman-dreams-of-becoming-the-president-2216ee71.

Horowitz, Juliana Menasce, and Nikki Graf. "Most U.S. Teens See Anxiety and Depression as a Major Problem Among Their Peers." Pew Research Center. February 20, 2019. https://www.pewresearch.org/social-trends/2019/02/20/most-u-s-teens-see-anxiety-and-depression-as-a-major-problem-among-their-peers/.

Hu, Jane. "The Second Act of Social-Media Activism." *New Yorker.* August 3, 2020. https://www.newyorker.com/culture/cultural-comment/the-second-act-of-social-media-activism.

Hunt, Paula D. "Sybil Ludington, the Female Paul Revere: The Making of a Revolutionary War Heroine." *New England Quarterly* 88, no. 2 (2015): 187–222.

Hunt, Samantha. "What Is a Teenage Girl?" *New York Times.* January 22, 2021. https://www
.nytimes.com/2021/01/22/opinion/kamala-harris-girls.html.

Hurley, Lawrence. "Dakota Access Pipeline Suffers U.S. Supreme Court Setback." Reuters.
February 22, 2022. https://www.reuters.com/business/energy/us-supreme-court-turns
-away-dakota-pipeline-operators-appeal-2022-02-22/.

Husband, Julie. "'The White Slave of the North': Lowell Mill Women and the Reproduction
of 'Free' Labor." *Legacy* 16, no. 1 (1999): 11–21.

Jackson, Jada. "Seventeen's First Black Cover Model, Joyce Walker-Joseph, Is Still Breaking
Barriers." *Oprah Daily.* https://www.oprahdaily.com/life/a36697337/joyce-walker-joseph
-interview/.

Jacobs, Harriet A. "Letter from a Fugitive Slave: Slaves Sold under Peculiar Circumstances."
New-York Daily Tribune. June 21, 1853. https://docsouth.unc.edu/fpn/jacobs/support16
.html.

Jamieson, Amber. "Teens Wore Quinceañera Dresses to Protest Texas' Immigration Law."
BuzzFeed. July 20, 2017. https://www.buzzfeednews.com/article/amberjamieson/these
-teens-wore-quinceanera-dresses-to-protest-an.

Jarrett, Valerie. "Yes, Dolores Can: The 90-Year-Old Activist on Speaking Up, Raising Hell,
and Doing the Work." *Glamour.* October 13, 2020. https://www.glamour.com/story/dolores
-huerta-women-of-the-year-2020.

Jarvis, Brooke. "The Teenagers at the End of the World." *New York Times Magazine.* July 21,
2020. https://www.nytimes.com/interactive/2020/07/21/magazine/teenage-activist
-climate-change.html.

Johnson, Alexis McGill. "I'm the Head of Planned Parenthood. We're Done Making Excuses for Our Founder." *New York Times.* April 17, 2021. https://www.nytimes.com/2021
/04/17/opinion/planned-parenthood-margaret-sanger.html.

Jones, Arthur, II, and Aaron Navarro. "This Year on Pace to See Record Anti-Transgender
Bills Passed by States, Says Human Rights Campaign." CBS News. April 22, 2022.
https://www.cbsnews.com/news/2022-anti-transgender-legislation-record-human
-rights-campaign/.

Jones, Carolyn. "Girls Draw Even with Boys in High School STEM Classes, but Still Lag in
College and Careers." EdSource. March 12, 2017. https://edsource.org/2017/girls-now
-outnumber-boys-in-high-school-stem-but-still-lag-in-college-and-career/578444.

Josephson, Hannah. *The Golden Threads: New England's Mill Girls and Magnates.* New York:
Duell, Sloan and Pearce, 1949.

Kahn, Mattie. "All the Light They Cannot See." *Elle.* June 2017.

Kahn, Mattie. "The World According to Greta." *Glamour.* October 22, 2019. https://www
.glamour.com/story/women-of-the-year-2019-greta-thunberg.

Karabel, Jerome. *The Chosen: The Hidden History of Admission and Exclusion at Harvard, Yale, and
Princeton.* Boston: Houghton Mifflin, 2005.

Kenngott, George Frederick. *The Record of a City: A Social Survey of Lowell, Massachusetts.* New
York: Macmillan Company, 1912.

Kiester, Edwin, Jr. "What's Happening in the Rest of the Country." *Chicago Tribune.* September 10, 1972.

Kilgore, Ed. "Gen Z May Break the Deadlock Over Abortion Rights." *New York Magazine.*
June 1, 2022. https://nymag.com/intelligencer/2022/06/gen-z-may-break-the-deadlock
-over-abortion-rights.html.

King, Martin Luther, Jr. Research and Education Institute. Online King Records Access (OKRA) database. http://okra.stanford.edu/transcription/document_images/undecided /550302-001.pdf.

King, Martin Luther, Jr. *The Papers of Martin Luther King, Jr., Volume IV: Symbol of the Movement, January 1957–December 1958.* Edited by Clayborne Carson, Susan Carson, Adrienne Clay, Virginia Shadron, and Kieran Taylor. Berkeley: University of California Press, 2000.

Kiraly, S. J. "Psychological Effects of the Threat of Nuclear War." *Canadian Family Physician* 32 (1986): 170–74.

Kluger, Richard. *Simple Justice: The History of* Brown v. Board of Education *and Black America's Struggle for Equality.* 1975. Reprint, New York: Vintage Books, 2004.

Kramer, Jane. "Road Warrior." *New Yorker.* October 12, 2015. https://www.newyorker.com /magazine/2015/10/19/road-warrior-profiles-jane-kramer.

Ladner, Joyce. "Standing Up for Our Beliefs." In *Hands on the Freedom Plow: Personal Accounts by Women in SNCC,* edited by Faith S. Holsaert, Martha Prescod Norman Noonan, Judy Richardson, Betty Garman Robinson, Jean Smith Young, and Dorothy M. Zellner. Urbana: University of Illinois Press, 2012.

Lanza, Alexis. "Young Women Are Using Instagram to Fight for the Future of the Planet." The 19th. November 25, 2020. https://19thnews.org/2020/11/young-women-climate -activists-instagram-future-planet/.

Larcom, Lucy. "A New England Girlhood." In *Written by Herself: Autobiographies of American Women: An Anthology,* edited by Jill Ker Conway, 312–22. New York: Vintage, 1992.

Larcom, Lucy. *A New England Girlhood: Outlined from Memory.* New York: Houghton Mifflin Company, 1889.

Larcom, Lucy. *Idyl of Work.* Boston: James R. Osgood and Company, 1875. https://quod.lib .umich.edu/a/amverse/BAD5902.0001.001/1:14?rgn=div1;view=fulltext.

Lee, Mabel Ping-Hua. "China's Submerged Half." Transcript of speech delivered at the Suffrage Shop of the Women's Political Union. New York. 1915. https://timtsengdotnet.files .wordpress.com/2013/12/mabel-lee-speech-china_s-submerged.pdf.

Lee, Mabel Ping-Hua. "Meaning of Women's Suffrage." *The Chinese Students' Monthly* 9, no. 7 (May 1914): 526–31.

Leventhal, Willy S., ed. *The Children Coming On: A Retrospective of the Montgomery Bus Boycott and the Oral Histories of Boycott Participants.* Montgomery, AL: River City Publishing, 1998.

Levine, Ellen. *Freedom's Children: Young Civil Rights Activists Tell Their Own Stories.* 1993. Reprint, New York: Puffin Books, 2000.

Lewis, Nicole Lynn. *Pregnant Girl: A Story of Teen Motherhood, College, and Creating a Better Future for Young Families.* Boston: Beacon Press, 2021.

Li, Katelyn X. "When Harvard Met Radcliffe." *Harvard Crimson.* May 27, 2019. https://www .thecrimson.com/article/2019/5/27/harvard-radcliffe-1969/.

Liang, Hua. "Fighting for a New Life: Social and Patriotic Activism of Chinese American Women in New York City, 1900 to 1945." *Journal of American Ethnic History* 17, no. 2 (1988): 22–38.

Long, Michael G. *Kids on the March: 15 Stories of Speaking Out, Protesting, and Fighting for Justice.* New York: Workman Publishing, 2021.

Lovell, Kera. "Girls Are Equal Too: Education, Body Politics, and the Making of Teenage Feminism." *Gender Issues* 33, no. 2 (2016): 71–95.

Lovett, Edward. "How Did Guy Fawkes Become a Symbol of Occupy Wall Street?" ABC News. November 5, 2011. https://abcnews.go.com/blogs/headlines/2011/11/how-did-guy-fawkes-become-a-symbol-of-occupy-wall-street.

MacDonald, Allan. "Lowell: A Commercial Utopia," *New England Quarterly* 10, no. 1 (1937): 37–62.

Macdonald, Dwight. "A Caste, a Culture, a Market—II." *New Yorker.* November 21, 1958.

Malkiel, Nancy Weiss. "'Keep the Damned Women Out': The Struggle for Coeducation in the Ivy League, the Seven Sisters, Oxford, and Cambridge." *Proceedings of the American Philosophical Society* 161, no. 1 (2017): 31–37.

Mallett, Kandist. "What to Know before Heading to a Protest." *Teen Vogue.* May 29, 2020. https://www.teenvogue.com/story/how-to-prepare-protest.

Mants, Joann Christian. "We Turned This Upside-Down Country Right Side Up." In *Hands on the Freedom Plow: Personal Accounts by Women in SNCC,* edited by Faith S. Holsaert, Martha Prescod Norman Noonan, Judy Richardson, Betty Garman Robinson, Jean Smith Young, and Dorothy M. Zellner. Urbana: University of Illinois Press, 2012.

Margolick, David. "Through a Lens, Darkly." *Vanity Fair.* September 2007. https://www.vanityfair.com/news/2007/09/littlerock200709.

Markusen, Eric. "Education and the Threat of Nuclear War." *Educational Perspectives* 21, no. 3 (1982): 32–36.

Marquand, Cynthia B. "Children's Peace Committee Helps Educate Peers about World Issues." *Christian Science Monitor.* March 28, 1983. https://www.csmonitor.com/1983/0328/032834.html.

Massoni, Kelley. *Fashioning Teenagers: A Cultural History of* Seventeen *Magazine.* 2010. Reprint, New York: Routledge, 2016.

May, Elaine Tyler. *Homeward Bound: American Families in the Cold War Era.* 1988. Reprint, New York: Basic Books, 2009.

McIntire, Suzanne. *Speeches in World History.* New York: Infobase Publishing, 2009.

McWhorter, Diane. "The Enduring Courage of the Freedom Riders." *Journal of Blacks in Higher Education* no. 61 (2008): 66–73.

Meltzer, Françoise. *For Fear of the Fire: Joan of Arc and the Limits of Subjectivity.* Chicago: University of Chicago Press, 2001.

Merish, Lori. *Archives of Labor: Working-Class Women and Literary Culture in the Antebellum United States.* Durham, NC: Duke University Press, 2017.

Metz, Nina. "Eva Maria Lewis Has Found Her Voice as an Organizer, in On the Ground Chi." *Chicago Tribune.* June 5, 2020. https://www.chicagotribune.com/social-justice/ct-faces-of-fallout-george-floyd-eva-maria-lewis-0604-20200605-45uru2hte5fprnhbls4lurp25a-story.html.

Miao, Hannah. "Young Voters Are Poised to Be a Decisive Factor Even as Coronavirus Creates Obstacles." CNBC. October 27, 2020. https://www.cnbc.com/2020/10/26/2020-election-young-voters-could-be-a-decisive-force-despite-coronavirus.html.

Michals, Debra. "Lucretia Mott." National Women's History Museum. 2017. https://www.womenshistory.org/education-resources/biographies/lucretia-mott.

Michels, Tony. "Uprising of 20,000 (1909)." In *Shalvi/Hyman Encyclopedia of Jewish Women.* Jewish Women's Archive. December 31, 1999. https://jwa.org/encyclopedia/article/uprising-of-20000-1909.

Miller, David. "A Loss for Dr. King—New Negro Roundup: They Yield." *New York Herald Tribune.* December 19, 1961.

Miller, Leslie J. "Children's Hot Cold War." *New York Times.* June 12, 1982. https://www.nytimes.com/1982/06/12/opinion/childrens-hot-cold-war.html.

Mintz, Steven. *Huck's Raft: A History of American Childhood.* Cambridge, MA: Harvard University Press, 2004.

Montrie, Chad. "'I Think Less of the Factory Than of My Native Dell': Labor, Nature, and the Lowell 'Mill Girls.'" *Environmental History* 9, no. 2 (2004): 275–95.

Moody, Anne. *Coming of Age in Mississippi: The Classic Autobiography of Growing Up Poor and Black in the Rural South.* New York: Random House, 2011.

moon girl jesse (@tinderdistrict). "ladies! here is my secret for a perfect cut crease . . ." Twitter post. March 23, 2021, 3:10 p.m. https://twitter.com/tinderdistrict/status/1374438403979153408.

Moran, William. *The Belles of New England: The Women of the Textile Mills and the Families Whose Wealth They Wove.* New York: Thomas Dunne Books, 2002.

Morgan, Robin, ed. *Sisterhood Is Powerful: An Anthology of Writings from the Women's Liberation Movement.* New York: Vintage Books, 1970.

Morris, Monique W. *Pushout: The Criminalization of Black Girls in Schools.* New York: New Press, 2016.

Mueller, Tabitha. "Gen Z, Millennial Vote Organizers Hope to Channel Youth Energy into Historic Turnout." *Nevada Independent.* October 30, 2020. https://thenevadaindependent.com/article/gen-z-millennial-vote-organizers-hope-to-channel-youth-energy-into-historic-turnout.

Murray, Melissa. "Sex and the Schoolhouse." Review of *The Schoolhouse Gate: Public Education, the Supreme Court, and the Battle for the American Mind,* by Justin Driver. *Harvard Law Review* 132, no. 5 (2019): 1445–88.

Naggiar, Stacey. "Victims of Forced Sterilization to Receive $10 Million from North Carolina." NBC News. July 25, 2013. https://www.nbcnews.com/nightly-news/victims-forced-sterilization-receive-10-million-north-carolina-flna6c10753957.

Nash, Diane. "Address to the National Catholic Conference for Interracial Justice." Transcript of speech delivered in Detroit, Michigan. August 25, 1961. https://awpc.cattcenter.iastate.edu/2019/08/09/address-to-the-national-catholic-conference-for-interracial-justice-august-25-1961/.

Nelson, Angela. "Young Voters Were Crucial to Biden's Win." Tufts Now. November 12, 2020. https://now.tufts.edu/2020/11/12/young-voters-were-crucial-bidens-win.

Nieto del Rio, Giulia McDonnell. "Darnella Frazier, the Teenager Who Recorded George Floyd's Murder, Speaks Out." *New York Times.* May 25, 2021. https://www.nytimes.com/2021/05/25/us/darnella-frazier.html.

North, Anna. "Young Female Activists Like Greta Thunberg Have the World's Attention." *Vox.* December 11, 2019. https://www.vox.com/2019/12/11/21010936/greta-thunberg-time-magazine-cover-person-year.

Nudelman, Franny. "Harriet Jacobs and the Sentimental Politics of Female Suffering." *ELH* 59, no. 4 (1992): 939–64.

Olson, Lynne. *Freedom's Daughters: The Unsung Heroines of the Civil Rights Movement from 1830 to 1970.* New York: Scribner, 2001.

Painter, Nell Irvin. *Sojourner Truth: A Life, A Symbol.* New York: W. W. Norton & Company, 1996.

Palladino, Grace. *Teenagers: An American History.* New York: Basic Books, 1996.

Parks, Rosa, and Jim Haskins. *Rosa Parks: My Story.* New York: Puffin Books, 1992.

Parson, Harvey. "Brenda Travis Took a Stand and Was Ordered to Leave State at 17 or Forfeit Her Freedom." *Mississippi Today.* August 17, 2018. https://mississippitoday.org/2018/08/17/brenda-travis-took-a-stand-and-was-ordered-to-leave-state-at-17-or-forfeit-her-freedom/.

Payne, Elizabeth Anne, Martha H. Swain, and Marjorie Julian Spruill, eds. *Mississippi Women: Their Histories, Their Lives.* Vol. 2. Athens: University of Georgia Press, 2010.

Pike, Lili. "Why So Many Young People Showed Up on Election Day." *Vox.* November 7, 2020. https://www.vox.com/2020/11/7/21552248/youth-vote-2020-georgia-biden-covid-19-racism-climate-change.

Powledge, Fred. *Free at Last?: The Civil Rights Movement and the People Who Made It.* New York: Little, Brown and Company, 1990.

Prickett, Sarah Nicole. "Jigsaw Youth." *Artforum.* March 14, 2014. https://www.artforum.com/film/sarah-nicole-prickett-on-matt-wolf-s-teenage-45709.

Pruitt-Young, Sharon. "Young People Are Anxious about Climate Change and Say Governments Are Failing Them." NPR. September 14, 2021. https://www.npr.org/2021/09/14/1037023551/climate-change-children-young-adults-anxious-worried-study.

Quinn, Mae C. "Black Women and Girls and the Twenty-Sixth Amendment: Constitutional Connections, Activist Intersections, and the First Wave Youth Suffrage Movement." *Seattle University Law Review* 43, no. 4 (2020): 1238–70.

Rampersad, Arnold. *Ralph Ellison: A Biography.* New York: Vintage Books, 2007.

Ransby, Barbara. *Ella Baker and the Black Freedom Movement: A Radical Democratic Vision.* Chapel Hill: University of North Carolina Press, 2003.

Ray, David. "Brave Times at Burglund High." *Jackson Free Press.* February 19, 2014. https://www.jacksonfreepress.com/news/2014/feb/19/brave-times-burglund-high/.

Reagon, Bernice Johnson. "My Black Mothers and Sisters or On Beginning a Cultural Autobiography." *Feminist Studies* 8, no. 1 (1982): 81–96.

Record, Angela R. "Born to Shop: Teenage Women and the Marketplace in the Postwar United States." In *Sex & Money: Feminism and Political Economy in the Media,* edited by Eileen R. Meehan and Ellen Riordan. Minneapolis: University of Minnesota, 2002.

Reyburn, Susan. "The Private Cost of Public Heroism: On Rosa Parks' Life in Detroit." *Lit Hub.* January 28, 2020. https://lithub.com/the-private-cost-of-public-heroism-on-rosa-parks-life-in-detroit/.

Reyes, Haley. "'Shame on You': 16-Year-Old in Texas Refuses to Be Silent about Her Reproductive Rights." *Ms.* magazine. February 16, 2022. https://msmagazine.com/2022/02/16/teenager-texas-abortion-reproductive-rights/.

Rhoden, William C. "Black and White Women Far from Equal under Title IX." *New York Times.* June 10, 2012. https://www.nytimes.com/2012/06/11/sports/title-ix-has-not-given-black-female-athletes-equal-opportunity.html.

Robinson, Harriet H. *Loom and Spindle: Or Life Among the Early Mill Girls with a Sketch of 'The Lowell Offering' and Some of Its Contributors.* Boston: Thomas Y. Crowell & Company, 1898.

Robinson, Jo Ann Gibson. *The Montgomery Bus Boycott and the Women Who Started It.* Knoxville: University of Tennessee Press, 1987.

Robinson, Thomas A., and Lanette D. Ruff. *Out of the Mouths of Babes: Girl Evangelists in the Flapper Era*. New York: Oxford University Press, 2012.

Rodriguez, Barbara. "Girls Are Being Socialized to Lose Political Ambition—and It Starts Younger Than We Realized." The 19th. September 23, 2021. https://19thnews.org/2021/09/study-girls-socialized-lose-political-ambition-younger-age/.

Rodriguez, Barbara. "The Country Needs Poll Workers. Young Women Are Stepping Up." The 19th. October 21, 2020. https://19thnews.org/2020/10/poll-workers-young-women-stepping-up/.

Rosenberg, Chaim M. *Child Labor in America: A History*. Jefferson, NC: McFarland & Company, 2013.

Rosenblatt, Kalhan. "A Gen Z Organization Is Enlisting People to Flood Anti-Abortion Websites Following Leak of Draft Opinion That Would Overturn Roe." NBC News. May 3, 2022. https://www.nbcnews.com/news/us-news/gen-z-organization-enlisting-people-flood-anti-abortion-websites-leak-rcna27117.

Roth, Benita. *Separate Roads to Feminism: Black, Chicana, and White Feminist Movements in America's Second Wave*. Cambridge: Cambridge University Press, 2004.

Rowan, Carl. "Quiet Mississippi Decision Important for U.S. Poor." *Toledo Blade*. July 16, 1969.

Ruane, Michael E. "Vietnam Critic's End Was the Start of Family's Pain." *Washington Post*. November 1, 2015. https://www.washingtonpost.com/local/vietnam-critics-end-was-the-start-of-familys-pain/2015/11/01/b50e1d54-7cdf-11e5-b575-d8dcfedb4ea1_story.html.

Rudell, B. J. "Will Young Voters Be the Difference Makers in 2020." *The Hill*. September 24, 2019. https://thehill.com/opinion/campaign/462837-will-young-voters-be-the-difference-makers-in-2020/.

Sarkissian, Arek. "Florida Court Says Teen Isn't Mature Enough to Get an Abortion." *Politico*. August 16, 2022. https://www.politico.com/news/2022/08/16/parentless-teen-cant-have-an-abortion-under-state-parental-consent-law-00052211.

Savage, Jon. "The Columbus Day Riot: Frank Sinatra Is Pop's First Star." *Guardian*. June 10, 2011. https://www.theguardian.com/music/2011/jun/11/frank-sinatra-pop-star.

Savage, Jon. *Teenagers: The Prehistory of Youth Culture: 1875–1945*. New York: Penguin Books, 2008.

Schaller, Thomas F. "50 Years Ago, the U.S. Ratified the 26th Amendment; Don't Expect It to Ratify Another—Ever." *Baltimore Sun*. June 30, 2021. https://www.baltimoresun.com/opinion/op-ed/bs-ed-op-0701-last-amendment-eve-20210630-ucn5ctsxbjbbljiq5kdjqnbad4-story.html.

Schatz, Robert T., and Susan T. Fiske. "International Reactions to the Threat of Nuclear War: The Rise and Fall of Concern in the Eighties." *Political Psychology* 13, no. 1 (1992): 1–29.

Schrum, Kelly. "'Teena Means Business': Teenage Girls' Culture and *Seventeen* Magazine." In *Delinquents and Debutantes: Twentieth-Century American Girls' Cultures*, edited by Sherrie A. Inness. New York: New York University Press, 1998.

Schrum, Kelly. *Some Wore Bobby Sox: The Emergence of Teenage Girls' Culture, 1920–1945*. New York: Palgrave Macmillan, 2004.

Schwebel, Milton. "Effects of the Nuclear War Threat on Children and Teenagers: Implications for Professionals." *American Journal of Orthopsychiatry* 52, no. 4 (1982): 608–17.

Seeger, Pete, and Bob Reiser. *Everybody Says Freedom*. New York: W. W. Norton & Company, 1989.

Segarra, Lisa Marie. "Naomi Wadler, 11, Captures Nation's Heart with Powerful Speech about Violence Against Black Women." *Time.* March 24, 2018. https://time.com/5214363/naomi-wadler-march-for-our-lives-speech-black-women/.

Shapiro, Laurie Gwen. "How a Thirteen-Year-Old Girl Smashed the Gender Divide in American High Schools." *New Yorker.* January 26, 2019. https://www.newyorker.com/culture/culture-desk/how-a-thirteen-year-old-girl-smashed-the-gender-divide-in-american-high-schools.

Shaw, Stephanie J. *What a Woman Ought to Be and to Do: Black Professional Women Workers During the Jim Crow Era.* Chicago: University of Chicago Press, 1996.

Shteir, Rachel. "Why We Can't Stop Talking About Betty Friedan." *New York Times.* February 3, 2021. https://www.nytimes.com/2021/02/03/us/betty-friedan-feminism-legacy.html.

Sinha, Manisha. *The Slave's Cause: A History of Abolition.* New Haven, CT: Yale University Press, 2016.

Slayton, Tom. "Wondering If They'll Be Alive in 20 Years Led Children on Campaign Against Nuclear Arms." *Rutland Daily Herald.* August 2, 1981.

Snyder, Thomas D., ed. *120 Years of American Education: A Statistical Portrait.* Washington, D.C.: Center for Education Statistics, 1993.

Sobey, Rick. "Elizabeth Warren Wants to Expand Youth Voting, Her Bill Would Require States to Have Pre-Registration for Those 16, 17 Years Old." *Boston Herald.* July 11, 2022. https://www.bostonherald.com/2022/07/11/elizabeth-warren-wants-to-expand-youth-voting-her-bill-would-require-states-to-have-pre-registration-for-those-16-17-years-old/.

Solantaus, T., M. Rimpela, and V. Taipale. "The Threat of War in the Minds of 12-18-Year-Olds in Finland." *Lancet* 323, no. 8380 (1984): 784–85.

Soong, T. V. "Eastern Conference at Amherst, Mass." *The Chinese Students' Monthly* 10, no. 1 (October 1914): 30–32.

Stauffer, Rainesford. "How Democrats Can Win the Youth Vote in November." *New York Times.* July 8, 2020. https://www.nytimes.com/2020/07/08/opinion/election-democrats-youth.html.

Stein, Julie Solow. "Youthful Transgressions: Teenagers, Sexuality, and the Contested Path to Adulthood in Postwar America." PhD diss., University of California, Berkeley, 2013.

Steinem, Gloria. "The Moral Disarmament of Betty Coed." *Esquire.* September 1, 1962. https://classic.esquire.com/article/1983/6/1/the-moral-disarmament-of-betty-coed.

Stevens, Elisabeth. "When Abortion Was Illegal: A 1966 *Post* Series Revealed How Women Got Them Anyway." *Washington Post.* June 9, 2019. https://www.washingtonpost.com/history/2019/06/09/when-abortion-was-illegal-post-series-revealed-how-women-got-them-anyway/.

Stewart, Doug. "Proud to Be a Mill Girl." *American Heritage.* Spring 2012. https://www.americanheritage.com/proud-be-mill-girl.

Student Nonviolent Coordinating Committee. *Freedom School Poetry.* New York: Packers Press, 1966.

Talbot, Margaret. "Girls Just Want to Be Mean." *New York Times Magazine.* February 24, 2002. https://www.nytimes.com/2002/02/24/magazine/girls-just-want-to-be-mean.html.

Taylor, Kate. "In New Class of Young Lawmakers, a Former Girl Scout Goes to the Statehouse." *New York Times.* November 13, 2018. https://www.nytimes.com/2018/11/13/us/young-candidates-elections.html.

Tecson, Brandee J. "Abercrombie Pulls T-Shirts After Teen Girls Launch Boycott." MTV News. November 7, 2005. http://www.mtv.com/news/1513153/abercrombie-pulls-t-shirts-after -teen-girls-launch-boycott/.

Tetrault, Lisa. *The Myth of Seneca Falls: Memory and the Women's Suffrage Movement, 1848–1989.* Chapel Hill: University of North Carolina Press, 2014.

Theoharis, Jeanne. *A More Beautiful and Terrible History: The Uses and Misuses of Civil Rights History.* Boston: Beacon Press, 2018.

Theoharis, Jeanne. *The Rebellious Life of Mrs. Rosa Parks.* Boston: Beacon Press, 2013.

Theoharis, Jeanne, and Say Burgin. "Pitting Rosa Parks Against Claudette Colvin Distorts History." *Washington Post.* October 19, 2022. https://www.washingtonpost.com /made-by-history/2022/10/19/rosa-parks-documentary/.

Thompson, Natalia. "Confessions of a Teenage Feminist." *Off Our Backs* 37, no. 4 (2007): 37–40.

Travis, Brenda, with John Obee. *Mississippi's Exiled Daughter: How My Civil Rights Baptism Under Fire Shaped My Life.* Montgomery, AL: NewSouth Books, 2018.

Travis, Brenda. Interview with Bruce Hartford. Civil Rights Movement Archive. February 2007. https://www.crmvet.org/nars/travisb.htm#btlbt.

Trickey, Erick. "'Why Is Child Marriage Still Legal?': A Young Lawmaker Tackles a Hidden Problem." *Politico.* January 9, 2022. https://www.politico.com/news/magazine/2022/01 /09/cassie-levesque-new-hampshire-child-marriage-524159.

Trollope, Anthony. *North America.* New York: Harper & Brothers Publishers, 1862.

Ura, Alexa. "Despite Losing Bathroom Bill Fight, a Texas Girl Gets Her Two Minutes." *Texas Tribune.* July 22, 2017. https://www.texastribune.org/2017/07/22/transgender-girl -gets-her-two-minutes-bathroom-bill/.

Velocci, Carli. "Why Protesters Love Costumes." *Racked.* March 2, 2018. https://www .racked.com/2018/3/2/17042504/protest-costumes.

Visvanathan, Susan. "Representing Joan of Arc." *India International Centre Quarterly* 24, no. 4 (1997): 22–32.

Wade-Gayles, Gloria Jean. *Pushed Back to Strength: A Black Woman's Journey Home.* Boston: Beacon Press, 1993.

Wallis, Claudia. "Women Face the '90s." *Time.* December 4, 1989. https://content.time.com /time/subscriber/article/0,33009,959163,00.html.

Wamsley, Laurel, and Vanessa Romo. "With Speeches and Bright Dresses, Quinceañeras Protest Texas Sanctuary City Ban." July 19, 2017. https://www.npr.org/sections/thetwo -way/2017/07/19/538112799/with-speeches-and-bright-dresses-quincea-eras-protest -texas-sanctuary-city-ban.

Warzel, Charlie. "The Pro-Trump Media Has Met Its Match in the Parkland Students." *BuzzFeed.* February 21, 2018. https://www.buzzfeednews.com/article/charliewarzel /parkland-school-shooting-survivors-crisis-actors-pro-trump.

Watts, Jonathan. "Greta Thunberg, Schoolgirl Climate Change Warrior: 'Some People Can Let Things Go. I Can't.'" *Guardian.* March 11, 2019. https://www.theguardian.com /world/2019/mar/11/greta-thunberg-schoolgirl-climate-change-warrior-some-people -can-let-things-go-i-cant.

Waxman, Olivia B. "'I Was Not Going to Stand.' Rosa Parks Predecessors Recall Their History-Making Acts of Resistance." *Time.* March 2, 2020. https://time.com/5786220 /claudette-colvin-mary-louise-smith/.

Weber, Evan, and Varshini Prakash. "Sunrise Movement's General Election Impact." Sunrise Movement. October 31, 2020. Updated November 6, 2020. https://www.sunrise-movement.org/press-releases/sunrise-movements-general-election-impact/.

Weeden, Kim A., Dafna Gelbgiser, and Stephen L. Morgan. "Pipeline Dreams: Occupational Plans and Gender Differences in STEM Major Persistence and Completion." *Sociology of Education* 93, no. 4 (2020): 297–314.

Weinraub, Bernard. "The Brilliancy of Black." *Esquire.* January 1, 1967.

Wells, Georgia, Jeff Horwitz, and Deepa Seetharaman. "Facebook Knows Instagram Is Toxic for Teen Girls, Company Documents Show." *Wall Street Journal.* September 14, 2021. https://www.wsj.com/articles/facebook-knows-instagram-is-toxic-for-teen-girls -company-documents-show-11631620739.

White, Annette Jones. "Expression of My Discontent." In *Hands on the Freedom Plow: Personal Accounts by Women in SNCC,* edited by Faith S. Holsaert, Martha Prescod Norman Noonan, Judy Richardson, Betty Garman Robinson, Jean Smith Young, and Dorothy M. Zellner. Urbana: University of Illinois Press, 2012.

Willard, Frances Elizabeth, and Mary Ashton Rice Livermore. *A Woman of the Century: Fourteen Hundred-Seventy Biographical Sketches Accompanied by Portraits of Leading American Women in All Walks of Life.* Buffalo, NY: Charles Wells Moulton, 1893. https://archive.org/details /bub_gb_zXEEAAAAYAAJ/page/241/mode/2up.

Williams, Juan. *Eye on the Prize.* 1987. Reprint, New York: Penguin Books, 2013.

Woodward, Aylin. "Greta Thunberg Addressed World Leaders through Tears: 'How Dare You! You Have Stolen My Dreams and My Childhood With Your Empty Words.'" *Business Insider.* September 23, 2019. https://www.businessinsider.com/greta-thunberg -tearful-speech-un-climate-action-summit-2019-9.

Wright, Nazera Sadiq. *Black Girlhood in the Nineteenth Century.* Urbana: University of Illinois Press, 2016.

Young, James Harvey. "Anna Elizabeth and the Civil War: For and Against Lincoln." *Mississippi Valley Historical Review* 31, no. 1 (1944): 59–80.

Young, Jean Smith. "Do Whatever You Are Big Enough to Do." In *Hands on the Freedom Plow: Personal Accounts by Women in SNCC,* edited by Faith S. Holsaert, Martha Prescod Norman Noonan, Judy Richardson, Betty Garman Robinson, Jean Smith Young, and Dorothy M. Zellner. Urbana: University of Illinois Press, 2012.

Younge, Gary. "She Would Not Be Moved." *Guardian.* December 15, 2000. https://www .theguardian.com/theguardian/2000/dec/16/weekend7.weekend12.

Yurcaba, Jo. "Texas Has Considered Dozens of Anti-Trans Bills. These Moms Have Helped Stop Them." NBC News. September 30, 2021. https://www.nbcnews.com/nbc-out/out -politics-and-policy/texas-considered-dozens-anti-trans-bills-moms-helped-stop -rcna2355.

Zaveri, Mihir. "Body Camera Footage Shows Arrest by Orlando Police of 6-Year-Old at School." *New York Times.* February 27, 2020. https://www.nytimes.com/2020/02/27/us /orlando-6-year-old-arrested.html.

Zelizer, Viviana A. *Pricing the Priceless Child: The Changing Social Value of Children.* 1985. Reprint, Princeton, NJ: Princeton University Press, 1994.

INDEX